A Romano-British Roadside Settlement at Beanacre, Wiltshire

Cai Mason

A Romano-British Roadside Settlement at Beanacre, Wiltshire

Cai Mason

with contributions by
Phil Andrews, Elina Brook, Dana Challinor, Nicholas Cooke, Kirsten Egging Dinwiddy
Phil Harding, Richard Henry, L. Higbee, Inés López-Dóriga
J. M. Mills and Rachael Seager Smith

Illustrations by
Rob Goller and Nancy Dixon

Wessex Archaeology Occasional Paper
2018

Published 2018 by Wessex Archaeology Ltd
Portway House, Old Sarum Park, Salisbury, SP4 6EB
www.wessexarch.co.uk

British Library Cataloguing in Publication Data
A catalogue record for this book is available from the British Library

ISBN 978-1-911137-08-5

Typeset and designed by Kenneth Lymer
Cover design by Rob Goller
Copy edited by Philippa Bradley
Printed by Lightning Source UK

Front cover
Stone altars (ONs 39 and 40)

Back cover
Enamelled plate brooch (ON 70), typical oven, locally produced oxidised ware flagon, and central part of site crossed by Roman road

Wessex Archaeology Ltd is a company limited by guarantee registered in England, company number 1712772. It is also a Charity registered in England and Wales number 287786, and in Scotland, Scottish Charity number SC042630. Our registered office is at Portway House, Old Sarum Park, Salisbury, Wiltshire, SP4 6EB.

Contents

List of Figures

List of Plates

List of Tables

Acknowledgements

The project was commissioned by J. Murphy and Sons Ltd on behalf of National Grid. We would like to thank Douglas Smith, Robbie Griggs and John-Paul Heggie from National Grid, Henry Kavanagh of Murphy and Sons Ltd and Jenny Wylie of Hyder Consulting for their assistance throughout the project. Thanks are also due to Melanie Pomeroy-Kellinger and Rachel Foster, who monitored the project on behalf of Wiltshire Council.

Our gratitude is also extended to Mr King for allowing access to his farmland, which provided the opportunity to undertake a geophysical survey of the surrounding fields. We would also like to thank Dave Crisp who conducted a metal detector survey of the site, without whom many of the coins and other metal finds would not have been recovered.

The excavation was directed by Cai Mason and Matt Kendall, with the assistance of Tom Blencowe, Ben Cullen and Phil Andrews. The excavation team comprised Bianca San-Martin, Bill Moffat, Dave Murdie, Ed Grenier, Frances Ward, George Morgan-Walcroft, Jamie McCarthy, John Sanigar, Kerrie Birnie, Lee Newton, Luke Jervis, Lynn Hume, Natalia Hunt, Owen Watts, Pete Capps, Pete Fairclough, Roy Krakowicz, Steve Froud, Stuart Wearing and Tom Burt. The geophysical survey was carried out by Laura Andrews and Diana Chard, and managed by Lucy Parker. Environmental samples were processed by Tony Scothern, sorted by Nikki Mulhall and assessed by Sarah F. Wyles. Inés López-Dóriga would like to thank Ruth Pelling (Historic England) for useful discussion on the analysis of the environmental remains.

The fieldwork was managed by Gareth Chaffey, and the post-excavation programme overseen by Phil Andrews and Gareth Chaffey. The illustrations are by Rob Goller and Nancy Dixon. This report has been edited by Philippa Bradley and typeset by Kenneth Lymer.

The project archive will be deposited at the Wiltshire Museum, Devizes.

Abstract

In 2015 archaeological monitoring during the construction of an electricity supply line for the Great Western Railway uncovered a large, and previously unknown, Romano-British settlement to the north of Beanacre, Wiltshire.

Finds of worked flint provide evidence for transient human activity from the Mesolithic/Neolithic onwards, whilst a small cluster of pits/postholes, two of which contained Bronze Age finds, suggest that there may have been more settled activity on the site by this date. There was no evidence of Iron Age occupation.

The Romano-British settlement straddled the main Roman road between the towns of *Aquae Sulis*, *Verlucio* and *Cunetio*, all of which existed by the second half of the 1st century AD. The earliest features within the Beanacre settlement were of a similar date, which suggests that it was probably established soon after the road between these towns had been laid out.

At its maximum extent, the roadside settlement probably continued for at least 0.9 km along the road frontage and encompassed 12–20 hectares. The most concentrated zone of activity was along the main road, with further areas of less-intensive activity within enclosures set back from the road frontage.

The earliest structure within the settlement was an unusual sunken-featured building dating from the late 1st or early 2nd century AD. This building contained two possible hearths and two infant burials; features which have parallels in similar Romano-British structures from Kent and Leicestershire. Two further inhumation burials were uncovered in other parts of the site. One was an adult found close to an enclosure boundary; the other was a neonate, which was buried within a building. Both burial contexts are typical of the period.

The most striking aspect of the settlement was the profusion of clay and stone-lined ovens, 41 in total, most of which date from the mid-Romano-British period. These appear to have been primarily used for cooking, which suggests that food provision – particularly roast pork and bread – was an important part of the settlement's economy. Although the emphasis on food production may have a prosaic explanation – ie, provisioning passing travellers – the density of ovens is much higher than has previously recorded in comparable settlements, which suggests that there may have been something unusual about the Beanacre site.

The most notable finds from the excavation were two small stone altars. These were found together, a few metres to the north of the main Roman road, and close to an unusual dog burial and a stone-lined well. The altars may indicate the position of a roadside shrine, which suggests that there was a religious aspect to the site, though it is unclear how significant this was in terms of the settlement's function.

During the late Romano-British period, stone-founded buildings and other structures were constructed using the locally quarried ragstone. It is unclear if the superstructure of these buildings were of stone or timber construction, but the depth of foundations suggest that they were probably more than one storey high. The near-absence of ceramic roof tiles and relatively small quantities of stone roof tiles, suggest that most of the buildings were probably thatched.

A heavily truncated crop drying oven was also recorded; this feature produced a similar assemblage of charred plant remains to those recovered from the cooking ovens and is a typical example of its type.

The Romano-British settlement appears to have been abandoned in the 4th century, and the site subsequently reverted to purely agricultural use. The Roman road did however continue to be used until the post-medieval period, by which time wear and natural erosion had turned the former road into a hollow-way.

Chapter 1
Introduction

The electrification of the Great Western Main Line railway from London to Bristol necessitated the installation of a twin 25KV power supply from National Grid's Westlands Lane Substation (NGR ST 901000 708000) to a newly constructed Automatic Trackside Feeder Station at Thingley Rail Junction (NGR ST 896000 662000). Construction of the power line entailed stripping a 15–20 m wide easement along a 5.2 km corridor between the two substations (Fig. 1.1). Within this easement, cables were laid in two 3 m wide trenches, set either side of a 6 m wide haul road.

To mitigate the impact of the construction works on any buried archaeological remains, Wiltshire Council Archaeology Service (WCAS) requested that the stripping of topsoil and the initial excavations along the line of the cable trenches be monitored by means of an archaeological watching brief. The agreed methodology (Wessex Archaeology 2014a) stipulated that any archaeological remains uncovered during the monitoring would be excavated and recorded in advance of the construction work. WCAS also identified three areas of particular archaeological interest, where intensive monitoring was needed: Area 1 was focused either side of a Roman road that followed the boundary between Melksham Without and Lacock parishes, Area 2 was focused on a series of earthworks and cropmarks to the east of Wick Farm, near Lacock, Area 3 was located close to a group of cropmarks to the south of Thingley Junction. The archaeological fieldwork was undertaken between January and April 2015, and the post-excavation assessment produced later that year (Wessex Archaeology 2015a).

Topography and Geology

The cable route followed a generally north–south course through gently undulating farmland broadly parallel and immediately to the west of the Chippenham branch of the Wessex Main Line railway, and approximately 1 km to the west of the River Avon. Ground levels ranged between 43 m and 65 m above Ordnance Datum (OD). Area 1 was situated at the foot of a low hill on the western edge of the Avon floodplain. Here, the former Roman road crossed the easement at approximately 44 m OD. The land to the south of the Roman road sloped downhill slightly, whilst the land to the north sloped downhill towards a small unnamed stream at approximately 42 m OD.

The solid geology at the northern end of the cable route is Late Jurassic Limestone of the Cornbrash Formation, interspersed with bands of Mudstone of the Forest Marble Formation, and Sandstone, Siltstone and Mudstone of the Kellaways Formation. To the south of Area 2, the Cornbrash gives way to Late Jurassic Mudstone of the Oxford Clay Formation. The high ground to the west of the Avon valley is bisected by four small east–west tributaries of the main river, the largest of which, the Ladbrook, is flanked by superficial deposits of alluvium. There are also extensive river terrace deposits of sand and gravel towards the southern end of the cable route (British Geological Survey Online Viewer).

The gravel terraces flanking the River Avon have freely draining lime-rich loamy soils. Beyond the gravel terraces, the Avon Valley has slowly permeable, seasonally wet loamy and clayey soils. The limestone geology on the higher ground to the west of the Avon Valley gives rise to freely-draining shallow and lime-rich loamy soils, whilst the high areas with less-permeable geology have lime-rich loamy and clayey soils with impeded drainage. All of these soil types have historically been used for both arable and pasture, with some woodland in areas with poorer drainage.

Archaeological Background

Prehistoric

Neolithic, Bronze Age and Iron Age occupation sites have been uncovered in several locations to the south-west of Chippenham, notably on the gravel terraces near Showell Farm and Milbourne Farm (eg, Bateman and Enright 2000; Cotswold Archaeological Trust 1999; Cotswold Archaeology 2003; 2014; Oxford Archaeological Unit 1991). An assemblage of Neolithic pottery, Bronze Age spearheads and a dirk was also found during construction of the A350 bridge to the west of Melksham (McMahon 2004, 6). Between Melksham and Chippenham, the evidence for prehistoric activity is very sparse and largely

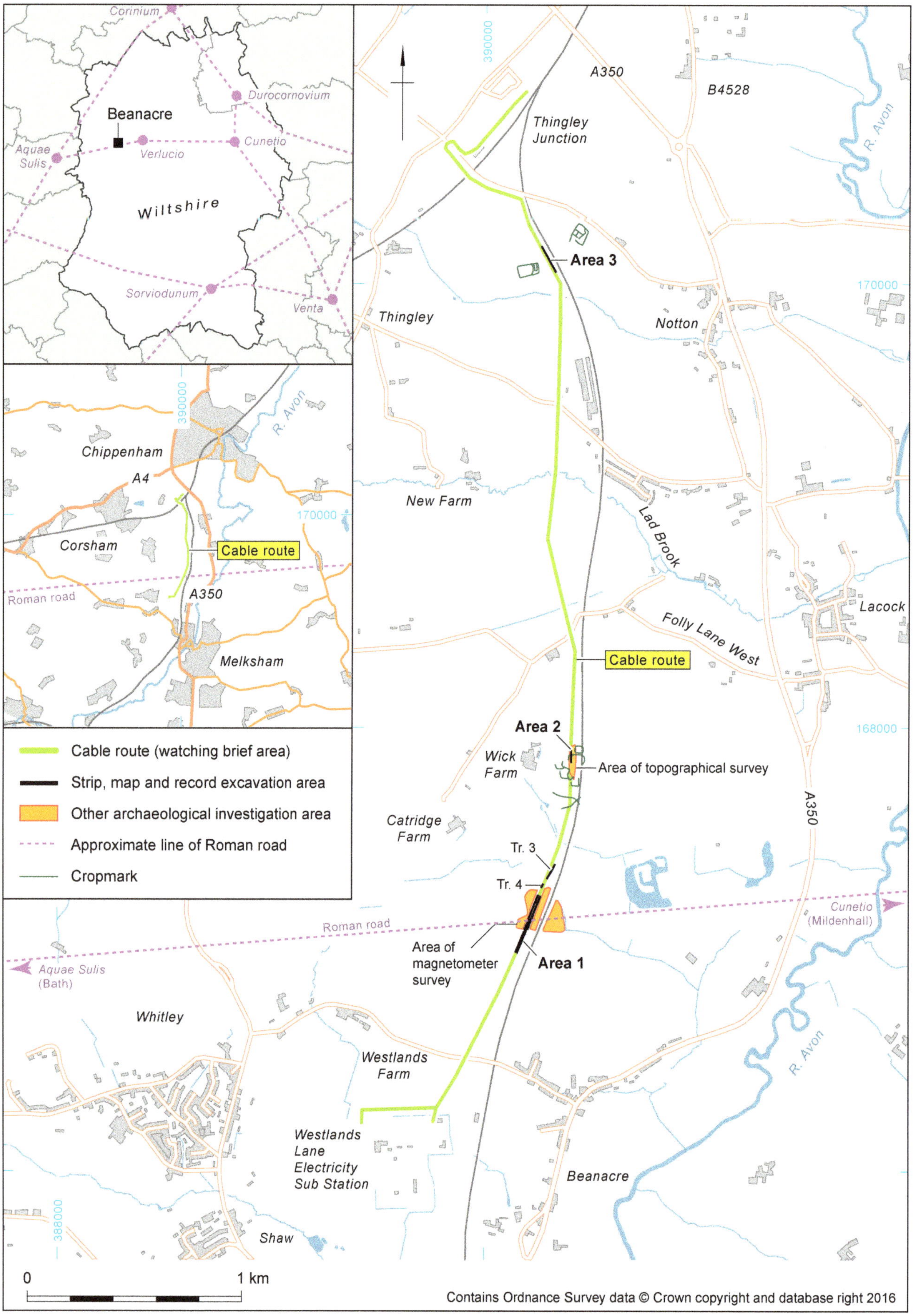

Figure 1.1 Site location, showing cable route and areas of archaeological investigation

restricted to isolated finds and diffuse scatters of Mesolithic and later worked flint, and there are no known prehistoric finds within 1 km of the cable route. However, this apparent paucity of prehistoric activity may simply reflect a lack of archaeological investigations beyond the areas affected by modern development.

There is widespread cropmark evidence for Bronze Age funerary monuments in the area, notably a probable barrow cemetery at Berryfield, to the south of Melksham. Probable barrows have also been identified at Lacock Abbey and near Shurnhold Farm and Frying Pan Farm, to the west of Melksham. There are a further three possible barrows at Thingley Farm and Thingley Junction, both within 150 m of the northern end of the cable route (Wiltshire Council 2018).

Romano-British

There is more evidence for Romano-British activity in the area, most notably a Roman road that crosses the cable route within Area 1. The Roman road linked settlements of *Aquae Sulis* (Bath) and *Cunetio* (Mildenhall), via the small town of *Verlucio*. The line of the Roman road is defined by extant field boundaries, earthworks and cropmarks, which are clearly visible for several kilometres to the east and west of the cable route. The Roman road crossed the River Avon 1.5 km to the east of the excavation area. Underwater archaeological investigations in this location uncovered substantial stone footings (CBA Wessex and CBA South West 1969, 49), which may be the remains of a bridge.

There are several known Roman rural settlements in the surrounding area (Fig. 1.2), including villas at Nuthills Farm (Marquess of Lansdown 1929), possibly Bromham (Oliver 1881) and Atworth (Shaw Mellor and Goodchild 1942; Erskine and Ellis 2008). Lower status farm sites have been identified at Showell Farm (Cotswold Archaeological Trust 1999; Young and Hancocks 2006), Milbourne Farm (Oxford Archaeological Unit 1991), Pockeridge Farm (Burn 1944; Wessex Archaeology 2000) and Bath Road, Melksham (Powell 2018). Nuthills Farm and Bromham villas are both located in the hinterland of *Verlucio*, approximately 6 km to the east of Area 1, whilst Atworth villa is situated to the south of the Roman road, 4.5 km west of the cable route. Showell Farm and Milborne Farm are both located on the gravel terrace overlooking the River Avon, 1 km to the east of Thingley Junction.

In addition to the known Romano-British settlement sites, the Wiltshire Historic Environment Record (WHER) and Portable Antiquities Scheme (PAS) record numerous finds of Roman material within 1 km of the cable route, many of which were found near Area 1.

Roman finds are particularly numerous in Lacock village and to the south of Folly Lane West, which suggests possible settlement activity in both locations. There are also concentrations of finds along the line of the Roman road, notably within a broad swathe that extends for up to 0.9 km to the east of Area 1. There is a further scatter of Roman finds 0.5 km to the west of Area 1, which may indicate the location of a separate settlement. Prior to the commencement of the archaeological work in 2015, a silver Roman finger-ring had been found within Area 1 (Hinds 2007). Finds from the fields to the east of Area 1 include Roman pottery and numerous coins (Ellis 2001) and a hoard of 93 late 3rd-century Barbarous Radiates (Ghey 2015). Most of the other coins from this area also date from the late 3rd or 4th century. Three Roman brooches and a bronze mount in the form of a human bust were recovered from the area to the east of the site. One of the brooches dates from the 1st century AD (Hinds 2008). Tellingly, perhaps, the coin hoard was found in a field named 'Blacklands' on the 1839 Melksham tithe apportionment. This name, probably derived from the colour of the soil, is frequently associated with Romano-British settlement sites (eg, Richardson 1996, 459; Wessex Archaeology 2007; Barber *et al.* 2013; Wilkinson 2013). Since 2015, there have been further finds of coins and metalwork, which are discussed by Henry in Chapter 3.

Saxon

There are no known Saxon remains in the immediate vicinity of the cable route. The villages of Lacock and Whitley are, however, both recorded in the *Domesday* Survey of AD 1086 (Williams and Martin 1992, 163, 177), which indicates that they were in existence by the late Saxon period. The *Domesday* Survey also records two mills in Corsham, both of which were probably situated near Thingley (Wiltshire Council 2011a). Extensive areas of woodland are also recorded in the manors of Lacock, Chippenham and Melksham (Darby and Welldon Finn 1967, 39; Williams and Martin 1992, 163, 177).

Medieval documents refer to part of the Roman road between Bath and western end of the East Wansdyke as the *Wadensdich* or *Wodenes Ditch*, which suggests that it was considered to be part of the early medieval boundary of the same name (Harvey 1998, 76–89; Grundy 1939, 576–9). The identification of the Roman road with the Wansdyke persisted into the post-medieval period and the name appears on a 1775 map of the Methuen Estate (Wiltshire Records Office 1742/8663).

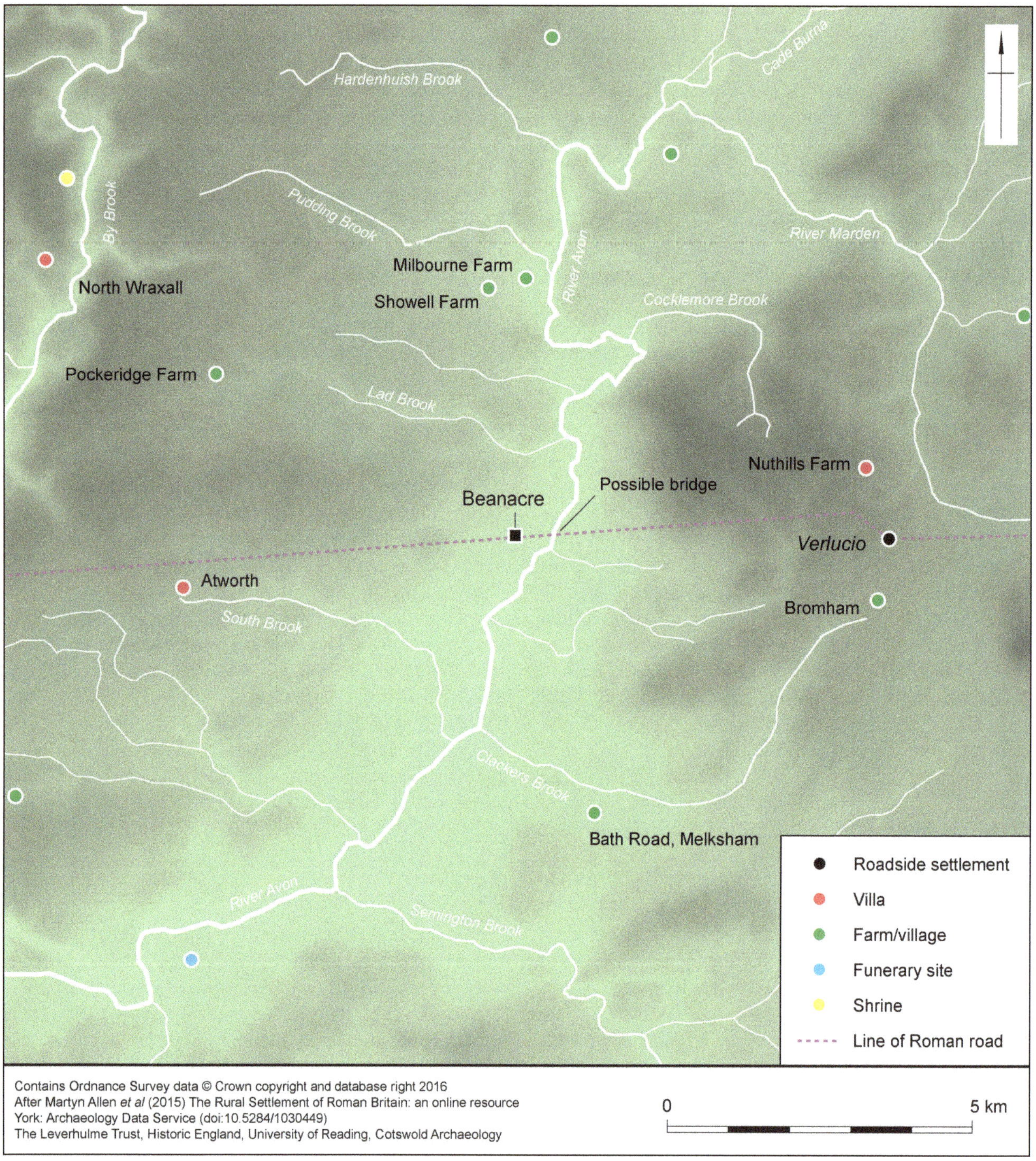

Figure 1.2 Location of the site in relation to selected nearby Romano-British settlements, villas and other sites

Medieval and Later

After the Norman Conquest, Lacock manor was granted to Edward of Salisbury and by the 13th century it was held by Ela, Countess of Salisbury. In 1229, Ela granted the manor to the church, and in 1232 she founded the Augustinian Nunnery of Lacock. The manor remained a monastic possession until the Dissolution. In 1540, the manor was purchased by William Sharington; it then passed by marriage to the Talbot family, who retained ownership of the estate until 1944 (Wiltshire Council 2011b).

Melksham manor was a royal possession from the late Saxon period to the 13th century. It was subsequently held by Amesbury Priory. From 1275 onwards, Melksham Beanacre is recorded as a separate manor, which was also held by Amesbury Priory. Melksham Beanacre was subsequently taken by the Crown, who sold it to the first of a succession

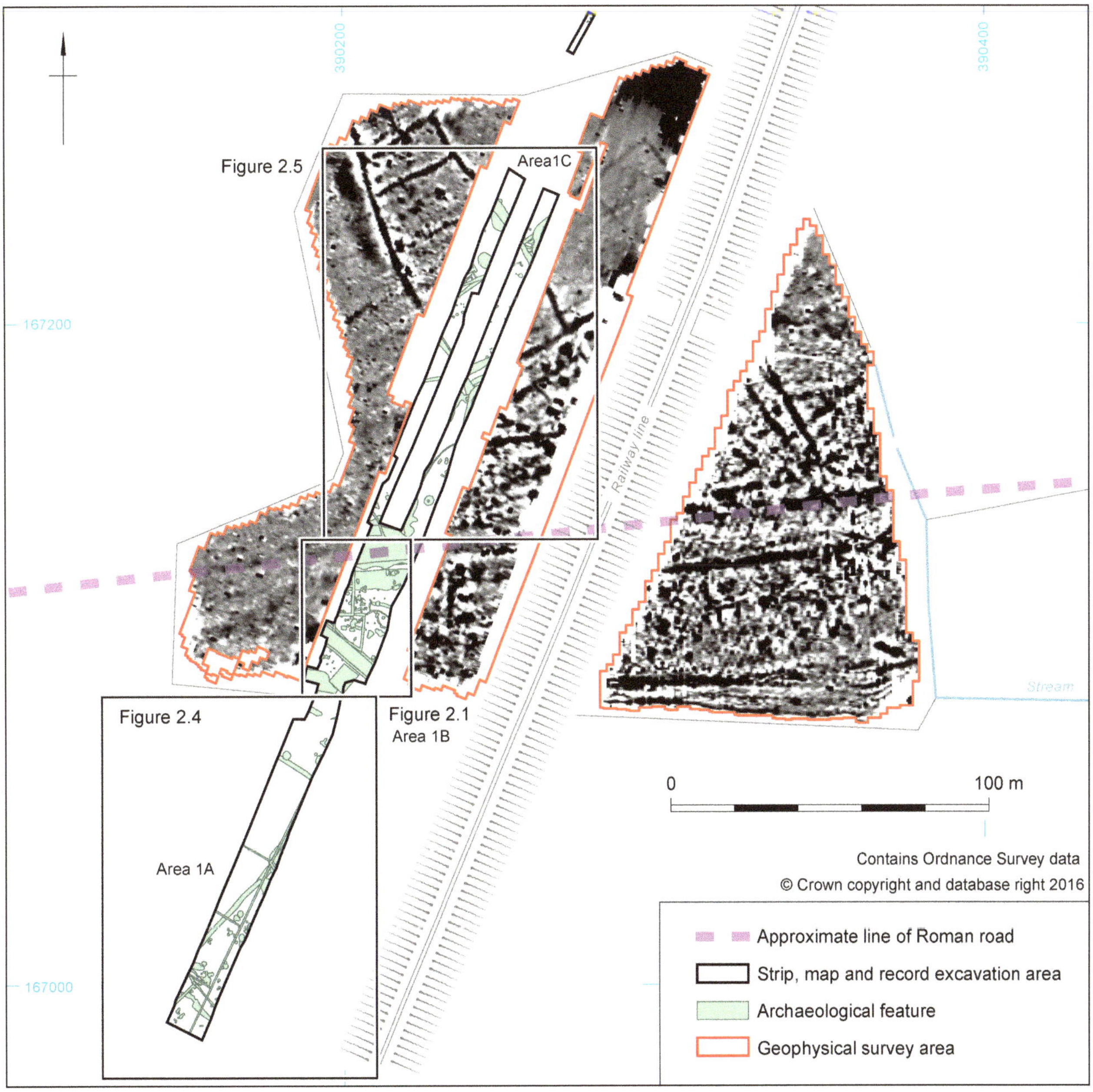

Figure 1.3 Archaeological features shown in relation to geophysical survey areas

of secular owners. In the late 17th century the manor was purchased by Paul Methuen, and it remained part of the Methuen estate until the 20th century (Chettle *et al.* 1953).

There are no known medieval remains within the cable route. However, the nearby villages of Shaw, Beanacre and Thingley all have medieval origins (Chettle *et al.* 1953; Wiltshire Council 2011a), as do Wick Farm and Little Notton Farm (Gover *et al.* 1939, 104; Lake and Edwards 2014). Catridge Farm existed by the 16th century (Historic England 2017a), whilst Upper Beanacre Farm, Westlands (formerly West Knolls) Farm and New Farm all date from the 18th century (Historic England 2017b–d).

During the medieval period, large parts of Melksham and Chippenham manors lay within the royal forests of Pewsham and Melksham, much of which were wooded. There would also have been extensive areas of agricultural land, particularly around the villages and farms that are known to have existed during this period.

Two fields to the south and east of Wick Farm and Catridge Farm are identified on 1764 and 1841 maps as 'The Grange' and 'Grange Mead' (Wiltshire Records Office 2664/1/2E/19/L; T/A). This name could indicate the presence of a medieval monastic grange immediately to the west of the cable route. Indeed, there are a number of undated earthworks and cropmarks in this location, some of which extended into Area 2. These features are indicative of former hollow-ways, field boundaries or possibly more extensive settlement activity (Wessex Archaeology 2006, 11). The form of these features and their proximity to Wick Farm suggests that they are medieval.

The only significant modern development in the immediate vicinity of the cable route was the construction of the Great Western Railway Main Line in 1841 and the Wilts, Somerset and Weymouth Railway branch line in 1848 (Maggs 1982). Both lines remain in use.

The Site

Area 1

During the initial topsoil stripping, a large quantity of Romano-British pottery was found close to the line of the Roman road in Area 1. As a result, WCAS requested that a 100 m long section of the easement to the north and south of the Roman road be subject to a strip, map and record excavation. Once the subsoil had been stripped, it became clear that the course of the Roman road, which was most clearly defined by a (later) hollow-way, was flanked by a large, and previously unknown, Romano-British settlement that extended beyond the initial area of excavation in both directions. Thus WCAS asked that the area of investigation be enlarged to determine the extent of the settlement within the easement. This eventually entailed stripping a 277 m long by 15 m wide area, which was subsequently excavated under controlled archaeological conditions. The excavation area was subdivided into three 'zones' of activity: 1A, 1B and 1C (see Fig. 1.3), and investigated according to an agreed methodology (Wessex Archaeology 2014b). In order to determine the northern extent of the settlement a further two evaluation trenches, measuring 70 m by 2 m and 13 m by 2 m respectively, were excavated in the field immediately to the north of the main excavation area; these proved to be largely sterile and, therefore, no further work was undertaken in these locations. Wessex Archaeology also voluntarily undertook a geophysical survey of two fields adjacent to Area 1 (Fig. 1.3). The geophysical survey demonstrated that the exposed archaeological remains formed part of a larger settlement that extended for at least 200 m along the Roman road.

Area 2

Several undated (but possibly medieval) earthworks and cropmarks lay in this area, at least two of which extended into Area 2 (see Fig. 1.1). After the topsoil had been removed, a topographic survey was undertaken and two 24 m x 2 m evaluation trenches were excavated along the line of the western cable trench. No archaeological remains were found in either trench and, therefore, no further work was undertaken in this area.

Area 3

Area 3 lay between two well defined but undated cropmark complexes (see Fig. 1.1), the grouping of the constituent enclosures suggesting farmsteads of perhaps later prehistoric or Roman date. The initial plan was to excavate an evaluation trench after the topsoil had been removed. However, it became apparent during the initial strip that the topsoil directly overlay undisturbed natural geology, with no archaeological features present and no finds.

Chapter 2
The Excavations

Prehistoric

The earliest evidence of human activity on the site is a small assemblage of worked flint blades and a microdenticulate of Neolithic or possibly Mesolithic date, all of which were found as residual finds in later contexts. Whilst the quantities of early prehistoric worked flint are small, their presence does indicate that the area was at least occasionally visited during this period.

There is slightly more evidence of Bronze Age activity comprising posthole 1521 and pit 1525. These features were associated with a further four undated postholes, probably of a similar date, which were clustered together in the centre of Area 1C (see Fig. 2.5). The pit and posthole contained a few abraded sherds of Bronze Age pottery and some struck flint, though none of the finds were particularly diagnostic or closely datable. The features formed no clear pattern and their function remains uncertain, however they may indicate occupation on or near the site at some time during the second millennium BC.

Early Romano-British

There is a clear hiatus in activity on the site between the Bronze Age and the Roman period, which suggests that the Romano-British settlement was established on what was essentially a virgin site. Finds of mid-1st-century AD pottery and metalwork provide evidence for some form of activity, probably occupation, on the site by this date.

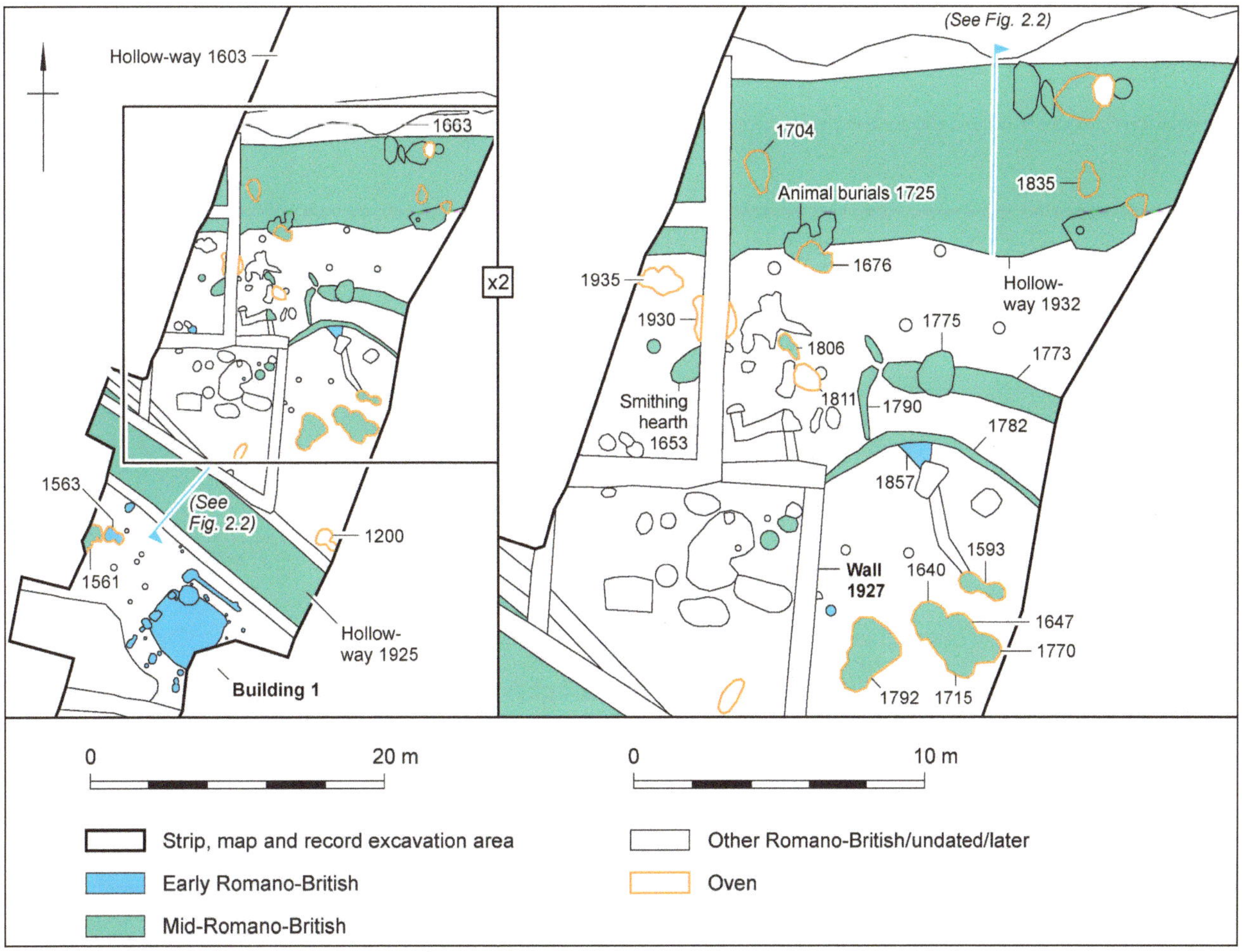

Figure 2.1 Plan of early and mid-Romano-British features in Area 1B

Plate 2.1 Hollow-way 1925, looking west

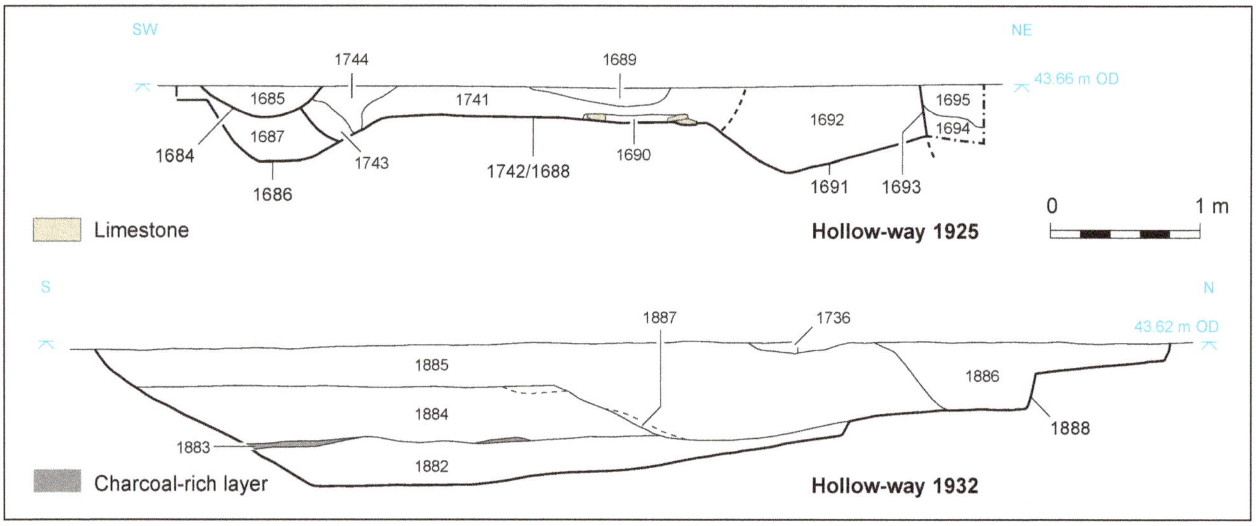

Figure 2.2 Sections of mid-Romano-British hollow-ways 1925 and 1932

Roads and Trackways

The excavation site lies along the line of the road between the Roman towns of *Aquae Sulis* (Bath) and *Cunetio* (Mildenhall). The line of this road is defined by extant hedge boundaries and cropmarks that extend for several kilometres to the east and west of the site. Within the easement, the line of the road corresponds with an east–west aligned, 7 m wide by 0.4 m deep, hollow-way (1603) flanked by thin spreads of gravel (1663) (Fig. 2.1). The hollow-way itself dates from the post-medieval period, whilst the patches of gravel probably represent heavily truncated remains of the Roman road surface. No finds were recovered from the gravel layers. The road is, however, likely to be broadly contemporary with the founding of the nearby settlement of *Verlucio*, which lies mid-way along the road between *Aquae Sulis* and

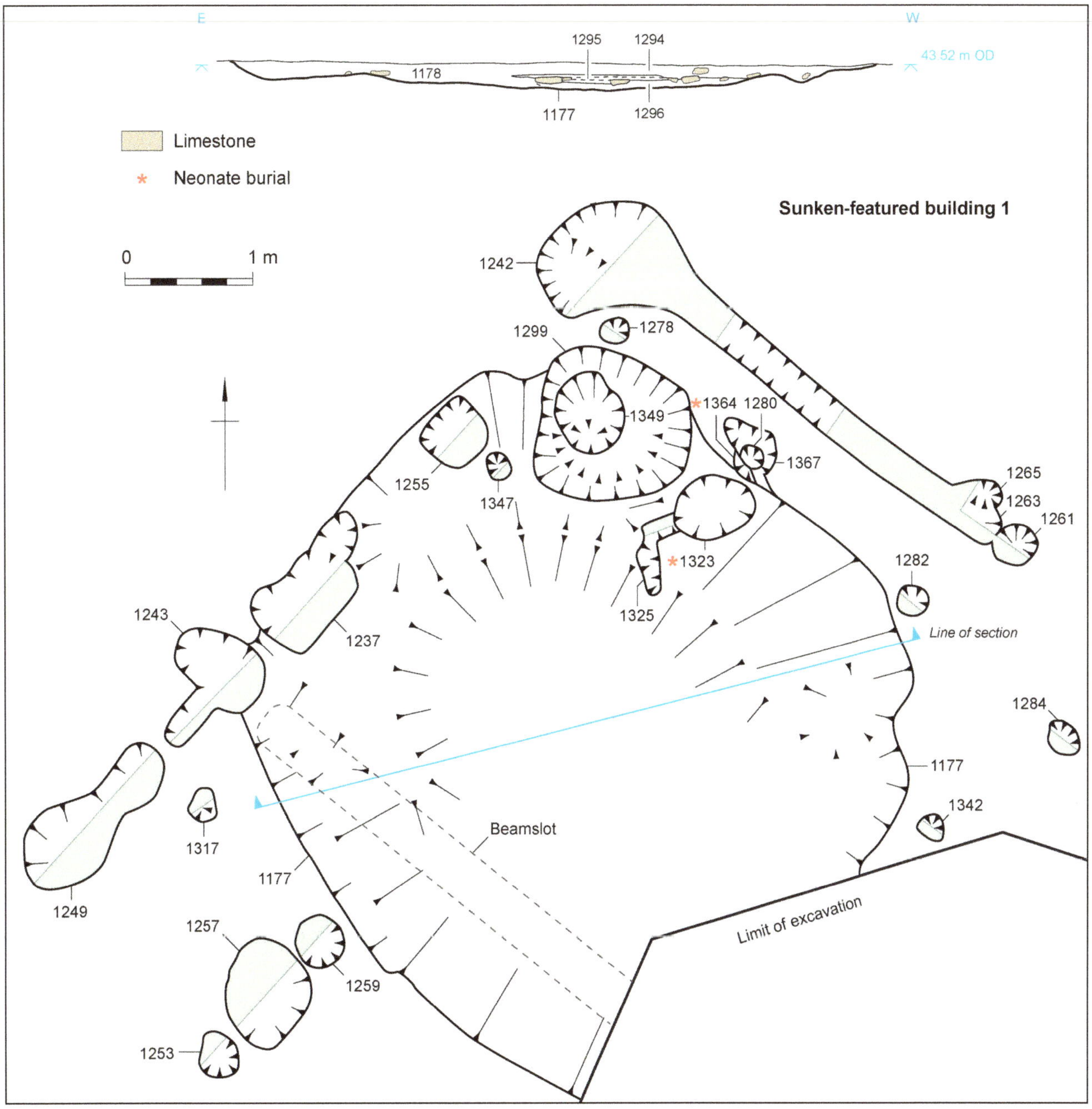

Figure 2.3 Plan and section of early Romano-British sunken-featured building

Cunetio. The origins of *Verlucio* are, at present, poorly understood, however the presence of mid-1st-century finds and analysis of coin data suggests occupation from at least AD 80 onwards (Wiltshire Council Archaeology Service (WCAS) 2004, 8).

Another hollow-way (1925; Pl. 2.1, Fig. 2.2), aligned north-west to south-east, was uncovered 20 m to the south of the inferred line of the main Roman road. Finds from the infill of the hollow-way suggest that it was backfilled and/or silted up in the mid-Romano-British period. However, the presence of a similarly-aligned early Romano-British building alongside the hollow-way (see Building 1, below) suggests that there was a thoroughfare along this line by the late 1st or early 2nd century AD.

There was a third, broad, linear cut (feature 1932) immediately to the south of the inferred line of the main Roman road. Interpretation of this feature, which was infilled with soil that contained mid–late 2nd-century finds, remains uncertain; it may have been another hollow-way, or it could have been a linear roadside quarry. Excavations across the line of the main Roman road between *Londinium* and *Camulodunum* in Old Ford, London, uncovered a similar arrangement of features. In that instance, a raised central 'carriageway' was flanked by two subsidiary trackways, the lower ones possibly for use by pedestrians/livestock. In some places, the subsidiary trackways were constructed over infilled gravel-extraction quarries that flanked the road

(Sheldon 1971, 42, fig. 2; Mills 1984, 26). If feature 1932 is interpreted a subsidiary trackway within a hollow-way, then it seems probable the route it followed would have existed by the early Romano-British period. Feature 1932 is discussed in more detail below.

Building 1

Immediately to the south-west of hollow-way 1925 was a small sunken-featured rectangular structure, defined by beam slots and postholes ranged around a sunken area (Building 1; Figs 2.1 and 2.3). The building appears to have had two phases of construction. The first comprised a sub-rectangular hollow with two rows of small postholes along its south-west and north-east sides. This phase of building encompassed an area of approximately 5.5 m x 5.5 m externally. During the second phase, the hollow was partially infilled, and a row of larger postholes was added along the north-west side of the building. Further large postholes and two beamslots were also added to the north-east and south-west sides of the building. The second phase of building extended its north-east to south-west alignment to approximately 7.3 m externally.

Finds from the basal fill of the sunken area include samian ware dated AD 60–120. Finds from the second phase of the building (later infill of the sunken area and postholes) include samian ware dated AD 50–110.

Charred plant remains (see López-Dóriga, Chapter 4) from the first phase of the building were very rich in hulled wheat and barley grains, many of which were germinated. This could indicate that the building was used for crop processing or possibly brewing, or that these types of activity were occurring nearby.

Two intercutting postholes/pits and two neonate burials (see below) lay in the north corner of the building. Pit/posthole 1349, which was 0.45 m deep and 0.4 m wide, was truncated by pit 1299. The latter had a heat-affected base, but there were no indications of burning on the sides, which suggests that the heating was caused by dumping hot material, such as hearth rakings, in the pit, rather than it being an indication of *in situ* burning. A substantial quantity of pottery, mostly derived from a single large storage jar, was recovered from the base of pit 1299. Most of the pottery from this feature could only be broadly dated to the Romano-Bristol period, but the more closely datable sherds were early Roman and, therefore, broadly contemporary with Building 1.

After the building went out of use, the internal hollow appears to have naturally silted up. Finds associated with the building's abandonment were of a similar date to those associated with its use. The presence of samian ware dated AD 70–110 provides a *terminus post quem* for its abandonment.

Human Burials

There were two neonate burials along the north-eastern edge of Building 1, lying at relatively shallow depth, one in grave 1364 (skeleton 1365), the other in pit 1323 (skeleton 1324) (see Egging Dinwiddy, Chapter 3 for details). The latter feature, which had heat-affected sides, is interpreted as a small hearth that was subsequently cut into by the grave.

Other Features

A north-west to south-east aligned, 1.4 m long by 1 m wide keyhole-shaped oven (1563) was uncovered 4.5 m to the north-west of Building 1 (Fig. 2.1). The oven had a hearth at the southern end and a rake-out pit to the north. The charred plant assemblage from the oven was very similar to that from Building 1, which may indicate that they were contemporary and related.

A heavily truncated ENE–WSW aligned gully (1334) and two shallow pits (1385 and 1857) are also tentatively dated to the early Roman-British period (Figs 2.1, 2.4 and 2.5). The function of these features remains unclear, but the fact that they were widely scattered and few in number suggests that there was relatively little activity away from the road frontage during this period. Samian ware provides a *terminus post quem* of AD 110–130 for gully 1334, AD 50–120 for pit 1385, and AD 50–100 for pit 1857.

Mid-Romano-British

Roads and Trackways

The roads and trackways that were established in the early Romano-British period continued to be used in the mid-Romano-British period. By this date, the route defined by hollow-way 1925 (Fig. 2.1) had been eroded into a 4.8 m wide by 0.35 m deep linear depression. A sequence of shallow ditch cuts was recorded along both flanks of the hollow-way, probably dug to define the route and facilitate drainage. A crude surface of coarse gravel and small stones was recorded in the base of the hollow-way, but there is no evidence that it was ever formally metalled (Fig. 2.2). There were no cart ruts in the trackway, which suggests that it was primarily used by pedestrians and livestock. During the mid-Romano-British period, hollow-way 1925 was infilled with a

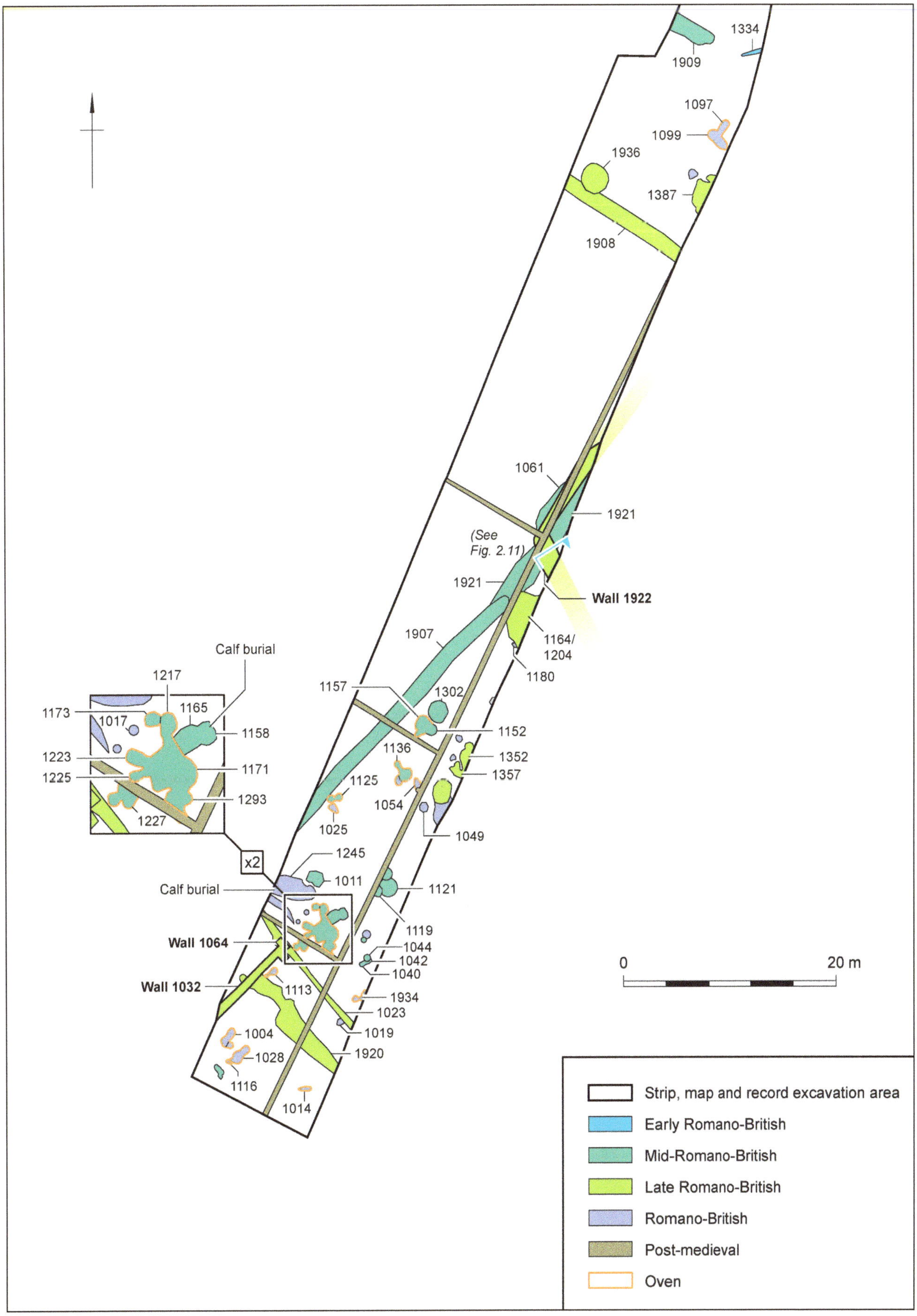

Figure 2.4 Plan of archaeological features in Area 1A

Figure 2.5 Plan of archaeological features in Area 1C

mixture of dumped material and natural silting. It did not, however, go out of use at this date, and during the late Romano-British period the line of the trackway was re-defined by ditches along the same line as their mid-Romano-British precursors. Finds from the infilled hollow-way suggest that it was backfilled and/or silted-up after AD 160, but probably no later than the mid-3rd century AD. Irrespective of the deposition processes involved, the fact that deposits were accumulating in the hollow-way rather than eroding, suggest that it was not as heavily used in the 2nd–3rd century as it was during the 1st–2nd century.

Feature 1932 was a 6 m wide by 0.9 m deep linear cut that ran parallel to the inferred line of the main Roman road. This feature had moderately sloping sides and a slightly sloping, stepped base (Figs 2.1 and 2.2). There was no evidence for any form of surfacing or cart ruts in the base of the cut. There are two possible interpretations of feature 1932: firstly, that it was a subsidiary trackway to the main Roman road; secondly, that it was a roadside quarry. One full section and five smaller slots were excavated across this feature, all of which showed a broadly consistent depth and profile; this could be interpreted as supporting the subsidiary trackway interpretation. If the interpretation of this feature as a trackway, perhaps used for herding livestock, is correct, then the absence of cart ruts would be expected. The absence of a surface is however less easy to explain, as small stones and gravel are likely to have accumulated in any regularly-used thoroughfare. In summary, at present, there is insufficient evidence to determine exactly how or why this feature was created. All that can be determined with any certainty is that it was clearly associated with the adjacent Roman road. Feature 1932 became infilled with what appears to have been a mixture of dumped material and natural silting. Pottery from the infill deposits provides a date of AD 140–200 for its disuse, which in turn provides a *terminus post quem* for the overlying features (see ovens and Building 2, below).

Enclosures

During the mid-Romano-British period two new foci of activity developed. One lay within a north-east to south-west aligned strip across the southern end of the site (Fig. 2.4), the other covered a 40 m wide, north-west to south-east aligned band towards the northern end of the site (Fig. 2.5). Both areas were defined by substantial enclosure ditches.

The north-western extent of the southern zone of activity was defined by ditches 1061, 1907 and 1921. To the south of this line the area was subdivided into a series of rectilinear enclosures that extended beyond

Plate 2.2 Mid-Romano-British ditch 1443, Romano-British ovens 1490 1494 and late Romano-British ditch 1913 and burial 1485, looking north-east

the limits of excavation. Finds and features within these enclosures (ovens, pits and stone-built structures) are indicative of occupation, which suggest that the enclosures were gardens/yards for dwellings or other buildings located immediately to the south-east of the excavated area. The earliest ditch (1921) was up to 2.8 m wide and 0.8 m deep; its fill contained pottery that could only be broadly dated to the Romano-British period. The enclosure could, therefore, conceivably have been laid out in the early Romano-British period. However, the absence of any other early features in this area suggests that it is more likely to be mid-Romano-British. Ditch 1907, which was up to 1.6 m wide and 0.75 m deep, was probably a re-cut of ditch 1921. Ditch 1061, which was over 1 m wide and 0.3 m deep, defined the corner of an enclosure that followed the same alignment as late Romano-British wall 1922. Samian ware from ditches 1907 and 1061 provides a *terminus post quem* for their infilling of AD 140–200 and AD 145–65 respectively. However, the fact that the line of these ditches continued to be respected by other, late Romano-British features suggests that the boundary they defined remained extant in the 3rd–4th century, probably in the form of a hedge and/or bank.

The northern zone of activity was defined by two parallel ditches (1422/1938 and 1516/1914) which formed part of a 'ladder' field system that extended to the north-east beyond the limits of excavation (Fig. 2.5). These ditches, which were 1.4–3.2 m wide and 0.6–1.1 m deep, were re-cut and maintained into the late Romano-British period, however finds from the lower fills, which included a coin of AD 117, suggest that the initial silting occurred in the 2nd–3rd century AD. The geophysical survey showed that the field system extended for at least 85 m along a north-west to south-east alignment (see Fig. 1.3). The individual enclosures measured 23–34 m north-east to south-

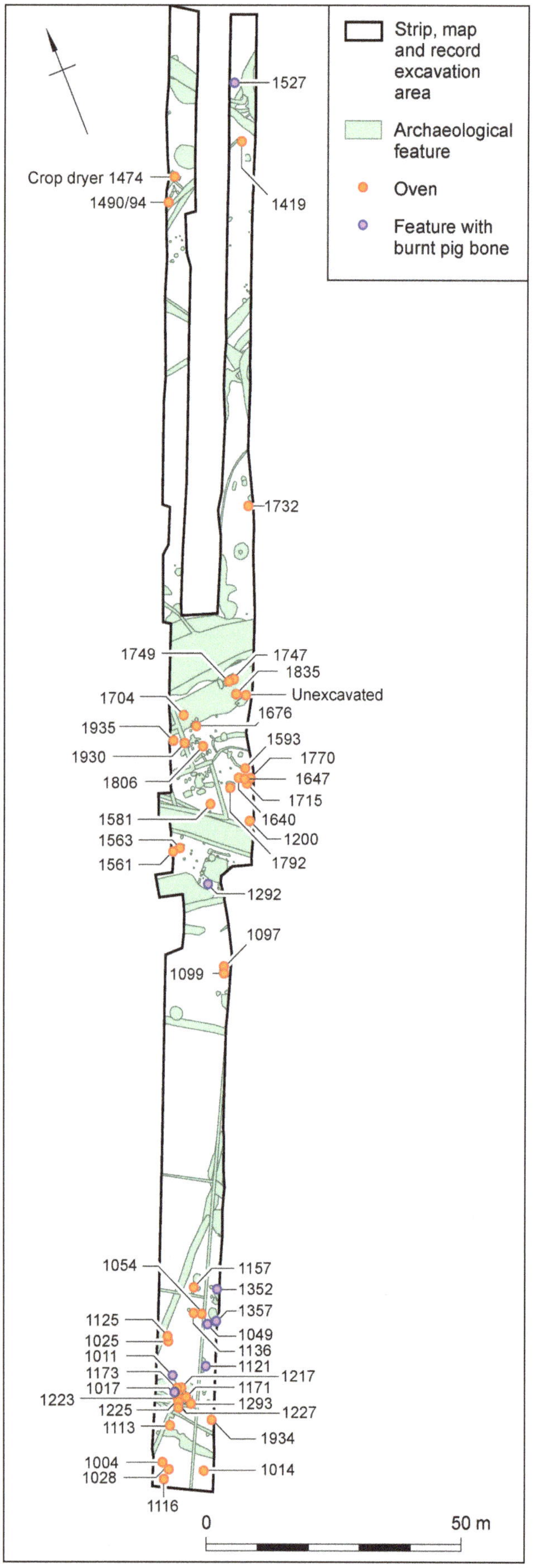

Figure 2.6 Plan of Romano-British ovens and features containing burnt pig bones

Plate 2.3 Mid-Romano-British oven 1792, looking north-east

west, by 10–25 m south-east to north-west (approximately 0.23–0.85 ha each). Although various postholes and post-pads were recorded within the enclosures, there was no conclusive evidence for buildings. This, and the size of the enclosures, suggests that they were primarily for horticulture or animal husbandry.

North-east to south-west aligned ditches 1410 and 1443 (Pl. 2.2) measured 2.3 m wide, 0.6 m deep and 1.1 m wide, 0.72 m deep respectively. Finds from their fills indicate a similar, 2nd–3rd century AD date for their infilling. Samian ware from 1443 provides a *terminus post quem* of AD 120–200 for this event. Ditch 1499, which was parallel to ditch 1410 and measured 1.6 m wide and 0.75 m deep, pre-dated ditch 1938, but could only be broadly dated to the Romano-British period on finds evidence. However, given the date of the adjacent features, a mid-Romano-British date seems probable.

Ditch 1503 was 0.45 m wide and 0.3 m deep, and was the earliest of a cluster of ditches towards the northern end of Area 1C; it may have been a continuation of ditch 1443. Finds suggest a probable 2nd–3rd-century date for its silting. Ditch 1503 was cut by mid-/late Romano-British ditch 1506 and late Romano-British ditches 1914 and 1937.

In Area 1A ditch 1909, which was parallel to, and 16 m to the south-west of hollow-way 1925, appears to have formed a boundary to an area of intense

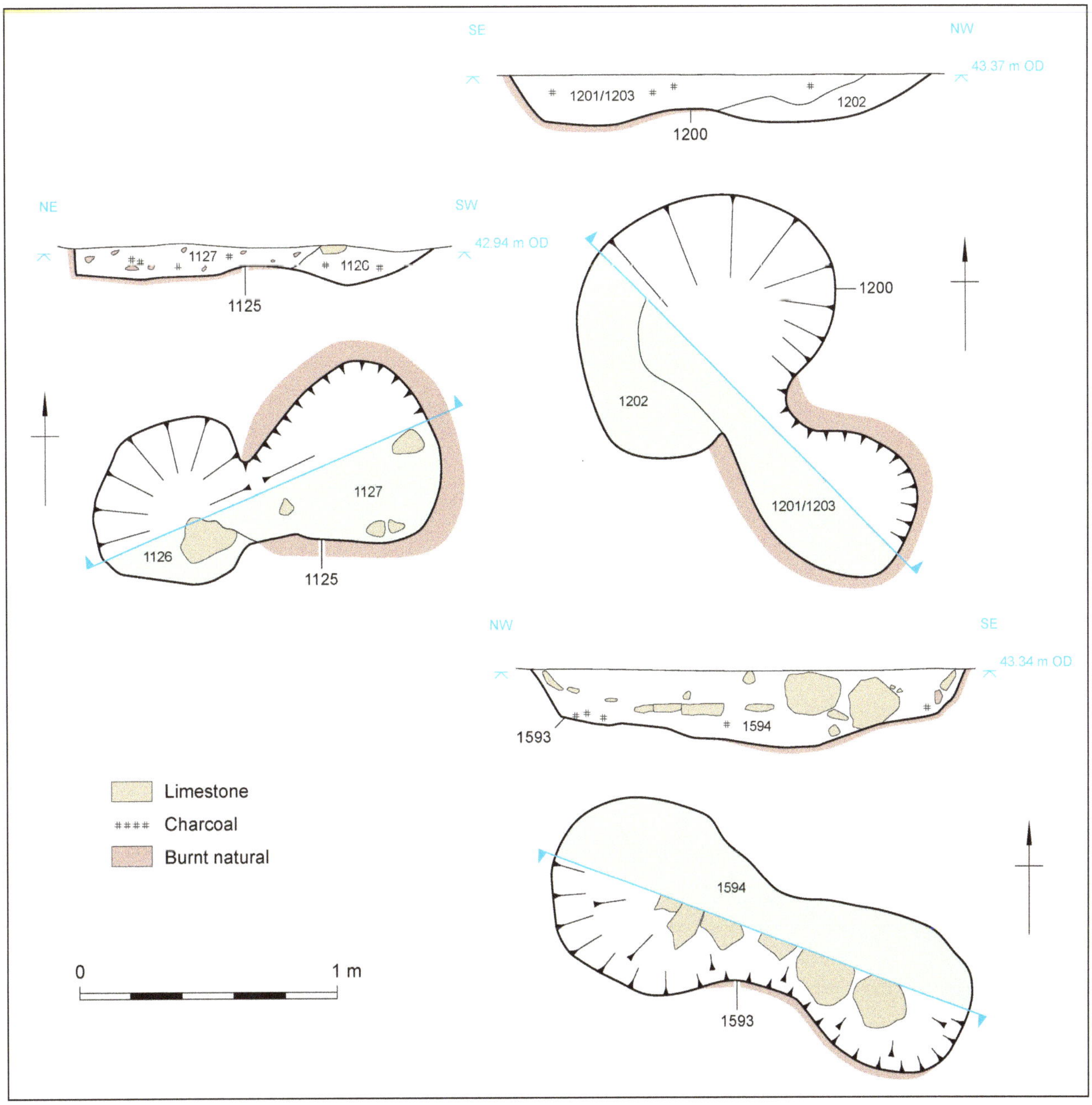

Figure 2.7 Plans and sections of Romano-British ovens 1125, 1200 and 1593

activity along the roadside (Fig. 2.4). Ditch 1909 was 1.5 m wide, but only survived to a depth of 0.15 m, which suggests that this area had been heavily truncated by later agricultural activity. The ditch appears to have silted up in the 2nd–3rd century.

Ovens

One of the most characteristic features of the Beanacre site was the profusion of ovens, 41 in total, all but two of which appear to date from the mid-Romano-British period (see Figs 2.6–2.8; Pls 2.3–7, Table 2.1). Most of the ovens were clustered in two distinct areas: one in Area 1A, to the south of ditch 1907; the other in Area 1B, between ditch 1908 and hollow-way 1603. There were a further three ovens scattered across Area 1C.

Most of the ovens were keyhole- or hourglass-shaped, and comprised a sunken hearth linked to an ash rake-out pit via a short flue. Thirteen of the ovens had some form of locally-quarried ragstone lining, though in four instances the lining was only present in the flue or base. Oven 1792, the largest example, was notable in that it was the only example with a stone-floored rake out pit. It was 2.47 m long, 1.1 m wide and 0.47 m deep (Fig. 2.8, Pl. 2.3), but most were 1.5–2.0 m long, 0.5–1.5 m wide and less than 0.4 m deep. The smallest oven (1116; Pl. 2.4) was only 0.4 m long, 0.25 m wide and 0.2 m deep. Oven 1116

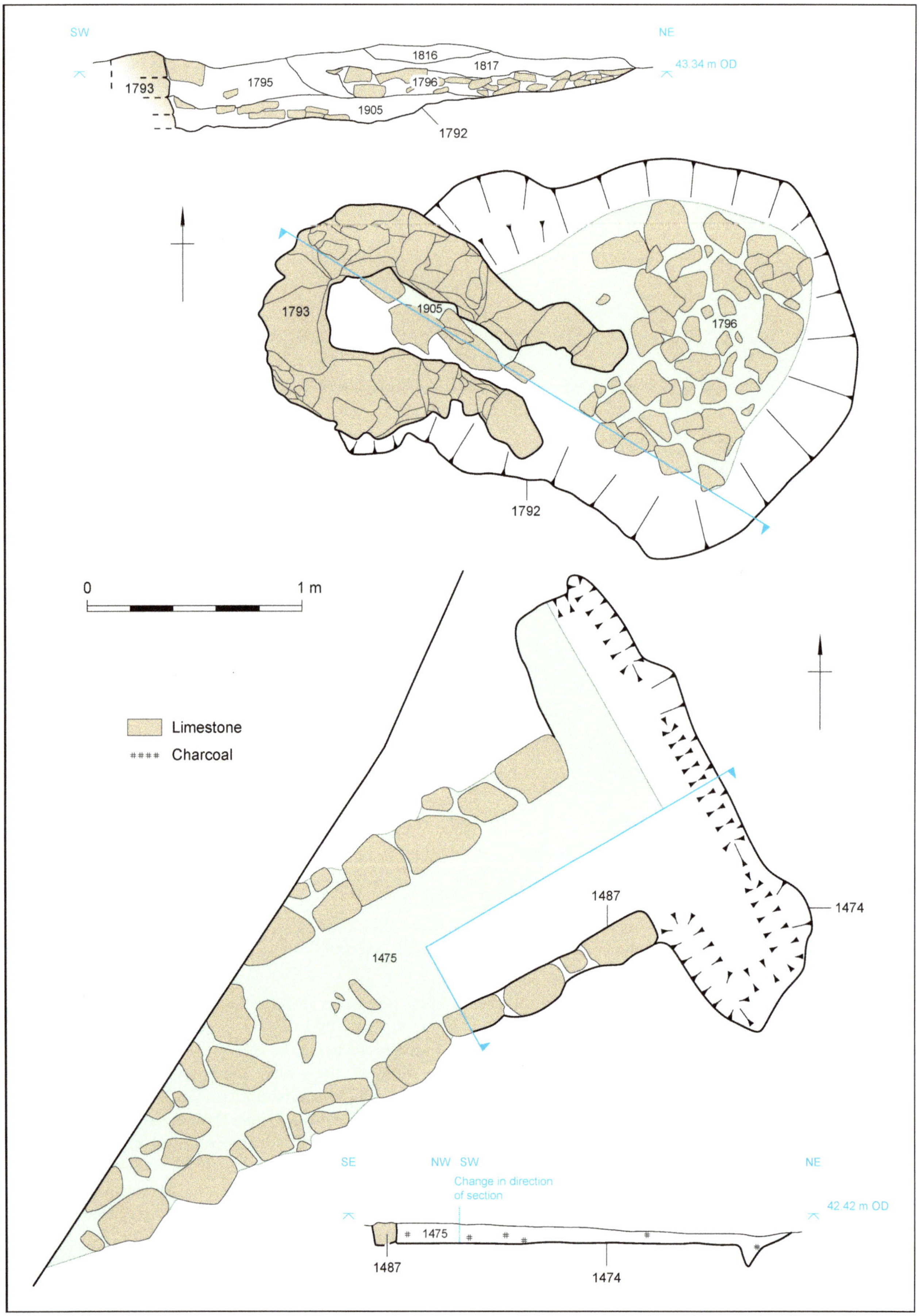

Figure 2.8 Plans and sections of Romano-British oven 1792 and crop drying oven 1474

Plate 2.4 *Mid-Romano-British oven 1116, looking west*

Plate 2.5 *Romano-British oven 1200, looking north*

Plate 2.6 *Mid-Romano-British ovens 1173, 1217, 1223, 1227 and 1293, and rake out pit 1171, looking north-west*

Plate 2.7 *Mid-Romano-British ovens 1640, 1647, 1715 and 1770, looking east*

could only ever have been used to cook very small amounts of food, and given this apparent impracticality, a plausible interpretation is that this could have been a 'practice oven', perhaps constructed by, or for, a child. Oven 1200 (Pl. 2.5) provides a good example of one of the unlined ovens, in this case with only slight evidence for burning. A copper alloy ear scoop was recovered from the oven (Fig. 3.12, 12).

There were two clusters of ovens that appear to have been ranged around common working/rake-out areas. Some, though not all, of the ovens in these clusters appear to have been in contemporary use. One of these clusters (Pl. 2.6), which comprised ovens 1217, 1225, 1223, 1217 and 1293 and rake out pit 1171, was situated to the south of ditch 1907 in Area 1A (Fig. 2.4). The other group (Pl. 2.7), comprising ovens 1593, 1640, 1647, 1715, 1770 and 1792, was located in a 'working hollow' in Area 1B, between hollow-way 1925 and a group of shallow (0.15 m deep) ditches/gullies (1773, 1782 and 1790) (Fig. 2.1). These ditches probably flanked a bank that helped shelter and/or divert water around the 'working hollow'. Samian ware from the ditch fills provides a *terminus post quem* of AD 120–200 for their silting. The ovens in the second group, near hollow-way 1925, were sealed by an extensive soil layer (1602) that contained a large assemblage of 2nd–3rd-century pottery, including samian ware dated AD 125–200, and a coin of AD 140.

Table 2.1 A summary of the Romano-British ovens

Cut	*Orientation*	*Length (m)*	*Width (m)*	*Depth (m)*	*No. of fills*	*Stone-lined (Y/N)*	*Pottery (no/g)*	*Animal bone (g)*	*Fired clay (g)*	*Slag (g)*	*Other*	*Charred plant taxa from environmental samples*
1004	NNE–SSW	1.97	0.76	0.18	4	Y (base only)	–	–	16	–	–	n/a
1014	W–E	1.15	0.5	0.19	2	N	2/18	–	–	–	–	n/a
1025	(SE–NW)	1.28	0.45	0.09	2	N	8/19	5/2	–	–	–	n/a
1028	NE–SW	2.1	0.9	0.25	2	Y	–	3/14	–	–	–	n/a
1054	SSE–NNW	0.88	0.44	0.12	2	N	1/1	–	52	–	–	n/a
1097	SW–NE	1	0.5	0.15	1	N	9/41	7/12	234	743	–	n/a
1099	SE–NW	1.4	0.6	0.15	1	N	23/141	5/3	234	–	–	n/a
1113	SW–NE	1.3	0.66	0.15	1	N	1/8	10/83	1	–	–	n/a
1116	SE–NW	0.4	0.25	0.2	1	N	2/12	1/6	–	–	–	n/a
1125	SW–NE	1.39	0.7	0.14	2	N	17/333	2/2	–	606	–	n/a
1136	SE–NW	2	0.6	0.34	6	N	61/473	28/88	14	–	2 Fe hobnails/tacks, 2 vessel glass	n/a
1157	NE–SW	1.44	0.98	0.45	5	N	64/920	16/262	-	–	ON 6 (Cu al. brooch), 1 Fe nail	n/a
1173	E–W	1.4	0.6	0.35	3	N	39/310	21/34	94	–	1 Pb scrap	n/a
1200	NW–SE	1.64	1.23	0.19	3	N	12/173	8/22	80	–	ON 21 (Cu al. ear scoop), 1 Fe nail	n/a
1217	S–N	1.1	0.55	0.15	1	N	16/88	1/2	–	–	1 Fe	n/a
1223	SE–NW	1.4	0.6	0.4	4	Y	18/163	23/61	77	–	1 Fe hobnail/tack	n/a
1225	ENE–WSW	1.35	0.46	0.31	6	Y (flue only)	–	–	159	–	–	n/a
1227	ENE–WSW	1.4	1.3	0.25	5	N	43/368	4/5	–	–	–	n/a
1293	NNE–SSW	1.1	0.8	0.19	2	Y (flue only)	15/148	6/13	218	–	1 Fe hobnail/tack, 1 Fe nail	n/a
1419	SE–NW	1.18	0.32	0.31	2	N	11/110	28/43	–	–	1 CBM	n/a
1490	(S–N)	0.5	0.35	0.12	1	N	–	–	–	–	–	n/a
1494	SW–NE	1.22	0.58	0.26	2	Y	4/34	1/8	–	55	–	*Vicia/Lathyrus*, *Avena/Bromus*, *Trifolium/Medicago*, *Triticum* sp.
1561	NE–SW	1.9	1.1	0.22	1	N	4/25	14/10	–	–	–	*Rumex* sp., *Galium* sp., *Triticum* sp.
1563	NW–SE	1.35	0.9	0.1	1	N	9/30	–	–	–	–	*Vicia/Lathyrus*, *Poa/Phleum*, *Rumex* sp., *Trifolium/Medicago*, *Triticum* sp., *Hordeum vulgare*
1581	(NE–SW)	1.6	0.6	0.13	3	Y	4/100	1/1	–	–	1 Fe nail	*Vicia/Lathyrus*
1593	NW–SE	1.7	0.65	0.28	1	N	28/680	2/2	34	33	ON 83 (Fe nail)	*Avena/Bromus*, *Vicia/Lathyrus*, *Trifolium/Medicago*, *Rumex* sp., *Triticum* sp. *Crataegus* sp., *Chenopodium* sp., *Plantago* sp.
1640	NW–SE	1.9	0.87	0.19	5	Y	10/50	1/1	–	–	1 Fe nail	n/a
1647	NW–SE	2.2	1.4	0.3	4	Y	2/14	15/27	–	1	ON 98 (Cu al. scrap), 1 Fe hobnail/tack	*Avena/Bromus*, *Vicia/Lathyrus*, *Rumex* sp., *Brassica* sp., *Triticum* sp.
1676	NW–SE	1.12	0.35	0.11	2	N	–	8/9	101	82	1 Fe disc	*Brassica* sp., *Avena/Bromus*, *Hordeum vulgare*
1704	S–N	1.48	0.7	0.06	2	Y	1/6	–	–	6	–	*Vicia/Lathyrus*
1715	NW–SE	1.4	0.7	0.2	7	Y	15/42	19/11	28	–	1 Fe	*Avena/Bromus*, *Triticum* sp.
1732	SE–NW	1.68	0.58	0.22	3	N	10/43	2/2	–	14	–	*Triticum* sp.
1747	(E–W)	0.94	0.6	0.24	1	N	6/76	1/6	28	–	–	–
1749	(E–W)	1.8	1.3	0.22	2	N	–	–	–	–	–	n/a
1770	SE–NW	1.15	0.95	0.25	1	Y	–	–	–	–	–	n/a
1792	NNE–SSW	2.47	1.1	0.43	6	Y	29/322	2/9	153	53	–	*Lolium/Festuca*, *Trifolium/Medicago*, *Triticum* sp.
1806	SE–NW	0.99	0.53	0.22	3	N	13/189	3/7	–	49	–	*Vicia/Lathyrus*, Triticeae
1835	N–S	1.15	0.65	0.28	1	N	16/96	3/5	–	105	-	*Avena/Bromus*, *Bromus* sp., *Triticum* sp.
1930	SE–NW	1.76	1.64	0.1	4	N	11/21	3/3	–	23	1 Fe	–
1934	NE–SW	1.7	1	0.26	4	N	26/150	9/24	–	871	1 Fe hobnail/tack, 1 Pb scrap	–
1935	(W–E)	1.6	1	0.2	3	N	8/13	26/38	–	–	1 Fe nail	*Avena/Bromus*, *Vicia/Lathyrus*, *Trifolium/Medicago*, *Heather type stem*, *Triticum* sp.

KEY: Orientation: stokehole-chamber (in brackets if uncertain); Fe – iron; Cu al. – copper alloy; Pb – lead; CBM – ceramic building material

Ovens 1676, 1704, 1747 and 1835 were all constructed in the top of infilled hollow-way 1932 (Figs 2.1 and see 2.9); samian ware from the hollow-way provides a *terminus post quem* of AD 140–200 for their construction. It therefore seems probable that most the ovens in Area 1B date from the second half of the 2nd century AD and many of those in Area 1A are likely to be of a similar date.

Analysis of environmental samples from the ovens and their associated rake-out pits produced a relatively rich assemblage of charred plant remains, charcoal and burnt pig bones, which suggests mixed uses including cooking, probably their primary function, but possibly also malting. The evidence for the use of the ovens is discussed in more detail by Challinor, Higbee and López-Dóriga in Chapter 4.

Smithing Hearth

The main evidence for metalworking on the site during the mid-Romano-British period was a 1.4 m by 0.8 m wide by 0.35 m deep hearth (1653, Fig. 2.1) in Area 1B, the base of which had clearly been subjected to intense heat. The backfill of the pit, which was also heat-affected, contained iron smithing slag, burnt clay and charcoal, some hammerscale and pottery of probably 2nd–3rd-century date. The hearth was truncated by the foundations of Building 3, which suggests that the metalworking activity was broadly contemporary with the adjacent ovens. The evidence for metalworking is discussed in more detail by Andrews in Chapter 3.

Pits

A small number of pits of mid-Romano-British date were recorded across the site. Most were fairly shallow sub-circular or amorphous features of indeterminate function. A much larger, oval pit (1414), measuring at least 4.6 m by 3.3 m and 0.5 m deep, was recorded in Area 1C (Fig. 2.5). The function of this feature remains unclear, but clay extraction for construction purposes (eg, for daub for walls or oven-lining) is a possibility. Finds from the backfill include 2nd–3rd-century pottery and a silver *denarius* issued in AD 192.

In Area 1A were two relatively large pits (1302 and 1165) with steep straight sides (Fig. 2.1). Pit 1302 was sub-circular in plan and measured 1.7–1.9 m wide by 1 m deep; its backfill contained 2nd–3rd century pottery, including a fragment from a possible face pot (Fig. 3.6, 26), and a copper alloy nail cleaner (Fig 3.12, 11). Pit 1165 was sub-rectangular and measured 1 m by 1.2 m wide and 0.85 m deep. Pit 1165 truncated oven 1217 and rake out pit 1171, and was itself cut by mid-Romano-British calf burial 1158 (Pl. 2.8). Finds from the backfill of pit 1165 include samian ware dating to AD 150–200 and other 2nd century or later pottery, and a copper alloy spoon (Fig. 3.12, 14). The function of pits 1165 and 1302 is unknown, though refuse disposal and/or use as latrines are both possibilities, and the environmental evidence for use was inconclusive.

Shallow pit/scoop 1011 in Area 1A was notable for the presence of large quantities of burnt pig bones and charcoal in its fill. The pig bones have been interpreted as the remains of roasted meat being cooked in the nearby ovens (see Higbee, Chapter 3). Pit 1527 in Area 1C was filled with a similar deposit of ash and burnt pig bones. An enamelled plate brooch of probable 2nd-century date (ON 70, Fig. 3.12, 4, and see back cover) was also recovered from this feature. The upper edges of pit 1527 were heat affected, though this may simply reflect the temperature of the ash deposited there rather than it being an indication that it was used as a hearth.

Postholes and Post-pads

Various scattered postholes have been dated to the mid-Romano-British period. Although there were no coherent patterns evident, a concentration of postholes in the centre of Area 1B could potentially indicate the position of a building (Fig. 2.1). Three small ragstone-filled pits were recorded in the centre of Area 1C, two of which (1472 and 1476) were excavated (Fig. 2.5). Pit 1472 was dated to the mid-Romano-British period by pottery of probable 2nd–3rd century date; there were no finds in pit 1474, but it is likely to be of a similar date. The function of the features, which appear to have been post-pads, remains unclear, but they could have formed part of a structure (that extended beneath the unexcavated central haul road).

Plate 2.8 Mid-Romano-British calf burial 1158, looking north-west

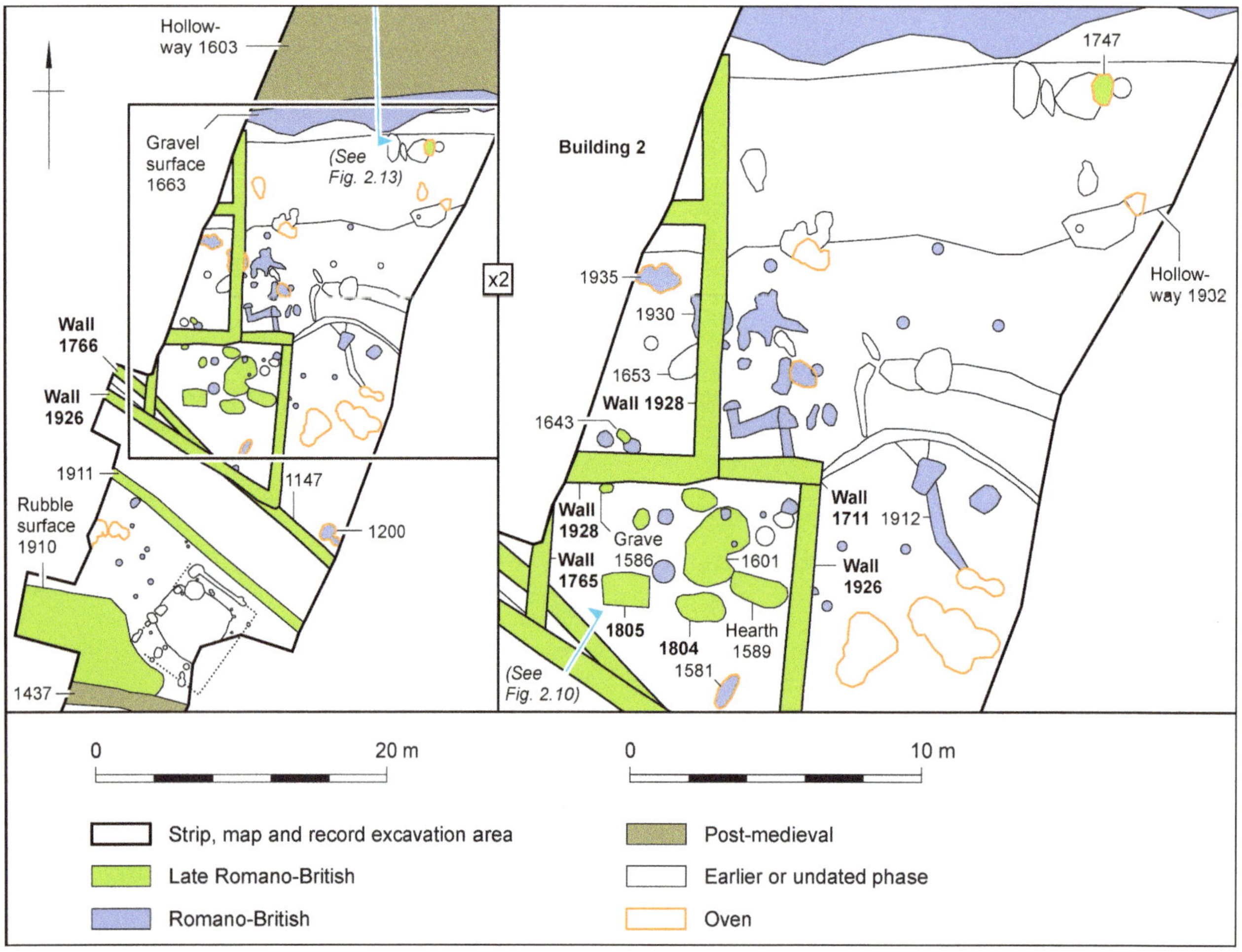

Figure 2.9 Plan of late Romano-British features in Area 1B

Plate 2.9 Late Romano-British rubble surface 1910, looking north-west

Animal Burials

Two animal burials were dated to the mid-Romano-British period; a calf (1158) in Area 1A (Fig. 2.4), and a sheep/goat (1725) in Area 1B (Fig. 2.1). Calf burial 1158 (ABG 1160; Pl. 2.8) was placed in a shallow sub-circular pit that truncated the upper fill of late 2nd-century pit 1165. The backfill of the burial pit contained 2nd-century or later pottery, including samian ware dating to AD 120–50. Pit 1725 contained the disarticulated remains of a near-complete sheep/goat, the partial remains of another sheep/goat and the partial remains of a small dog. The animal burials are discussed in more detail by Higbee in Chapter 3.

Late Romano-British

Roads and Trackways

During the late Romano-British period, the route previously defined by hollow-way 1925 was demarcated by two ditches (1147 and 1911; Fig. 2.9, Pl. 2.1) and the south-western walls of Building 3 (see below), all of which cut backfill/silts of the mid-Romano-British hollow-way. Late Roman pottery and a 3rd/4th-century coin, recovered from the fills of ditches 1147 and 1911, indicate that they silted up in the late 3rd–4th century.

The route defined by hollow-way 1603 (the main road through the settlement) also continued to be used throughout the late Romano-British period, though later erosion along the line of the thoroughfare had truncated any deposits associated with this phase of its use.

A further surface of ragstone rubble (1910; Pl. 2.9) was uncovered to the south of hollow-way 1925. This surface appears to have respected the footprint of early Romano-British Building 1, however, the pottery suggests that it was deposited, or at least remained in use, during the late Romano-British period. The rubble probably represents an external yard surface.

A spread of rubble within shallow linear hollow 1404 in Area 1C probably represents the line of a crudely surfaced pathway (Fig 2.5). The rubble layer within this feature extended north-eastwards across the upper fill of late 3rd–4th-century ditch 1933 and appears to follow the alignment of two parallel features (probably ditches) that were identified by the geophysical survey to the east of the excavation area (see Fig. 2.3). These probable ditches were set 7 m apart, and appear to define a north-east to south-west aligned trackway that extended beyond the limits of the survey.

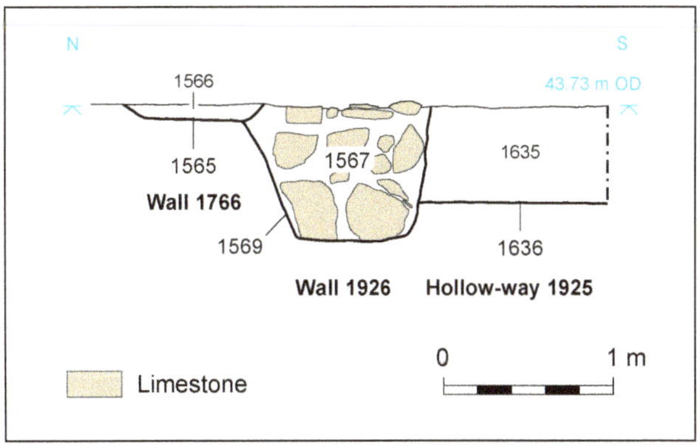

Figure 2.10 Section of late Romano-British walls 1766 and 1926

Enclosures

The spatial distribution of late Romano-British features suggests that most of the boundaries that were established in the mid-Romano-British period were still extant in the 4th century (see Figs 2.4–2.5). By this date, most of the ditches appear to have been allowed to silt up, which suggests that the boundaries they defined were probably also demarcated by upstanding features such as banks and/or hedges.

In Area 1A, two new parallel ditches (1023 and 1920), measuring 0.8 m wide by 0.09 m deep and 2.4 m wide by 0.6 m deep respectively, were laid out 2.8 m apart and at right angles to ditch 1907. The spacing between these ditches suggests that they may have flanked a narrow trackway or an upstanding boundary such as a bank and/or hedge. Ditch 1920 truncated oven 1113 and was in turn cut by the foundation trench for wall 1032/1064, which also cut ditch 1023.

In Area 1C, a shallow, 0.32 m wide by 0.2 m deep, north-east to south-west aligned ditch (1398) appears to have been dug to define an area of activity around well 1678. The northern end of the ditch curved towards the east, and it may have formed part of a boundary, visible on the geophysical survey (see Fig. 1.3), parallel and 25–30 m to the north of the Roman road. High levels of geophysical 'noise' (caused by ferrous objects, slag or burning) to the south of this line are indicative of intensive activity, probably occupation, along the roadside.

A further ditch (1937) at the northern end of Area 1C, 2.4 m wide by over 1.1 m deep, appears to have defined the corner of a late Romano-British rectilinear enclosure that extended beyond the limits of excavation. Late Romano-British pottery was recovered from the secondary fill of ditch 1937, whilst its tertiary fill contained pottery assigned a broad AD 240–400 date and five mid-4th-century coins, the latest of which were struck AD 337–4 and AD 330–45. The geophysical survey showed that this enclosure was laid out at right angles to the existing mid-Romano-British 'ladder' field system (see Fig. 1.3), and measured 51 m north-east to south-west by 30 m south-east to north-west. The geophysical survey appears to show that the enclosure was subdivided into two smaller paddocks, measuring 0.63 ha and 0.87 ha respectively. The geophysical survey shows far less 'noise' in this area than is evident alongside the Roman road. This suggests that the enclosures defined by ditch 1937 were probably used for agricultural purposes.

Structures

Building 2

Building 2 (Figs 2.9–2.10, Pls 2.10–2.12), which was situated immediately to the south of the main Roman road in Area 1B, had at least two phases of construction. The earliest phase post-dated the infilling of hollow-way 1932 and the use of smithing hearth 1653 and is, therefore, late 2nd–3rd century AD or later in date. The earliest part of Building 2 was a rectangular structure, 1928, measuring 14.3 m north–south. The western extent of the building lay beyond the limits of excavation, however given the available size of the plot between the intersecting lines of hollow-ways 1925 and 1603, it is probable that the building measured no more than 13 m east–west. Structure 1928 was divided into two rooms by an east–west partition, with north–south internal dimensions of 3.9 m (north room) and 7.7 m (south

Plate 2.10 Late Romano-British Building 2, showing walls 1565, 1765, 1766 and 1926, stone pads 1804 and 1805, and robber trench 1927, looking north-west

room). No contemporary floor surfaces survived and most of the wall foundations had been systematically robbed. The foundations, which only survived along the south side of the building, comprised a 0.3 m thick layer of tightly-packed pitched ragstone set within a 0.85 m wide by 0.6 m deep construction trench (Pl. 2.12). The foundations along the eastern side of the building had been entirely robbed, but the dimensions of the robber trench indicate that they would have been of similar size to those along the south side. The depth of the foundations suggests that the building probably had a second storey. The foundations were constructed in the same manner as those of late 3rd–4th-century walls 1032 and 1922 in Area 1A (Fig 2.4), and it seems probable that building 1928 is of a similarly late date. Support for this suggestion is provided by the presence of a pit (1643) within the building, which contained five coins dating from the period AD 270–93. It seems probable that this pit, along with most, if not all of the cut features within the building pre-date its construction. However, it is impossible to confirm this, as there were no stratigraphic relationships between these features and the walls of the building.

Wall 1565/1766 formed a continuation of the boundary defined by late 3rd–4th-century roadside ditch 1147, and was probably contemporary with structure 1928. The wall was of insubstantial construction (0.6 m wide by 0.1 m deep), which indicates that it was probably a relatively low, non-load bearing structure – probably a yard boundary. Wall 1565/1766 was cut by walls 1765 and 1926, which suggests that it was demolished prior to their construction. Two coins were recovered from the surface of the demolished wall, one of which dates from AD 270–96, the other is 4th century. This provides a possible date for its demolition, though the provenance is not considered secure given the shallow depth of the feature.

The earliest part of Building 2 – wall 1928 – was abutted to the south by an irregular extension measuring 11.5 m north–south by over 14 m east–west (contexts 1711, 1728, 1926 and 1927), the foundations of which cut through late 3rd–4th-century ditch 1147 and wall 1565/1766. The extension partially encroached onto the trackway defined by hollow-way 1925, but it respected its alignment, which suggests that the route remained in use. The partially robbed wall foundations (Pl. 2.13) were 0.95 m wide by 0.75 m deep along the south-west side of the building, 0.6 m wide by 0.5 m deep along the north side, and 0.86 m wide by 0.2–0.5 m

Plate 2.11 Late Romano-British Building 2, showing walls 1565, 1765, 1766 and 1926 looking south

deep along the east side. The disparity between the depth of the south-western foundations and those along the north and east sides suggests that the former was designed to carry more weight; a possible interpretation being that there was a gable at the south-western end of the building, though this could have caused structural problems through uneven roof load distribution.

There were two east–west aligned pitched-ragstone pads (1804 and 1805; Pl. 2.14) and a north–south aligned foundation (1765) within the extension to Building 1. The pads, which were 0.25 m thick, and measured 1.7 m by 0.95 m and 1.6 m by 1.15 m respectively, may represent the foundations of piers, perhaps used to support first-floor joists or roof timbers. Foundation 1765, which was 0.6 m wide, but only 0.1 m deep, was probably an internal partition.

A shallow scoop (1601) within the building's extension was filled with a deposit of sandstone roof tiles and a small assemblage of late 3rd–4th-century pottery. This material appears to have been dumped to infill a hollow and may be associated with the construction of the extension.

Building 2 was demolished in two phases. The extension was probably demolished first, followed by the main building. The demolition of the building entailed the near complete robbing of the foundations, which suggests that the building materials were salvaged, presumably for use in a

Plate 2.12 Section through late Romano-British wall 1928, looking north

nearby structure. Robber cut 1927 (robbing of wall 1926), which was probably the earlier of the two, contained two fills. The lower fill comprised small fragments of stone, gravel and soil, which probably accumulated while the foundations were being robbed out. Roman pottery was recovered from the lower fill, but none of it was closely datable. The upper fill, which was very dark and appears to have accumulated over a longer period, contained a moderately large assemblage of late 3rd–4th-century pottery and a coin of AD 330–5. Robber cut 1929 (robbing of wall 1928) was backfilled with a

Plate 2.13 Section through late Romano-British walls 1766 and 1926, looking south-east

Plate 2.15 Section through late Romano-British wall 1922, looking south-east

Plate 2.14 Section through late Romano-British stone pad 1804, looking south

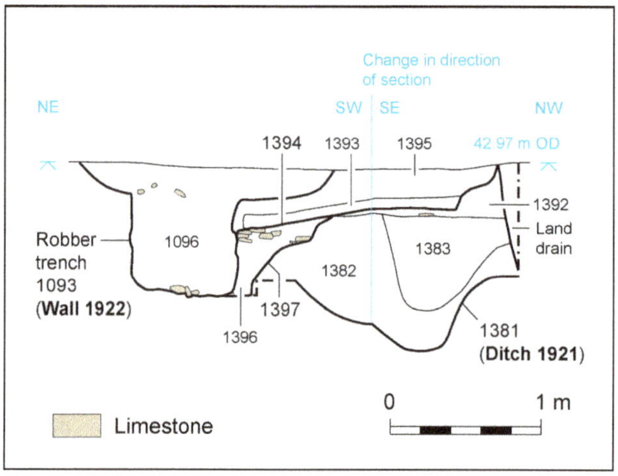

Figure 2.11 Section of robbed late Romano-British wall 1922 and ditch 1921

homogenous dump of material, which was similar to the lower fill of robber cut 1927. Four coins were recovered from the surface of the robber trench fill during hand cleaning and metal detecting, the latest of which dates from the period AD 367–75. A 4th-century coin was also recovered near the base of the robber trench.

Wall foundation 1922

In Area 1A wall foundation 1922 (Figs 2.4 and 2.11, Pl. 2.15) formed the corner of a north-east to south-west aligned structure that measured over 11 m north-east to south-west by at least 3 m north-west to south-east. The corner of the structure was set at an angle of 110°. The partially robbed foundations survived as a 0.25 m thick layer of tightly-packed pitched ragstone set within a 0.65 m wide by 0.8 m deep construction trench. There were no surviving surfaces associated with the wall. The construction trench for wall 1922 truncated late 2nd–3rd-century ditch 1061/1921 and was backfilled with soil and rubble that contained late 3rd–4th-century pottery, which provides a date for its construction. Most of the structure defined by wall 1922 lay beyond the limits of excavation and it is, therefore, impossible to be certain if it was part of a building or a very substantial boundary wall. What is clear, however, is that the foundations were clearly designed to support a significant amount of weight, and if it was a building then it is likely to have had more than one storey. Wall 1922 was truncated by robber trench 1923, the backfill of which contained late 3rd–4th century pottery.

Wall foundation 1032/1064

Wall foundation 1032/1064 (Fig. 2.4) was situated near the southern end of Area 1A, and extended for over 8 m on a north-east to south-west alignment. The wall survived as a layer of pitched-ragstone set within a 0.8 m wide and 0.22 m deep construction trench. There was a 0.7 m long north-west to south-east aligned return at the north-east end of the wall, which was abutted by a 1.15 m long by 0.65 m wide length of wall (1064) that extended 0.45 m towards the north-west; both these elements may have been foundations for buttresses. The relatively shallow depth of the foundations suggests the wall supported by foundation 1032 was probably not particularly substantial and, given the absence of a return at its north-east end, it seems probable that it formed part of a boundary wall rather than a building. However, the exact function of this structure remains uncertain. Wall foundation 1032/1064 cut across two ditches (1023 and 1920) that contained pottery dating from the 2nd–3rd and late 3rd–4th centuries respectively. After the wall was demolished or collapsed, it was robbed down to its lowest course; the robber cut was backfilled with soil containing pottery that could only be broadly dated to the Romano-British period.

Crop drying oven

A heavily truncated crop drying oven, 1474 (Figs 2.5 and 2.8, Pl. 2.16), was partly exposed towards the northern end of Area 1C. This structure comprised a north-east to south-west aligned, 3.75 m long by 2.3 m wide, T-shaped cut. The sides of the long axis (the flue) were lined with ragstone rubble, but there was no lining evident at the north-east end of the cut (the cross-flue). Instead, there was a series of short, narrow (0.3–0.75 m x 0.08–0.18 m) slots around the edge of the cut; these may have been settings for upright stone slabs. The use of upright slabs in crop drying oven construction has previously been recorded at an exceptionally well-preserved example from High Post, near Salisbury (Powell 2011, 31). Evidence from High Post and other comparable structures (eg, Rawlings and Fitzpatrick 1996; Wessex Archaeology 2000a; Wainwright 1971) indicates that crop drying oven 1474 would have had a stoke pit for a fire at the south-west end (in this instance, situated beyond the limits of excavation), which would have provided heat that would have been directed along the flue, then upwards via the cross-flue at the north-east end to the upper (truncated) part of the structure.

There were no finds associated with the construction of the crop drying oven, but the fact that it shared an alignment with an adjacent late Romano-British ditch (1913) suggests that it is probably of a similarly late date, as is invariably the case with this type of structure. Finds from the backfill of the flue include samian ware dated *c.* AD 180–260. If this feature does date to the late Romano-British period, then these finds should be considered residual.

A review of the evidence for the use of crop drying ovens, also known as corn driers, concluded that they were multi-purpose structures used for parching or drying damp grain and for malting (van der Veen 1989). Later studies have supported this conclusion (Pelling 2011a, 84). A large assemblage of charred cereal and weed seeds was recovered from a charcoal-rich layer in the flue of crop drying oven 1474 – probably the remnants of the structure's last firing. The charred cereal remains included spelt and hulled/emmer wheat grains, but there was no germinated grains that might provide evidence for malting (see López-Dóriga, Chapter 4).

Plate 2.16 Late Romano-British crop drying oven 1474, looking south-west

Ovens and hearths

A large hearth (1589; Fig. 2.9, Pl. 2.17) was recorded within the extension to Building 2. This feature comprised a 2 m by 0.9 m wide, sub-rectangular area of heat-affected soil. Finds from the layer beneath the hearth indicate that it dates from the late 3rd century or later, which is broadly contemporary with the building. The exact function of the hearth is unclear, though the fact that the area of burning appears to have been relatively discrete could indicate that it was contained within an above ground structure such as a clay oven.

Oval-shaped oven (1747) has been tentatively dated to the late Romano-British period. This feature was located in a heavily disturbed part of Area 1B. Two sherds of late 3rd–4th-century pottery were recovered from the oven's fills, however, given the disturbance evident in this part of the site, it is possible that these are intrusive.

Pits

A small number of pits of late Romano-British date were recorded across all three areas of the site, most

Plate 2.17 Late Romano-British hearth 1589 under excavation, looking north-west

Plate 2.18 Late Romano-British well 1678, looking north-east

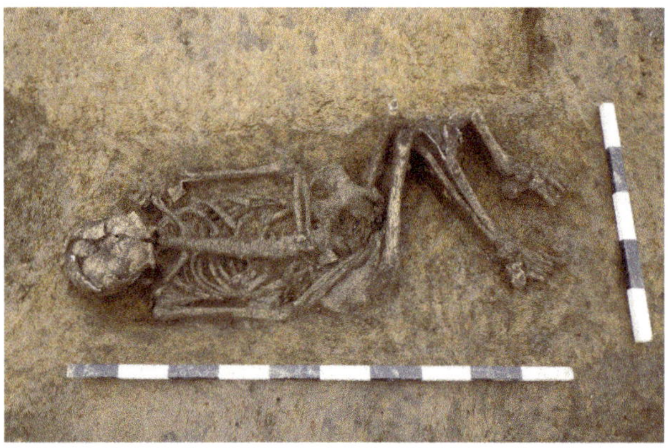

Plate 2.19 Late Romano-British adult burial 1440, looking south-west

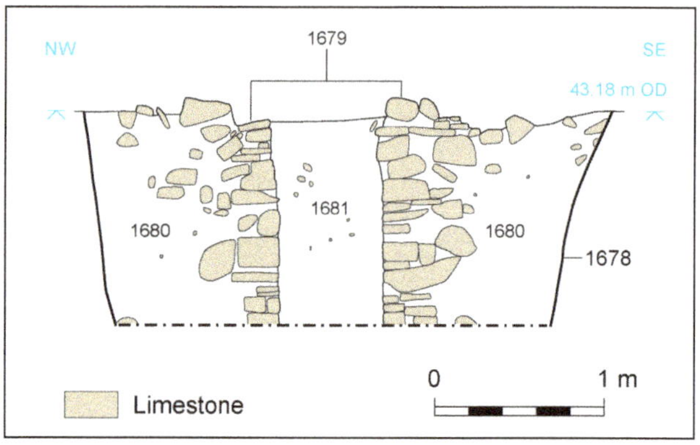

Figure 2.12 Section of late Romano-British well 1678

of which were shallow sub-circular or amorphous features of indeterminate function. Of note amongst these features, however, was a series of shallow pits and possible natural hollows (eg, 1352 and 1357) along the south-eastern edge of Area 1A, which were infilled with charcoal-rich soils that contained a large assemblage of burnt pig bones and a moderate quantity of late Romano-British pottery. Given the proximity of the features to a number of mid-Romano-British ovens, it seems probable that the bones represent incinerated food waste from the latter. If this interpretation is correct, then it seems probable that the pig bones are residual, possibly derived from a surface midden which subsequently became incorporated into the fills of later features.

Pit 1164, 4 m long, at least 1.85 m wide and 1 m deep, lay along the eastern edge of Area 1A, extending beyond the limits of excavation. Pit 1164 contained Romano-British pottery, some of which was early, and a worked bone toggle (ON 22, Fig. 3.12, 9). The partially filled northern end of the pit had been cut by another pit, 1204, measuring 1.1 m by at least 0.6 m and 0.8 m deep, the fill of which contained no datable finds. Both pits were then completely backfilled with a sequence of deposits that contained late 3rd–4th-century pottery. The function of these features remains uncertain, but clay extraction with subsequent refuse disposal is a possibility.

Wells

In Area 1C a large ragstone-lined well (1678; Figs 2.5 and 2.12, Pl. 2.18) lay 10 m to the north of the main Roman road and 11 m to the east of a possible roadside shrine (see below). The well was constructed within a near-vertical 3–3.2 m wide sub-circular pit, which was excavated to a depth of 1.2 m; subsequent auguring showed that it was at least 3 m deep. The construction cut was backfilled with clay and stone rubble that contained late 3rd–4th-century pottery.

The stone-lined shaft was circular, 0.6 m in diameter, and was backfilled with dark soil that contained late 3rd–4th-century pottery and a large semi-circular fragment of worked oolitic limestone (see Fig. 3.14, 18, Object Number (ON) 97), possibly part of a stone superstructure surrounding the top of the well.

A further possible well, 1936, was uncovered near the northern end of Area 1A (Fig. 2.4). This feature, which was circular, approximately 2.5 m in diameter and at least 1.2 m deep, was initially interpreted as a pit. However, further investigation showed that it was lined with clay that had subsequently slumped inwards, suggesting that the central shaft may have been originally lined with timber or wattle. The construction cut truncated the upper fills of an adjacent late 3rd–4th-century ditch (1908), and was backfilled with a sequence of deposits that contained pottery of the same date. Charred plant remains from the backfill were similar to those from the nearby ovens, though this may represent residual material.

Human Burial

A shallow grave (cut 1440, skeleton 1442; Fig. 2.5, Pl. 2.19) containing the remains of an older adult female (>50 years old) was uncovered within the Area 1C ladder enclosure. The grave followed the north-east to south-west alignment of an adjacent ditch. The burial was supine, with the head to the north-east, and the legs flexed and arms crossed over the abdomen. There were no nails or other evidence of a coffin. Twenty-four hobnails were found near the feet, which suggests that the individual was either buried wearing shoes, or that shoes were placed as grave goods in that location. Pottery, certainly residual, from the grave fill dates to the 3rd century AD or later.

There was a large (0.72 m by 0.6 m and 0.35 m deep) oval posthole (1485) immediately to the north-east of the grave. Finds from the fill of the posthole indicate that it dates from the 2nd–3rd-century or later. Whilst the location of this posthole is suggestive of a grave marker, this is by no means certain and its location may coincidental.

Plate 2.20 Late Romano-British dog 'grave' 1535, looking north-west

Plate 2.21 Romano-British neonate burial 1587, looking north

Dog Burial

A 'grave' (1537; Pl. 2.20) that contained a complete dog skeleton and the partial skeleton of another (ABGs 1535 and 1536) lay 10 m to the north of well 1678 in Area 1C. The dogs were buried in a small, rectangular, vertical-sided, north-east to south-west aligned pit. This was 1.65 m long, 0.65 m wide and 0.55 m deep, and resembled a grave for a human burial. Although there may be a practical explanation for the burials, their proximity to a possible roadside

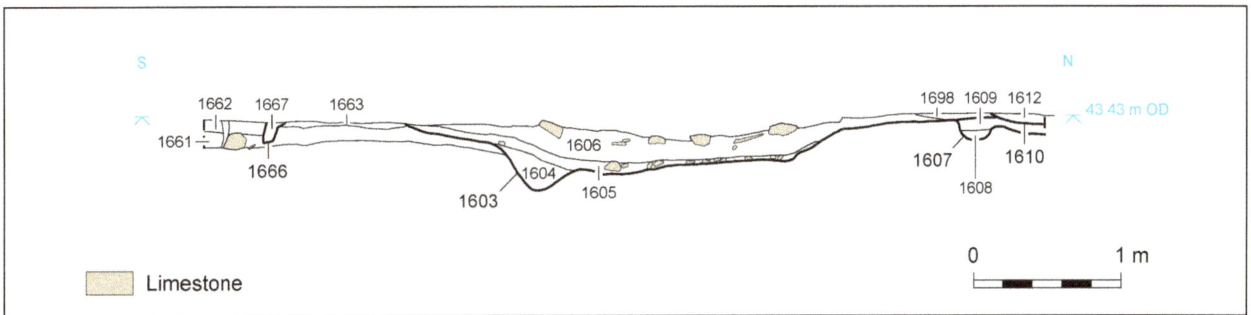

Figure 2.13 Section of post-medieval hollow-way 1603

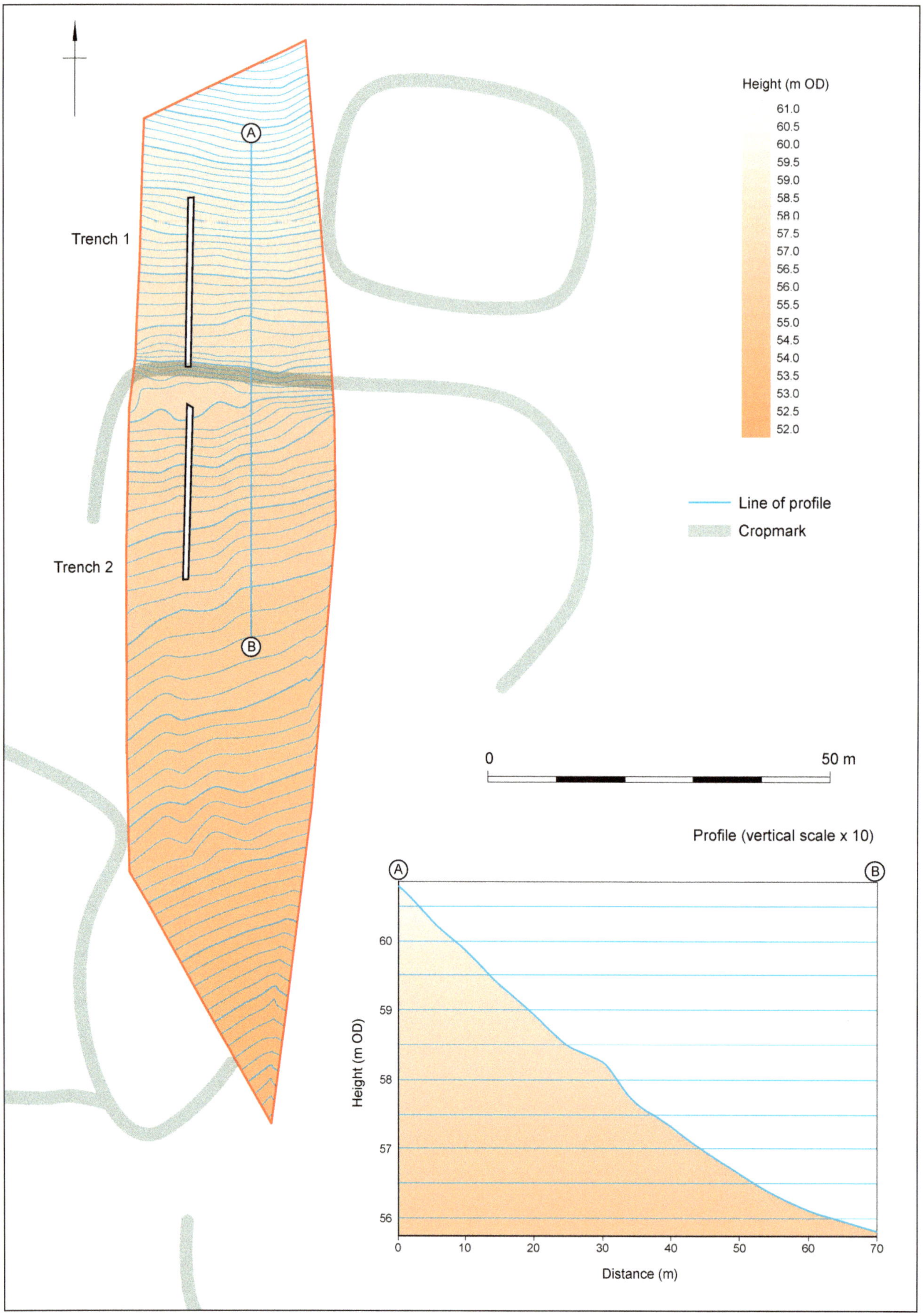

Figure 2.14 Topographical survey of Area 2

Plate 2.22 Post-medieval hollow-way 1603 crossing site in foreground, looking south

shrine (see below), raises the possibility that they may have been sacrificial offerings. Finds from the pit include 88 pieces of iron-working slag and a small quantity of Roman pottery, one sherd of which dates from the 3rd/4th century.

Romano-British (unphased)

Due to the broad production range of some Roman pottery wares, a few of the excavated features could only be broadly dated to the Romano-British period. Of note amongst this group are a cluster of pits and postholes in Area 1B and a possible roadside shrine at the southern end of Area 1C (Figs 2.1 and 2.5).

The pits and postholes in Area 1B were distributed across the area, but there was a notable concentration in and around Building 2. Although there were no clearly discernible patterns evident, it is possible that some of these features formed part of a post-built building, presumably predating the stone building.

Possible Roadside Shrine

Two small stone altars (ONs 39 and 40, see Figs 2.5, 3.15 and front cover) were uncovered during the mechanical stripping of the site. The altars were found close together, on the west side of the easement, and 7 m to the north of the main Roman road. The fact that they were found together suggests that they had probably not moved far from their original location. There were no structural remains associated with the altars, but their location near to well 1678, dog burial 1535 and a ragstone rubble surface, as well as the Roman road, may be significant. The rubble surface, which was uncovered between the former Roman road, well 1678 and the altars, appears to have been deliberately laid to create an area of hard standing. The original extent of the surface is uncertain (it extended beneath the central haul road as well as beyond the limit of excavation to the west), but it perhaps joined with pathway 1404 to the north.

Human Burial

A very shallow grave (1586; skeleton 1587) containing a neonate inhumation burial (Fig. 2.9, Pl. 2.21) lay immediately to the south of wall 1928 of Building 2 in Area 1B. The body was buried in a crouched position on its left-hand side, with the head to the east. It is unclear if the burial was placed outside building 1928 or if it was buried after the construction of the southern extension and, therefore, within the building.

Post-Roman Activity

Area 1

There is no evidence for occupation on the site after the late 4th century. However, the route of the main

Roman road appears to have continued in use until the post-medieval period, by which time wear and natural erosion had turned the former road into a 7 m wide and 0.4 m deep hollow-way (1603) (see Fig. 2.13, Pl. 2.22). There was a small ditch in the base, presumably dug to assist drainage. The ditch was sealed by a crude metalled surface which was in turn covered by an accumulation of soil that contained residual Roman finds and a few sherds of 17th–18th-century bottle glass. Historic mapping show that the south side of the hollow-way was defined by a hedged field boundary, which was removed between 1886 and 1900.

Area 2

A topographical survey within an area of cropmarks and earthworks to the east of Wick Farm (see Fig. 1.1) recorded the position of an undated east–west aligned lynchet (Fig. 2.14). Two 2 m wide trenches were opened in this area in order to assess the potential for buried archaeological remains, but no features were uncovered. Given the proximity of medieval remains at Wick Farm (Lake and Edwards 2014), it is probable that the undated lynchet is of a similar date, and may represent a former field boundary or trackway.

Chapter 3
Finds

Worked flint

by Phil Harding

The 35 pieces of worked flint were predominantly recovered from secondary contexts, with just four artefacts and a small fragment of burnt flint recovered from prehistoric features (posthole 1521, pit 1525 and probable later furrow 1406), all containing possible Bronze Age pottery. However, it is likely that some or all of this material may be residual. The worked flints are all unpatinated with limited amounts of edge damage. This is likely to have resulted from the post-depositional reworking of artefacts since their manufacture.

The assemblage includes two flake cores, 15 flakes and broken flakes, seven blades and broken blades, six scrapers, a microdenticulate, a fragment with miscellaneous retouch and a hammer stone, representing all phases of the production sequence. The hammer stone, which cannot be dated, comprises an elongated cylindrical nodule of water-worn flint with battered ends.

The quantities of material are small, but are nevertheless sufficient to indicate prehistoric activity in the area. It is possible that some of this activity is contemporary with the Bronze Age pottery but the quantity of well-made blades and a microdenticulate indicate that the area was visited, if not populated, at a much earlier date, if not during the Mesolithic, then certainly by the Neolithic period.

An additional 35 small, unworked fragments of flint gravel were recovered. Flint does not occur naturally in the area and the condition of this material suggests that it was probably introduced by natural fluvial activity. However, it is also possible that it was transported to the site as aggregate. This component was sufficiently plentiful to suggest that it probably provided the principal source of raw material for stone tool manufacture but irrespective of its origin or usage, this material contains no significant information.

A very small amount of burnt flint was recovered, from Bronze Age pit 1525 and an early Romano-British posthole within Building 1. This material type is intrinsically undatable, but is frequently associated with prehistoric activity.

Coins

Coins from the Excavation

by Nicholas Cooke

Seventy-five coins, comprising three of silver and 72 of copper alloy (Table 3.1), were recovered. All are of the Roman period and were found by hand excavation and through the systematic use of metal detectors (in the latter case as unstratified finds). In general, they are in good condition, with the majority (63 of the 75) identifiable to period. Some of the coins show signs of post-depositional corrosion, whilst others show evidence of pre-depositional wear. The 12 coins which could not be closely dated (ONs 4, 16, 59, 77, 139, 176, 182, 185, 195, 216, 222 and 223) were assigned rough dates based on their form – three (including ON 223, an illegible silver *denarius*) were broadly dated to the 1st to 3rd centuries AD, whilst the remainder were assigned dates in the late 3rd or 4th centuries AD.

The more closely datable coins range in date from the early 2nd century AD through to the late 4th century. A breakdown of these coins by period (using the coin periods set out by Reece (1995)) can be seen in Figure 3.1. The small number of 2nd-century and early 3rd-century coins indicate that there was coin

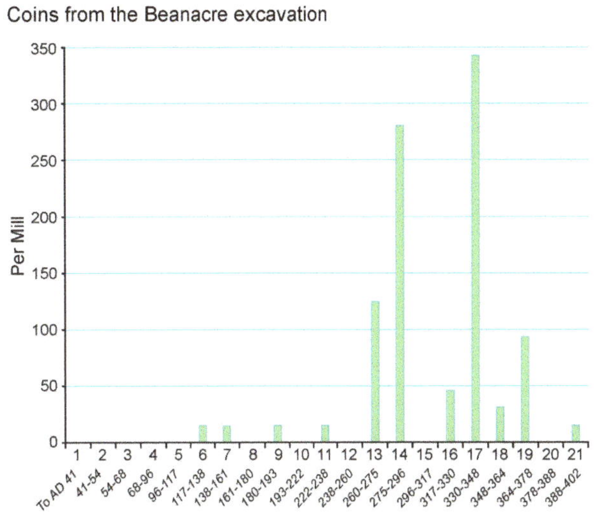

Figure 3.1 Analysis of the coins from the 2015 Beanacre excavation using Reece (1995) periods

Table 3.1 Catalogue of coins from the 2015 Beanacre excavation

Object Number	Context number	Metal	Denomination	Issuer	Diameter (mm)	Weight (g)	Obverse Comments	Reverse Comments	Issue Date	Notes
4	1148	Cu Alloy	AE 3	Unknown Emperor	14	0.41	Illegible	Illegible	C3–C4	Corroded and illegible. Pierced for suspension
7	1161	Cu Alloy	AE 3	Constantine I	14	1.16	Bust r, laureate. -NTI NVSMAXAVG	2 soldiers, 2 standards. (GLOR) IAEXERC ITVS	AD 330–335	?copy as LRBC I, 48
8	1161	Cu Alloy	*Antoninianus*	Irregular radiate	17	1.92	Bust r, radiate	Standing fig l with branch	AD 270–296	Portrait has hints of Claudius II.
10	1161	Cu Alloy	AE 3	Gratian	16	2.05	Bust r, pearl diadem. (DNGRAT) IAN VSAVGGAVG	Emperor r, dragging captive. GLORIAROMA NORVM. Mint mark: OF | II / | palm / -VGP."	AD 367–375	LRBC II, 331
12	1161	Cu Alloy	AE 3	Unknown Emperor	19	2.56	Bust l	Altar. (BEATA) TRAN QVILLITAS. Mint mark: PLN	AD 318–324	Corroded nummus of AD 318 - 324
13	u/s	Cu Alloy	*Antoninianus*	Irregular radiate	13	0.78	Bust r, radiate	?pax l. -XI below	AD 270–296	Irregular radiate. Almost rectangular flan. The XI below suggests a later coin, perhaps of Carausius being copied
14	u/s	Cu Alloy	AE 3	House of Valentinian	12	1.46	Bust r	Emperor r, with standard, dragging captive. (GLORIA RO) MANORVM	AD 364–375	Small flan? Copy as LRBC II, 78
16	u/s	Cu Alloy	AE 3	Unknown Emperor	14	0.85	Bust r	Illegible	C4	Small damaged flan
19	1161	Cu Alloy	As	Marcus Aurelius (Caesar)	25	8.83	Bust r, bare headed. AVRELIVS CAE (SAR AVG PII F COS)	Hilaritas standing, holding cornucopiae and long palm-branch. (HILAR) ITAS S.C	AD 140	RIC III (Ant Pius) 1236
20	u/s	Cu Alloy	AE 3	Valens	17	1.52	Bust r, pearl diadem. (DNV) ALEN SPFAVG	Winged victory l with wreath (SECVR) ITAS REIPVBLICAE. Mint mark: * | / K | Q / ASISCR	AD 367–375	LRBC II, 1362
26	1161	Cu Alloy	*Antoninianus*	Claudius II	20	3.27	Bust r, radiate. IMPCLAVDIVSAVG	Mars standing, holding branch and spear. VIRTVSAVG	AD 268–270	As RIC V (Part II) 109
47	u/s	Cu Alloy	*Antoninianus*	Gallienus	22	2.61	Bust r, radiate, bearded IMPGALLIENVSAVG	Doe walking right looking backwards. DIANAE CONS AVG. Mint mark: Epsilon	AD 260–268	RIC V (Part 1), Rome 176
50	1161	Cu Alloy	AE 3	Theodora	14	1.21	Female bust r, recognisably Theodora	Pax facing holding a branch. (PAX PV) BLICA	AD 337–341	As LRBC I, 104
51	1161	Cu Alloy	*Quinarius*	Allectus	19	2.42	Bust r, radiate, bearded. IMPCALLECTVSPFAVG	Galley. VIRTVS AVG. QC below	AD 293–296	RIC V pt. 2, 128
52	1161	Cu Alloy	*Antoninianus*	Irregular radiate	20	3.17	Bust r, radiate, bearded	Fig standing l (?Pax)	AD 270–296	V irregular flan
55	1423	Cu Alloy	*Sestertius*	Hadrian	34	18.63	Bust r, laureate. Clearly Hadrian	Concordia seated l. CONCORD- below	AD 117	As RIC II, 535
57	1449	Cu Alloy	AE 3	Constans	15	1.45	Bust r, pearl diadem 3 rosettes, cuirassed. CONSTAN SPFAVG	2 facing victories with wreaths VICTORIAEAVGGQNN. Mint Mark: D/TRS	AD 345	LRBC I, 148
58	1461	Cu Alloy	*Antoninianus*	Irregular radiate	14	0,80	Bust r, radiate	Illegible	AD 270–296	Irregular flan. Barbarous copy
59	u/s	Cu Alloy	AE 4	Unknown Emperor	12	0.45	Illegible	Illegible	C4	V small corroded flan. Prob a C4 copy
61	1484	Cu Alloy	AE 3	House of Constantine	16	1.71	Bust l, helmeted. VRBS ROMA	Wolf and Twins. Mint mark: Q B Q	AD 330–345	copy as LRBC I, 51
62	u/s	Cu Alloy	AE 3	House of Constantine	16	1.24	Bust l, helmeted. CONSTAN TINOPOLIS	Victory on prow. Mint mark: PLG	AD 330	LRBC I, 185
68	u/s	Silvered Cu Alloy	*Denarius*	Julia Soaemias	19	2.23	Bust r. -SO- -MIAS-	Female fig standing l. VEN-	AD 218–222	Appears to be silvered. ? copy of RIC III, 231
73	1161	Cu Alloy	AE 3	House of Valentinian	16	2	Bust r, pearl diadem	Emperor r with standard, dragging captive. Gloria Romanorum type	AD 364–378	As LRBC II, 78
74	1161	Cu Alloy	AE 3	House of Constantine	14	1.25	Bust r, pearl diadem with rosettes	2 soldiers, 1 standard. (GLOR) IAEXERC (ITVS)	AD 330–345	?copy as LRBC I, 87

77	1560	Cu Alloy	AE 3	Unknown Emperor	16	2.06	Bust r	Fig standing	C4	Corroded C4 coin
79	1606	Cu Alloy	AE 3	Constans	`14	0.72	Bust r. CONSTA- -FAVG	2 facing victories with wreaths.	AD 341–349	As LRBC I, 138
80	1612	Cu Alloy	AE 4	House of Theodosius	13	0.85	Bust r. -PFAVG	Victoriaeddauggqnn type Winged victory l with wreath. (VICTOR) IAAVGGG. Mint mark: LVGP	AD 388–402	As LRBC II, 389
87	1161	Cu Alloy	*Antoninianus*	Claudius II	20	2.48	Bust r, radiate. IMP CLAVDIVS-	Stylised fig standing. GENIVS-	AD 268–270	?copy as RIC V (Part II) 48
91	1644	Cu Alloy	*Antoninianus*	Claudius II	18	7	Bust r, radiate. IMPCLAVDIUS-	Providentia standing left, legs crossed, leaning on column, holding baton and cornucopiae. -ROVIDEN-	AD 268–270	As RIC V (Fart II) 91
92	1644	Cu Alloy	*Antoninianus*	Victorinus	17	1.88	Bust r, radiate, bearded. -VICTORINVS-	Figure l	AD 268–270	Antoninianus of Victorinus, uncertain reverse
93	1644	Cu Alloy	*Antoninianus*	Claudius II	19	2.59	Bust r, radiate, bearded. -DIVSAVG	Apollo, standing left, holding laurel-branch in right hand and lyre set on rock in left hand. APOLLI (CONS)	AD 268–270	struck off centre on an irregular flan. Copy as RIC V (Part II) 20
94	1644	Cu Alloy	*Antoninianus*	? Tetricus I	18	2.15	Bust r, radiate, bearded (?Tetricus I)	Salus feeding snake rising from altar. S (ALVS) A (VG)	AD 270–293	As RIC V (Fart II) Tetricus 126
95	1644	Cu Alloy	*Antoninianus*	Claudius II	18	2.21	Bust r, radiate. -IVSAVg	Aequitas standing, holding scales and cornucopiae. AEQVITA (SAVG)	AD 268–270	RIC V (Part II) Claudius II, 15
109	1761	Cu Alloy	*Antoninianus*	Unknown Emperor	17	2.21	Bust r, radiate, bearded	Female fig standing l	AD 270–296	Poss copy
110	1761	Cu Alloy	*Antoninianus*	Tetricus I	17	2.25	Bust r, radiate, bearded. -AVG	Fifes standing l with 2 military standards. F (IDES MILITVM)	AD 270–273	As RIC V (Fart II) Tetricus I 68
123	1002	Cu Alloy	*Antoninianus*	Tetricus I	16	1.11	Bust r, radiate, bearded	Spes l, holding flower. (SP) ES (PVBLICAt)	AD 270–296	?copy as RIC V (Part II) Tetricus I, 135
127	u/s	Cu Alloy	AE 3	House of Constantine	18	1.81	Bust l, helmeted. VRBS (ROMA)	Wolf and Twins. Mint mark: TRS	AD 330	Damaged flan. LRBC I, 51
132	1484	Cu Alloy	AE 3	House of Constantine	17	1.83	Bust l, helmeted. VRBS (R)OMA	Wolf and Twins	AD 330–335	As LRBC I, 51
133	1484	Cu Alloy	AE 3	House of Constantine	19	2.38	Bust l, helmeted. VRBS ROMA	Wolf and Twins. TRS.	AD 331	LRBC II, 58
135	u/s	Cu Alloy	AE 3	Theodora	14	1	Bust r, bare headed (Theodora)	Pietas facing with infants. PI (ETAS ROMANA)	AD 337–345	?copy as LRBC I, 105
136	1454	Cu Alloy	AE 3	Helena	15	1.1	Bust r, bareheaded	Pax standing holding branch. Pax Publica type	AD 337–341	As LRBC I, 104
137	1416	Silver	*Denarius*	Commodus	17	3.33	Bust r, laureate. L AEL AVREL COMM AVG P FEL	Liberalitas standing front, head left, holding coin counter & cornucopiae. LIB AVG VIII P M TR P XVII COS VII P P	AD 192	RIC III, 239
139	1002	Cu Alloy	*Antoninianus/nummus*	Unknown emperor	15	0.62	Illegible	Illegible	C3–C4	Possible copy. Oval flan. Probably a copy
140	u/s	Cu Alloy	AE 3	House of Constantine	15	0.92	Bust r, laureate, cuirassed. FLIVL-	2 soldiers, 1 standard Gloria Exercitus type	AD 335–341	As LRBC I, 89
144	1454	Cu Alloy	AE 3	Unknown Emperor	14	0.69	Bust l	Altar. Beata Tranquillitas type	AD 318–324	V thin flan.
149	1518	Cu Alloy	AE 3	House of Constantine	14	1.52	Bust l, helmeted. CONST-	Victory on prow. Mint mark: PLG	AD 330–345	?copy as LRBC 185
152	u/s	Cu Alloy	*Antoninianus*	Irregular radiates	20	1.42	Bust r, radiate	Fig standing	AD 270–296	Radiate copy.
156	u/s	Cu Alloy	AE 3	Constantius II	17	2.60	Bust r, pearl diadem. DNCONSTANTI VSPFAVG	Phoenix on pyre. FELTEMPREPARATIO	AD 348–350	As LRBC II, 32
165	u/s area B	Cu Alloy	AE 3	House of Valentinian	17	2.07	Bust r	Emperor r with standard, dragging captive. Gloria Romanorum type	AD 364–378	As LRBC II, 78

Table 3.1 continued

Object Number	*Context number*	*Metal*	*Denomination*	*Issuer*	*Diameter (mm)*	*Weight (g)*	*Obverse Comments*	*Reverse Comments*	*Issue Date*	*Notes*
166	1612	Cu Alloy	AE 3	House of Valentinian	17	1.54	Bust r, pearl diadem	Emperor r, with standard, dragging captive. Gloria Romanorum type	AD 364–378	As LRBC II, 78
176	1685	Cu Alloy	AE 2	Unknown Emperor	22	3.64	Bust l	Illegible	C1–C3	Dated on size alone
180	u/s Area B	Cu Alloy	*Antoninianus*	Irregular radiate	14	1.7	Bust r, radiate	Fig r	AD 270 –296	Barbarous copy
181	1002	Cu Alloy	*Antoninianus*	Irregular radiate	19	2.29	Bust r, bearded, radiate. -CVSPFAVG	Pax standing l with branch	AD 270–296	Probable radiate copy, possibly of a coin of Tetricus I
182	1002	Cu Alloy	AE 3	Unknown Emperor	15	0.84	Bust r	Illegible	C4	C4 coin. Thin flan
183	1002	Cu Alloy	*Antoninianus*	Carausius	18	2.35	Bust r, radiate. SIVSPFAVG	Fig l, ?Pax	AD 286–293	Corroded. As RIC V (Part II) 98
184	1002	Cu Alloy	*Antoninianus*	Carausius	22	4.20	Bust r, bearded. IMPCARAVSIVSPFAVG	Felicitas l, holding long caduceus & cornucopiae. ML-	AD 286–293	As RIC V (Part I') Carausius, 33
185	1002	Cu Alloy	AE 3	Unknown Emperor	18	2.59	Bust l	Illegible	C4	C4 coin
188	u/s area b	Cu Alloy	*Antoninianus*	Irregular radiate	19	1.99	Bust r, radiate	Pax l with branch	AD 270–296	Radiate copy. V stylised
190	1002	Cu Alloy	AE 3	Constantius II	15	1.62	Bust r, pearl diadem. CONSTANTI VSPFAVG	2 facing victories with wreaths (VI) CTORIAEDDAVGGQNN. Mint mark: Epsilon / ?	AD 341–348	As LRBC I, 151
191	1606	Cu Alloy	AE 4	House of Constantine	11	0.59	Bust r	Soldier spearing fallen horseman. Fel Temp Reparatio type	AD 350–360	Copy as LRBC II, 25
195	1606	Cu Alloy	AE 4	Unknown Emperor	11	0.59	Illegible	Illegible	C4	C4 copy
196	1606	Cu Alloy	AE 4	House of Constantine	14	1.16	Bust r	2 soldiers, 2 standards. Gloria Exercitus type	AD 330–345	?copy as LRBC I, 48
197	1606	Cu Alloy	*Antoninianus*	Aurelian	21	3.54	Bust r, radiate, bearded. IMPAVRELIANVSAVG	Emperor standing before Roma seated on shield, holding Victory and sceptre (ROM) AEAETE (RNAE)	AD 270–275	As RIC V (Part I; Aurelian 142
198	1606	Cu Alloy	AE 3	Constans	15	1.15	Bust r, pearl diadem. CONSTA NSPFAVG	2 facing victories with wreaths. Victoriaeddauggqnn type. Mint mark: Epsilon/?	AD 341–348	As LRBC I, 153
215	u/s area b	Cu Alloy	AE 4	House of Constantine	11	0.81	Bust l helmeted. V stylised - OPO-	Victory on prow	AD 330–345	V small flan, stylised engraving. Copy as LRBC I, 52
216	u/s area B	Cu Alloy	*Antoninianus/nummus*	Unknown Emperor	15	0.96	Illegible	Illegible	C3–C4	Badly corroded. Dated by size alone
217	u/s area B	Cu Alloy	AE 3	Crispus	18	2.33	Helmeted and cuirassed bust. DN CRISPO NOB CAES	Two captives seated below trophy. A-S across fields. Mint mark PLG	AD 320	RIC VII, Lyons 104
218	u/s Area B	Cu Alloy	AE 3	House of Constantine	15	1.07	Bust l, helmeted	Victory on prow	AD 330–335	Badly damaged. As LRBC I, 52
219	u/s Area B	Cu Alloy	*Antoninianus*	Irregular radiate	16	1.98	Bust r, radiate. Stylised	Fig standing l	AD 270–296	Radiate copy
221	u/s Area B	Cu Alloy	AE 3	Constantine I	19	2.06	Bust r, helmeted. CONSTA NTINVSAVG	Banner inscribed VOT XX standing between two captives. VIRTVS EXERCIT. Mint mark: PLN	AD 320–321	As RIC VII, 191
222	u/s Area B	Cu Alloy	*Antoninianus/nummus*	Unknown Emperor	18	1.65	Illegible	Illegible	C3–C4	C3 - C4
223	u/s Area B	Silver	*Denarius*	Unknown Emperor	19	2.82	Bust r, -VS-	Standing figure	C1–C3	denarius of C1 - C3
224	u/s Area B	Cu Alloy	AE 3	House of Constantine	15	1.27	Bust r, -PFAVG	2 facing victories with wreaths	AD 341–348	? Copy as LRBC I, 137
225	u/s area B	Cu Alloy	AE 3	Constans	15	1.49	Bust r, pearl diadem. CONSTANS PFAVG	2 soldiers, 1 standard (GLOR IAEXERC) ITVS. Mint mark: Y/PLG	AD 337–41	LRBC I, 251
226	u/s Area B	Cu Alloy	*Antoninianus*	Irregular radiate	15	1.23	Bust r, radiate	Providentia l with cornucopiae. PROVIDENTAAVG	AD 270–296	Probably a copy of a Providentia issue

Table 3.2 The number of coins from each site defined by Reece (1995) period

Reece period	Excavation	PAS metal detected	Combined	Lacock	Whitewalls	Silbury	Nettleton Scrubb	Wiltshire mean (PAS)
1 (to AD 41)	0	0	0	0	3	0	3	35
2 (41–54)	0	2	2	0	0	0	14	36
3 (54–69)	0	0	0	0	0	0	4	14
4 (69–96)	0	0	0	0	11	0	13	100
5 (96–117)	0	2	2	0	2	0	4	65
6 (117–138)	1	0	1	1	1	0	10	67
7 (138–161)	1	1	2	0	7	0	9	106
8 (161–180)	0	1	1	0	3	0	14	47
9 (180–192)	1	0	1	0	1	0	2	30
10 (193–222)	0	0	0	1	0	0	11	92
11 (222–238)	1	0	1	0	3	0	6	39
12 (238–260)	0	0	0	0	1	0	12	82
13 (260–275)	8	20	28	10	105	0	150	1204
14 (275–296)	18	7	25	11	55	1	111	737
15 (296–317)	0	2	2	0	10	0	12	286
16 (317–330)	3	8	11	1	20	0	34	581
17 (330–348)	21	34	55	13	99	5	448	1936
18 (348–364)	2	11	13	5	15	0	220	614
19 (364–378)	6	20	26	8	45	6	507	1914
20 (378–388)	0	1	1	0	1	0	4	49
21 (388–402)	1	1	2	0	7	4	202	223
Totals	**63**	**110**	**173**	**50**	**389**	**16**	**1790**	**-**

use on the site at this time – these include two of the three *denarii.* One of these, ON 68, is probably a plated copy of a *denarius* of Julia Soaemias, mother of the emperor Elagabalus. This appears to have a copper alloy core and to have been silvered.

The number of late 3rd (periods 13 and 14) and 4th (periods 15 to 21) century coins indicates that there was considerable coin use throughout this period. The peaks of coin loss in periods 13 and 14 are paralleled across British sites, and may mark the widespread adoption of coinage across the province. A number of the coins are irregular copies known as Barbarous Radiates. These contemporary copies of 'official' coinage were possibly struck to compensate for gaps in the supply of coinage to Britain and to provide sufficient small change for the province's needs. It is unclear whether these copies were officially sanctioned, if at all, but they are not uncommon as site finds, and seem to have circulated in the same fashion as officially struck coins.

The pattern of coin loss in the 4th century is largely as expected, with major peaks of coin loss in periods 17 and 19, and fewer coins of periods 15, 16, 18 and 20. Rather than reflecting differences in coin use and loss, these tend to reflect vagaries in the supply of coinage to the province, which may well have been a determining factor in the episodes of copying evident in the 4th century AD. The peak of coin loss in period 17 is, however, proportionally larger than expected for a British site, suggesting that there may have been a particular focus of coin use at this time. The single period 21 coin of the House of Theodosius (ON 80), which belongs to one of the last batches of coin sent to Britain, suggests that activity and coin use continued on site into the late 4th or early 5th century AD.

Coins Recorded by the Portable Antiquities Scheme

by Richard Henry

In addition to the 75 coins from the excavation, a further 110, mostly from an adjacent field, have been reported to the Portable Antiquities Scheme (see Table 3.2). No further assemblages are definitively from the site, although it should be noted that Moorhead (2001a) records 50 coins from a site along the Roman road to the south of Lacock found by D'Arcy Hunt (see Table 3.2). These coins share a similar profile to those definitely from the Beanacre field and their recorded location suggests that they may represent a further element of the Beanacre assemblage. There are two notable coins from the assemblage: a sestertius of Trajan dating to AD 103–111 (RIC 489) and a brockage of Valentinian I dating to AD 364–375. Brockages are caused when an already struck coin sticks to the coin die and impresses onto another blank that has not yet been struck, pressing an incuse image of the coin into the blank.

When the assemblage from Beanacre is compared to the Wiltshire average, the site follows the broad pattern expected. A limited number of coins belong to

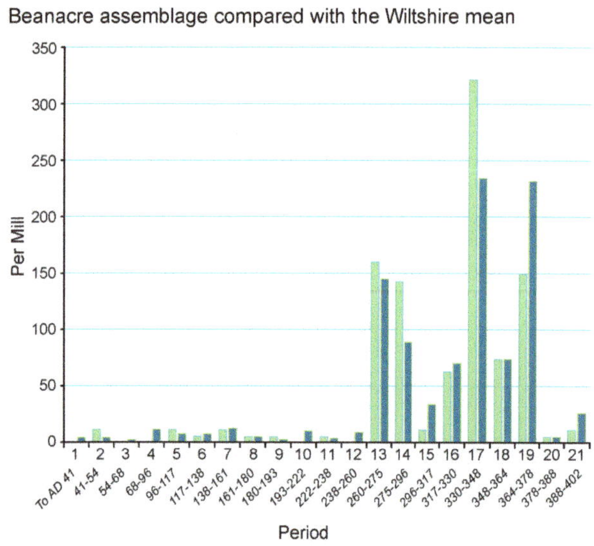

Figure 3.2 Comparison using Reece (1995) periods of the Beanacre excavation coin finds against the Wiltshire mean, the latter in dark green

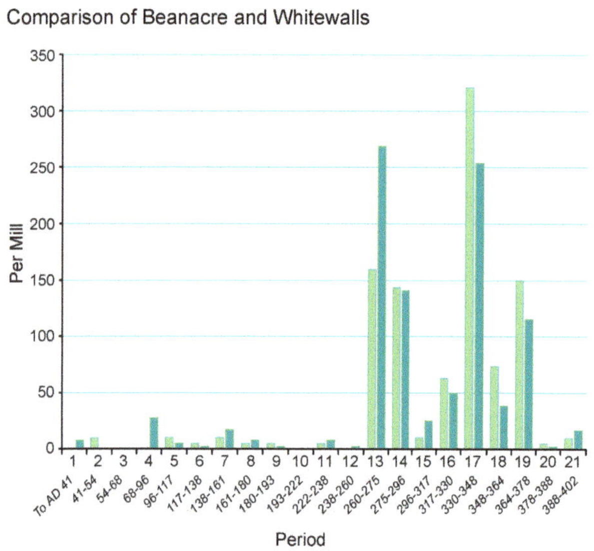

Figure 3.3 Comparison using Reece (1995) periods of the Beanacre excavation coin finds against the Whitewalls finds, the latter in dark green

the period prior to AD 260 when the currency system was tri-metallic with substantial coinage in gold, silver and bronze. These were struck regularly throughout the period and had a fixed relationship to each other. The vast majority of the issues are worn, indicating circulation for a considerable period of time. Evidence from hoards suggests that these issues were potentially in circulation for at least 70 to 130 years (Reece 1988). However, the sestertius of Trajan dating from AD 103–111 shows very limited wear, which highlights that it did not remain in circulation for a prolonged period before being lost. Bronze coinage in the 3rd century was primarily formed from old and worn issues with relatively few newer issues in circulation. These new issues entered Britain in such limited quantities in this period that they could not have made up for those examples leaving circulation.

Through statistical analysis and comparison of site assemblages, it is possible to not only date activity but also to suggest site function. Reece (1995) defined four broad categories: military, urban, rural and temple. When examining the majority of rural sites in Roman Britain, there is a substantial increase in coin loss from the AD 260s onwards. This is due to the fact that the radiate was so heavily debased that it was effectivly a copper alloy issue. The purchasing power of bronze issues was consequently reduced, a greater quantity of coins were required for transactions and, therefore, significant quantities were produced. Figure 3.2 compares the Beanacre assemblage against the county mean. In Reece period 13, the coin loss for the site is similar to the county mean, and there is another peak in Reece period 14 due to the quantity of Barbarous Radiates from the site. There is an above average peak in Reece period 17 and subsequently there is a significant decline in coin loss in Reece period 19. This is potentially notable as strong peaks in Reece period 19 are a trend seen throughout Wiltshire, particularly in the north of the county (Moorhead 2001a; Henry and Ellis-Schön 2017).

Late Roman Wiltshire was a productive and wealthy agricultural landscape, able to produce considerable quantities of grain and other goods for regional trade and/or export to the Continent (Moorhead 2001b; Draper 2006). It has been suggested that this Reece period 19 peak highlights an increase in rural activity possibly associated with the increased export of grain beginning in the reign of Julian the Apostate (AD 355–363) (Moorhead 2001b; Moorhead and Stuttard 2012; Brindle 2014). Furthermore, Moorhead (2009, 158) has proposed that it may have involved large numbers of public servants in the region ensuring production of commodities.

The Beanacre assemblage also provides us with the potential to assess Roman roadside settlement assemblages in the county in greater depth. Very few excavations of roadside settlements have provided the quantities of coins required to undertake statistical analysis. The most significant are Whitewalls (Wilmott and Shipp 2006), Silbury Hill (Moorhead 2011) and Nettleton Scrubb (Wedlake 1982) (see Table 3.2). The latter two sites have significant coin assemblages which, however, require careful consideration and cannot be taken at face value. The majority of coins from Silbury Hill are from two wells and a ditch rather than the settlement (Moorhead 2011), for example, although the roadside settlement assemblage itself is included in Table 3.2. This assemblage is too small for statistical analysis, but the most significant element is the four coins from Reece period 21, which highlight continuing coin use until the very end of the Roman period. The Nettleton Scrubb report (Reece 1982, 112–18) does not differentiate coins from the Roman temple and those from the roadside settlement, which distorts the data, particularly the significant peak in Reece period 18, which is regularly recorded at temple sites. The exact figure for coins from the Roman roadside settlement is not recorded.

When comparing the assemblages from Beanacre and Whitewalls, it is clear that both sites follow similar trends which might indicate a potential roadside settlement coin profile for the region (Fig. 3.3). Both have limited quantities of early issues, above average peaks in Reece periods 14 and 17 compared with the Wiltshire mean, and a significant decline in coin loss in Reece period 19. Both assemblages contain coins from the very last bronze issues to be circulated in Britain, as does that from Silbury Hill. That there is continued coin loss until the end highlights that, although there is a decline in coin loss in Reece period 19, this does not equate to abandonment. This potential roadside settlement coin profile for the region should be considered further when future assemblages from roadside settlements come to light.

Pottery

By Elina Brook and Rachael Seager Smith with a contribution by J. M. Mills

Introduction

A total of 6403 sherds of pottery, weighing approximately 102.8 kg, were recovered. The assemblage predominantly dates to the 1st to 4th centuries AD with smaller amounts of Bronze Age, medieval and post-medieval pottery. The medieval (6 sherds, 28 g) and post-medieval (1 sherd, 4 g) pieces are all unstratified and are not discussed further.

Methods

Sherds from each context were sub-divided into broad ware groups (eg, black/brown sandy ware; micaceous greyware) or known fabric types (eg, Oxfordshire colour-coated ware; South-east Dorset Black Burnished ware) and quantified by the number and weight of pieces in accordance with the standard Wessex Archaeology recording system for pottery (Morris 1992). A breakdown of the Romano-British assemblage by ware type is presented in Table 3.3. Established type series were used to record the South-east Dorset Black Burnished wares (Seager Smith and Davies 1993), the Oxfordshire wares (Young 1977), the New Forest wares (Fulford 1975) and Nene Valley wares (Perrin 1999). For the remainder of the assemblage, rims were recorded using broad form types (eg, ring necked flagon, dropped flange bowl and everted rim jar). Other variables, such asdecoration and evidence for use and repair, were also recorded. Material from a limited number of feature groups as well as other vessels of interest have been illustrated (Figs 3.4–3.11).

Two elements of the assemblage were subject to more detailed analysis; these comprise the samian – in an attempt to further refine dating, and the local oxidised sandy wares. These occur in relatively large quantities with a wide range of forms represented. Some of the forms (eg, mortaria) are known to have been traded beyond their immediate production zone but as a group, these wares are, as yet, without a detailed type series. Consequently, detailed fabric descriptions have been recorded for this group of wares (fabrics Q100–Q105) and an illustrated type series has been created.

Condition

Overall, the condition of the assemblage is moderately good with a mean sherd weight of 16.1 g. As expected, there is some variation in the condition of sherds between the chronological periods, for example 3.2 g for the Bronze Age and 16.1 g for the Romano-British material (Table 3.3). However, many of the softer, more lightly fired pieces have suffered from surface abrasion and edge damage, sometimes resulting in the loss of surface treatments, such as white slips or other colour-coatings. By contrast, however, the samian sherds are generally in good condition with little or no damage to the slip from the burial environment or post-depositional attrition, while the sherds are of moderate size (mean weight 11.8 g), with the later material surviving as larger pieces (Table 3.3).

Bronze Age

The earliest pottery is of probable Bronze Age date (22 sherds, 70 g). These consist of undiagnostic, abraded fragments in very poor condition (mean sherd weight 3.2 g) dated on fabric grounds alone. All are in a grog-tempered fabric, although two pieces contain additional rare flint inclusions. The majority came from posthole 1521 (14 fragments, 46 g) including two body sherds with finger-tip impressed decoration. A further six sherds (10 g) were found in pit 1525. These are the only ceramic finds from these features. The remaining two fragments (14 g) were residual within possible furrow 1406.

Table 3.3 Pottery totals by chronological period and ware type

Ware	*Fabric code*	*No.*	*% No.*	*Wt (g)*	*% Wt*	*MSW (g)*
Samian						
SG (La Graufesenque)	LGF SA	52	0.8	459	0.4	8.8
SG (Montans)	MON SA	2	<0.1	32	<0.1	16.0
C1st Lezoux	LEZ SA 1	1	<0.1	17	<0.1	17.0
Les Martres-de-Veyre	LMV SA	11	0.2	128	0.1	11.6
CG (Lezoux)	LEZ SA 2	135	2.1	1539	1.5	11.4
EG (La Madeleine)	MAD SA	1	<0.1	19	<0.1	19.0
EG (Rheinzabern)	RHZ SA	6	<0.1	158	0.2	26.3
EG (Trier)	TRI SA	5	<0.1	164	0.2	32.8
Samian sub-total		*213*	*3.3*	*2516*	*2.5*	*11.8*
Other imported wares						
Amphorae		160	2.5	7698	7.5	48.1
North Gaulish mortaria		7	0.1	684	0.7	97.7
Imported fineware		2	<0.1	6	<0.1	3.0
Other imports sub-total		*169*	*2.7*	*8388*	*8.2*	*49.6*
Regional wares						
SE Dorset Black Burnished ware	DOR BB1	486	7.6	7315	7.1	15.1
SE Dorset Black Burnished ware mortaria		1	<0.1	69	<0.1	69
Oxon colour-coated ware	OXF RS	22	0.3	316	0.3	14.4
Oxon whiteware mortaria	OXF WH (M)	15	0.2	672	0.7	44.8
Oxon colour-coated ware mortaria	OXF RS (M)	11	0.2	115	0.1	10.4
Oxon whiteware	OXF WH	3	<0.1	41	<0.1	13.7
Oxon white colour-coated ware	OXF WS	1	<0.1	9	<0.1	9.0
Oxon white colour-coated ware mortaria	OXF WS (M)	1	<0.1	10	<0.1	10.0
New Forest colour-coated ware		22	0.3	191	0.2	8.7
Verulamium region whiteware	VER WH	7	0.1	77	<0.1	11.0
Nene Valley ware mortaria		2	<0.1	472	0.5	236
Regional sub-total		*571*	*9.0*	*9287*	*9.0*	*16.3*
Local wares						
Mica-dusted ware		33	0.5	702	0.7	21.3
Miscellaneous colour-coated ware		4	<0.1	75	<0.1	18.8
Fine greyware		6	<0.1	28	<0.1	4.7
Fine whiteware		1	<0.1	5	<0.1	5.0
N. Wilts colour-coated ware		1	<0.1	15	<0.1	15.0
Lead glazed ware		1	<0.1	1	<0.1	1
Coarse oxidised sandy ware	Q101	1047	16.4	10065	9.8	9.6
Coarse, white-slipped oxidised sandy ware	Q103 / SOW WS	204	3.2	2656	2.6	13.0
Fine oxidised sandy ware	Q100	154	2.4	990	1.0	6.4
Red-brown oxidised ware	Q105	67	1.0	1215	1.2	18.1
Fine, white-slipped oxidised ware	Q102	7	0.1	115	0.1	16.4
Coarse, white-slipped sandy ware mortaria	Q104 / SOW WS (M)	48	0.8	3655	3.6	76.1
Fine oxidised ware		26	0.4	128	0.1	5.0
Oxidised ware		106	1.7	1080	1.1	10.2
Whiteware		35	0.5	365	0.4	10.4
White-slipped redware		11	0.2	385	0.4	35.0
Black/brown sandy ware		2690	42.2	24607	24.0	9.1
Savernake-type ware	SAV GT	762	12.0	31556	30.7	41.4
Blue-greyware		129	2.0	3178	3.1	24.6
Micaceous greyware		31	0.5	407	0.4	13.1
Glauconitic sandy greyware		23	0.4	432	0.4	18.8
Black micaceous ware		3	<0.1	75	<0.1	25.0
Flint-tempered ware		13	0.2	454	0.4	34.9
Sand and calcareous-tempered ware		12	0.2	107	0.1	8.9
Grog-tempered ware		4	<0.1	50	<0.1	12.5
Calcareous ware		1	<0.1	7	<0.1	7.0
Flint and grog-tempered ware		1	<0.1	128	0.1	128.0
Local wares sub-total		*5420*	*85.0*	*82481*	*80.3*	*15.2*
Total		**6373**		**102,672**		**16.1**

Roman

A total of 6373 sherds (102,672 g) are of Romano-British date. This material spans the entire period, from the 1st to 4th centuries AD, although the main focus occurred during the 2nd–3rd centuries AD. Despite the condition of sherds being moderately good (mean sherd weight 16.1 g), many rims are broken at the neck/shoulder junction thereby hindering further identification of specific form. Just 10 complete profiles were recorded.

Table 3.4 Quantification of samian by fabric (production centre) and phase

Phase	C1st Lezoux		SG (La Graufesenque)		SG (Montans)		Les Martres-de-Veyre		CG (Lezoux)		EG (La Mad)		EG (Rheinz)		EG (Trier)	
	No	Wt	No	Wt	No	Wt	No	Wt	No	Wt	No	Wt	No	Wt	No	Wt
ERB	1	17	13	82	–	–	1	5	1	4	–	–	–	–	–	–
MRB	–	–	19	252	2	32	8	111	79	993	–	–	1	9	–	–
LRB	–	–	11	56	–	–	1	5	35	389	1	19	2	103	2	93
M/LRB	–	–	1	1	–	–	–	–	2	25	–	–	1	12	–	–
R-B	–	–	7	62	–	–	1	7	5	31	–	–	–	–	–	–
PMed		–	–	–	–	–	–	–	1	4	–	–	–	–	–	–
U/S	–	–	1	6	–	–	–	–	12	93	–	–	2	34	3	71
Total	**1**	**17**	**52**	**459**	**2**	**32**	**11**	**128**	**135**	**1539**	**1**	**19**	**6**	**158**	**5**	**164**

Production Centre (Fabric)

Samian

by J. M. Mills

Imported fine and specialist wares collectively make up 6% of the Romano-British assemblage (Table 3.3), the majority being samian (3.3%).

The samian (213 sherds, 2516 g) is noteworthy for the range of production centres represented (Table 3.4). The majority of the South Gaulish pottery is, as is usual, of 1st century AD date and from La Graufesenque, although two pieces of 2nd century AD date from Montans were also identified. The bulk of the assemblage is from Central Gaul. Products from this region include a single sherd of the 1st century AD micaceous Lezoux fabric, as well as 11 pieces from the Trajanic-Hadrianic kilns of Les Martres-de-Veyre. Otherwise, the Central Gaulish samian is of Hadrianic and Antonine date and from Lezoux. The East Gaulish vessels include the standard Antonine to mid-3rd century AD wares from Rheinzabern and Trier, as well as one sherd from the Hadrianic to early Antonine kilns at La Madeleine. It is unusual for 1st century AD Lezoux ware and products from La Madeleine and Montans to occur in an assemblage of this size, as these are uncommon finds away from the large, urban centres. The 3rd century AD Trier mortarium (Pl. 3.1) is also an unusual find in rural Wiltshire, although one was recently recognised from Worcester (Mills forthcoming) suggesting a distribution beyond the south and east of Britain.

Unless specified otherwise, all forms mentioned below are from the Dragendorff series. The range of forms is wide (Table 3.5) for a small group, and includes less common forms such as Ritterling 8, Walters 81 and a form 42 dish alongside the more common bowl, dish, cup and decorated forms. Some forms, however, such as the cup/dish set form 35/36 and flanged bowl form 38, are perhaps under-represented in this assemblage. Similarly, given the presence of later vessels like the form 31R bowls and form 45 mortaria, the Walters 79/80 dish and cup set and, to a lesser extent, dishes of Curle 11 and 23 are few in number. Although in many instances the sherds are rather small and scrappy, there also appears to be a higher than usual percentage of decorated forms, especially within the fills of the mid-Romano-British pits and ovens.

The samian from the earliest Roman phase of activity (AD 50–150) amounts to just 16 sherds. Of these, 14 are from 1st century AD vessels; 13 are from La Graufesenque and one is in the early micaceous Lezoux fabric (Fig. 3.4, 4; Dec. Cat. No. 7). The earliest is a pre-Flavian Ritterling 8 cup base from beamslot 1270 of Building 1, while an example of decorated bowl form Drag 37, a Flavian introduction, came from the post-abandonment deposits associated with this structure (Fig. 3.4, 2; Dec. Cat. No. 5). Two other sherds, from a form 18/31 dish from Les Martres-de-Veyre (AD 100–125), and a Central Gaulish form 37 decorated bowl in the style of Potter X-9 (AD 110–130; Dec. Cat. No. 9) came from pit 1385 and gully 1334 respectively. The mean sherd weight for this group is less than 7 g, and a low sherd weight is often interpreted as suggesting deposition at a distance from the main focus of occupation. There is a high number of decorated bowl sherds among the group (cups: 4, platters/dishes: 5; decorated bowls: 7), but the significance of this, if any, cannot be ascertained from so few sherds.

Samian of the period AD 50–150 was also found residually across the site, with most of the La Graufesenque products, the Montans sherds, and most of the Les Martres vessels being from contexts assigned to later phases (Table 3.4). These, along with the single rim from a form 18/31 dish from La Madeleine in East Gaul (segment 1039 of late Romano-British ditch 1920), were manufactured before AD 150. Some of the Central Gaulish vessels from Lezoux will also belong within this early Roman group. Examples include the two sherds from bowls attributed to Austrus (Fig. 3.4, 5 and 6; Dec. Cat. No. 11 and 12), and a form 42 variant dish from ditch 1933, which all clearly pre-date AD 150, but few of

Table 3.5 Vessel forms (all Dragendorff unless specified otherwise) by fabric with rim EVES shown in brackets

		South Gaul		Central Gaul			East Gaul		
Vessel function	*Vessel form*	*La Grauf*	*Montans*	*C1st Lezoux*	*Les Martres*	*Lezoux*	*La Mad*	*Rhein*	*Trier*
Cup	Ritt 8	1	–	–	–	–	–	–	–
	27	9 (0.35)	–	–	–	1	–	–	–
	27g	1	–	–	–	–	–	–	–
	33	1 (0.13)	–	–	1	17 (0.81)	–	–	–
	40		–	–	–	–	–	1	–
Plate/dish	15/17	1 (0.22)	–	–	–	–	–	–	–
	15/17 or 18	1	–	–	–	–	–	–	–
	18	8 (0.46)	–	–	–	–	–	–	–
	18R	1	–	–	–	–	–	–	–
	18/31	2 (0.15)	–	–	2	2	1 (0.13)	–	–
	18/31 - 31	–	–	–	–	1	–	–	–
	18/31R	–	–	–	–	1	–	–	–
	18/31R or 31R	–	–	–	–	3 (0.06)	–	–	–
	18/31 or 31	–	–	–	–	1	–	–	–
	18/31ser	–	–	–	–	2 (0.08)	–	–	–
	31	–	–	–	–	15 (0.28)	–	–	–
	Lud Sa	–	–	–	–	–	–	–	1 (0.2)
	Curle 23	–	–	–	–	1 (0.09)	–	–	–
	36	–	–	–	–	3 (0.17)	–	–	–
	42 var	–	–	–	–	1 (0.05)	–	–	–
Plain bowl	Curle 11	1	–	–	–	–	–	–	–
	31R	–	–	–	–	5 (0.14)	–	–	–
	Lud Sb	–	–	–	–	–	–	1	3 (0.06)
	38	–	–	–	–	–	–	1	–
	Wa 81	–	–	–	–	–	–	1 (0.06)	–
Decorated bowl	29	4	–	1 (0.07)	–	–	–	–	–
	30	1	–	–	1	–	–	–	–
	37	9 (0.26)	1	–	2	24 (0.49)	–	1	–
	30 or 37	–	–	–	–	1	–	–	–
Mortaria	Curle 21	–	–	–	–	1	–	–	–
	45	–	–	–	–	–	–	–	1 (0.07)
Beaker/ closed	Dech 72	–	–	–	–	1	–	–	–
Total (max number)		**40**	**1**	**1**	**6**	**77**	**1**	**5**	**5**
Unspecified forms	cup	1	–	–	1	3	–	–	–
	dish/bowl	6 (0.05)	1	–	2	12 (0.25)	–	–	–
	bowl	–	–	–	–	6 (0.1)	–	–	–
	chips	4 sherds, 5g	–	–	–	25 sherds, 73g	–	–	–

the Lezoux vessels can be dated so closely. Forms such as the form 27 cup and 18/31 dish, and its rouletted counterpart 18/31R, which were not made after *c.* AD 160, are poorly represented in this assemblage, with just one Central Gaulish form 27 cup (late Romano-British well 1678) and two Drag 18/31 dishes, being noted. One of these dishes is stamped by Senonios (Stamp cat S2), while the other stamped by Cuccillus i (Stamp cat S1) is a form transitional between 18/31 and 31, which was probably not made later than AD 160. The low numbers of these forms suggests limited activity during this early period of occupation.

A little over half of the samian came from contexts assigned to the period AD 150–250, which spans the second half of the main period during which samian was imported into Britain. Among this group, there is much residual samian from South Gaul (La Graufesenque) and Les Martres-de-Veyre, as well as early 2nd century sherds from Montans (Table 3.4). Interestingly, except for one sherd, the latest samian (10 sherds from 2nd to mid-3rd century AD vessels from East Gaul), was residual, found in late Romano-British levels or unstratified.

This bias within the assemblage to the second half of the 2nd century AD may be further illustrated by comparing the incidence of 2nd century examples of cup form 27 with that of form 33 (1 and 17 examples respectively) and dishes of forms 18/31 (4 examples) and 18/31R (1 example) to forms 31 and 31R (15 and 5 examples respectively), which developed from them. The later forms are clearly more numerous and serve to indicate increased activity during the mid–late 2nd century AD.

The main events of this period (eg, the silting of hollow-way 1925 and trackway/quarry 1932, the infilling of the enclosure ditches and the building of many ovens), produced groups of samian that, in general, are very similar in date. A high proportion of decorated forms was apparent in various pits, ovens and in ditch 1773 associated with the ovens. Three of the six vessels from ovens 1336, 1157, 1123, 1227, 1293 and 1593, for example, are decorated bowls, probably all of form 37, with joining sherds from ovens 1227 and 1293. Samian representing 16 vessels was found in pits 1121, 1158, 1165, 1414, 1752 and 1879, and rake out pit 1171; of these, seven are form 37 bowls, including one decorated in the style of

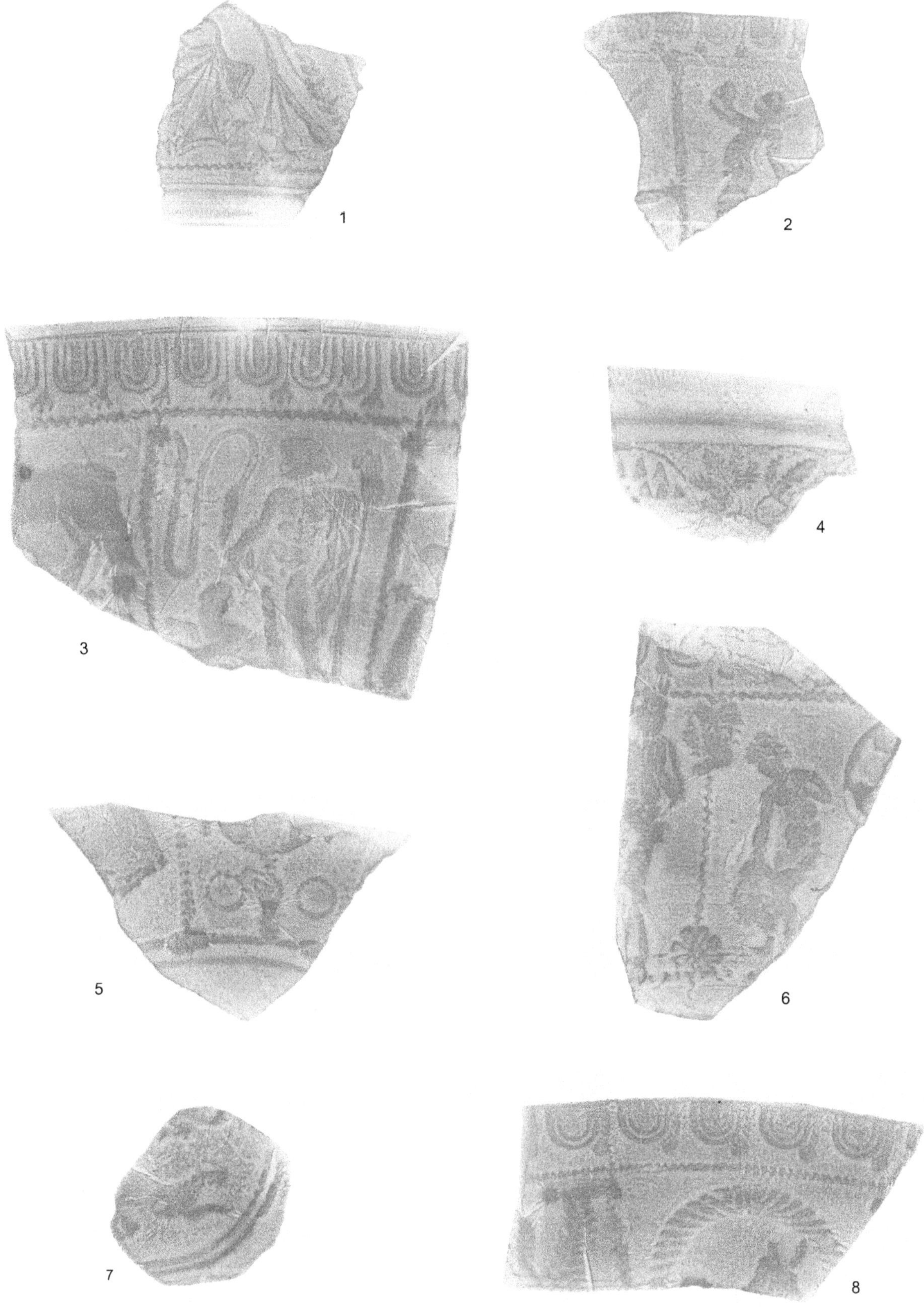

Figure 3.4 Decorated samian (nos 1–8) 1= Cat no. 1; 2 = Cat no. 5; 3 = Cat no. 6; 4 = Cat no. 7; 5 = Cat no. 11; 6 = Cat no. 12; 7 = Cat no. 24; 8 = Cat no. 26

Figure 3.5 Decorated samian (no. 9 = Cat no. 27)

Plate 3.1 Samian mortarium (Trier Drag 45)

Paternus II (Fig. 3.5, 9; Dec. Cat. No. 27), dated AD 160–190. This might be coincidental, but contrasts with the hollow-way fills where, from a maximum of 27 vessels, only three are form 37 bowls and two of these are residual South Gaulish vessels.

Overall, approximately 40% of the samian was found in late Romano-British (AD 250–410), unassigned or unstratified contexts (Table 3.4). Although some Central Gaulish vessels may well have remained in use into the 3rd century AD, it is not possible to identify any definite examples within this collection. At least two of the Trier vessels, however, were manufactured in the 3rd century AD. The mortarium has the bat-like spout (Pl. 3.1), characteristic of this period (Bird 1986, 183, 2.214), while the Lud Sb bowl rim from grain drier 1474 has a thin orangey slip and is also a 3rd century AD product. Samian exports to Britain ceased around AD 260 (Bird 1993, 2), so it is unlikely that much, if any, of the samian is contemporary with the late Romano-British activity at this site. The majority of sherds from features assigned to this period came from ditch fills, while four small sherds were found in the possible well 1936.

Samian Potters' Stamps

Potter's names and die numbers for the stamps are taken from NoTS Volumes 1–9 *Names on Terra Sigillata* (Hartley and Dickinson 2008–2012). Each entry gives: potters name (i, ii etc., where homonyms are involved), die, READING, production centre (fabric codes), form. Comment. Date. [excavation reference/context number]

S1. Cuccillus i, 2c, form 18/31, Lezoux. ϾVCϾILL·IM. This potters' dish forms are noted as being between 18/31 and 31 (Hartley and Dickinson 2008, 216). This example seems to have a high kick, but rises only in centre of the base so although a transitional form, it is dated as a form 18/31. A drilled hole through the base is probably evidence of repair although the hole is slightly larger than is usual

(6 mm in diameter). AD145–60. Context 1062, mid-Romano-British ditch 1061

S2. Senonios, 1a, Drag 18/31, Lezoux. [SE]NONIO[S] AD130–60. Layer 1161

S3. OFA[SG, dish, AD 50–110. Post-abandonment layer 1178 above Building 1

S4.]I or [I CG, form unknown, Hadrianic or Antonine. Context 1680, late Romano-British well 1678

S5.]NI CG, form 33 or 46, Hadrianic or Antonine. Layer 1602

S6 OII II OF form 31, anepigraphic/illiterate stamp Central Gaul. On the underside there is a lot of wear (removing the slip) in the centre. Antonine. Context 1037, late Romano-British ditch 1920

Decorated samian catalogue

South Gaul (La Graufesenque)

1. Form 30. Winding scroll of bifid leaves with palmate leaves and poppy seed heads and a zig-zag line at base of decoration. All these elements can be found on bowls with Masclus' mould signature. AD 50–65. Context 1449, late Romano-British ditch 1913. Fig. 3.4, 1
2. Form 29. From upper zone of decoration comprising festoons containing scrolls? with a pendant poppy head between. AD 50–85. Context 1295, group/structure 1328, phase 2 of Building 1
3. Form 37. Panelled decoration in the style of several of the bowls from Pompeii (Atkinson 1914), with a bifid wreath and panels above it extant, showing S-shaped gadroons and a running dog with leaf tips. AD 65–80. Context 1109, late Romano-British well 1936
4. Form 37. Bowl with a straight wreath of leaves below the ovolo (not surviving), a winding scroll, the lower lobe inhabited by a small boar (Hermet 1934, pl.27, 45 = O.1690) above rows of leaf tips. The wreath and boar are both on a bowl with a scrolled decorative scheme from the Cala Culip IV wreck (Neito and Puig 2001, bowl 410). Burnt. AD 70–85. Layer 1161
5. Form 37. Rim from a small bowl (diameter 160 mm); the ovolo has a long tongue with rosette terminal; the moulding is not clear and the borders appear as lines; rosettes at the junctions are evident. The only figure is a small one with one raised and one trailing arm (O.646). The ovolo occurs on small bowls including some with the PAS_ mould signature (Mees 1995, taf 160,1); several bowls from La Graufesenque have both the ovolo and figure (http://www.rgzm.de/samian/home/frames.htm, ser. nos 2001299, 2001983, 2001997). AD 75–100. Layer 1178, post-abandonment layer above Building 1. Fig. 3.4, 2
6. Form 37. Panelled decoration with an ovolo with bent, trident-tongue curving to the left and a narrow core above a wavy border. The panels have wavy line dividers with rosette terminals. The figure types include Bacchus with panther O.565, and a standing animal with a short tail, perhaps a stag or bear, facing left; only the rear legs extant. The Bacchus is on named bowls by Germanus and Calvus although the ovolo is not known for either potter. Flavian. Context 1887, mid-Romano-British trackway/quarry 1932. Fig. 3.4, 3

Central Gaul

7. Form 29. Micaceous Lezoux fabric. Scroll infilled with leaf tips and small, finely-detailed vine leaves. AD 50–85. Context 1296, group 1924, phase 1 of Building 1. Fig. 3.4, 4
8. Form 37. Les Martres-de-Veyre. Scrap of basal scroll of ram's horn motif (Rogers G377), used by Potter X-11 (Stanfield and Simpson 1990, 35, 414) in the same manner on a bowl from London. AD 100–125. Context 1774, mid-Romano-British ditch 1773

Lezoux

9. Form 37. Body sherd with part of an eagle (R.4033) and no other decoration. The eagle was used by Potter X-9. AD 110–130. Context 1335, early Romano-British gully 1334
10. Form 37. Burnt body sherd with ovolo (B204) above a bead row, an incomplete saltire of fine beads containing acanthus (Rogers K2) on an astragalus stalk (cf Stanfield and Simpson 1990, fig. 23, 13 and pl.85, 9 with mould stamp OF ATT) is all that survives of the decorative scheme. Probably Attianus. AD 120–145. Context 1172, mid-Romano-British rake out pit 1171
11. Form 37. Sherd from lower part of a bowl with two ridges delinenating the decorated zone. The vertical panels have beaded dividers with a terminal double D motif (Rogers B181), decoration includes an acanthus (Rogers K5) on a vertical astragalus flanked by plain rings. The panel to the left contains a plain square box which has not been identified. The acanthus and D motif were used by Austrus who also closed his decoration with a double ridge; all occur on a bowl from London attributed to Austrus (Stanfield and Simpson 1990, pl. 95, 21). AD 125–50. Layer 1161. Fig. 3.4, 5
12. Form 37. Body sherd from a bowl in Austrus' style – the wavy vertical divider with a mask (O.1216) at the top and rosette (Rogers C54) at the bottom is on a bowl from Castleford (Dickinson and Hartley 2000, fig. 35, 1014); figures Pan (O.709) and Venus (O.291) are both known for this potter. Although fragmentary, the ovolo is likely to be Rogers B244. AD 125–50. Layer 1602. Fig. 3.4, 6

Plate 3.2 Romano-British pottery spindlewhorls and 'discs'

13. Form 37. Incomplete ovolo with wavy border below. Hadrianic–early Antonine. Context 1148, late Romano-British ditch 1147
14. Form 37. Scrap with ovolo Rogers B24, small beads below the ovolo and as a panel divider. There is also the head of a figure, but it is not identifiable. The ovolo was used by several Lezoux potters including Docilis, Secundinus I and the Large S Potter. Hadrianic–early Antonine. Layer 1161
15. Form 37. Scrap with single-bordered ovolo (Rogers B74) with beaded border below. Used by several potters including the Quintilianus group and Cinnamus. Hadrianic–early Antonine. Layer 1741
16. Form 37. Ovolo (Rogers B17), with bead row below; the only extant elements of the freestyle decoration are the head of a large cat (probably rear facing panther O.1537) and infilling leaf tips (Rogers K2). The figure and motifs were all used by both Attianus II and Criciro. AD 120–165. Context 1168, mid-Romano-British pit 1165
17. Form 37. Ovolo (Rogers B231), used by several potters including Cinnamus ii, Sacer, Paternus III and Pugnus. Hadrianic–mid-Antonine. Context 1168, mid-Romano-British pit 1165
18. Form 37. 8-petalled rosette (Rogers C53). This rosette was used by several potters including Sacer, Cinnamus ii and Albucius. Hadrianic or Antonine. Context 1680, late Romano-British well 1678
19. Form 37. Standing figure but not identifiable. Hadrianic or Antonine. Context 1753, mid-Romano-British pit 1752
20. Form 37. Rim with ovolo (Rogers B52) with wavy line below; a beaded panel divider with open ring terminal suggests that this is Divixtus. Diana with deer (O.106) is on a form 30 bowl with the same ovolo and a Divixtus mould stamp from York (Stanfield and Simpson 1990, pl.115, 4). The use of a wavy border by Divixtus is unusual on form 37 vessels, but is seen occasionally on form 30 with his stamp. AD 135–165. Contexts 1228 and 1292, mid-Romano-British ovens 1227 and 1293 respectively
21. Form 37. Ovolo used by Tetturo, Tasgillus iii, and L. Immun(i)us with coarse wavy line below. AD 135–65. Unstratified
22. Form 37. Scrap with ovolo Rogers B144 and beads below. The ovolo was used by Sacer, Cinnamus ii and Cerialis ii and a few other potters. AD 135–70. Layer 1161
23. Form 37. Battered rim with an unclear ovolo with a bent tongue (could be Rogers B231), with a wavy border below and a pair of festoons, each containing seated bird (? O.2239). The festoons have a small trifid leaf terminal (Rogers G109), a feature seen on some of Pugnus' bowls (Stanfield and Simpson 1990, pl. 153, 4, 9). There is some kind of pendant, or perhaps a panel divider, between the festoons, but not enough survives to identify. The bird was used by several late Hadrianic and Antonine potters, but is not listed by Rogers (1999, 204), nor is any bird despite a seated bird being evident on his illustration pl.91, 6 (with ovolo B231). AD 140–170. Layer 1736, mid-Roman-British trackway/quarry 1932
24. Form 37. Panther (O.1518 or 1519) and another figure (possibly another large cat) above it in a double-bordered medallion. The sherd has been cut into a rough disc; the edges are very smooth although the shape is not regular; wear on the edges of the convex side suggests use as a gaming counter. Antonine. Context 1159, mid-Romano-British pit 1158, ON 240. Fig. 3.4, 7, Pl. 3.2
25. Form 37. Low pad-shaped foot-ring and base of decoration; a running goat above a plain line defining the lower edge of the decorated zone is all that remains. The goat (O.1842), was used by many potters. Antonine. Context 1467, mid-Romano-British ditch 1938
26. Form 37. Rim from a small bowl (180 mm diameter) with ovolo Rogers B231 and neat bead row below with a vertical beaded divider. Decoration comprises a festoon (Rogers F40) with mask (O.1214) placed horizontally and a small, cabled medallion containing seated deer (O.1704). The ovolo, mask, deer and festoon are all known for Cinnamus. The deer, and the mask placed horizontally are on a mould from Lezoux with Cinnamus 'advert' stamp, albeit with different motifs (ser. no. 0010830). The medallion could be Rogers E31 used by Attianus (Stanfield and Simpson 1990, pl. 87, 23). AD 150–175. Context 1088, late Romano-British robber trench 1923. Fig. 3.4, 8
27. Form 37. Four sherds from a vessel in Paternus II style, with ovolo (Rogers B105). The design is in panels with beaded dividers. Panels contain stand (Rogers Q16), Apollo (O.77) and triton (O.19) within a large, double-bordered medallion flanked by small plain rings, and Pudicitia (O.926A). The

motifs and figure types were used by several different potters, but only Paternus II is recorded as having used all of them. Pudicitia, the triton in a medallion and ovolo are all on a Paternus stamped bowl from the Wroxeter gutter group (Atkinson 1942; (http://www.rgzm.de/samian/home/frames.htm ser. no. 0012205). AD 160–90. Context 1172, mid-Romano-British rake out pit 1171. Fig. 3.5, 9

Other illustrated samian

Pl. 3.1. Form 45. East Gaul, Trier. Rim and applied mask/spout with very thin slip, little remains, version of Type d" (Bird 1986, 183, 2.214). AD 200–260. Unstratified

Other imported wares

The remainder of the imported wares (169 sherds, 8388 g) are dominated by 151 sherds from Dressel 20 olive oil containers from the Spanish province of Baetica. This was the most common amphora type imported into Britain during the late 1st through to the early 3rd centuries AD (Peacock and Williams 1986, 136). The largest quantity from a single feature came from pit 1387 (106 pieces, 4015 g), many of which are burnt. The assemblage also includes two deliberately removed Dressel 20 handle fragments (cleaning layer 1161 and tree-throw hole 1357). Of comparable date range are eight body sherds from Gallic (Pélichet 47) amphorae which were principally used to transport wine (Peacock and Williams 1986, 143). The remaining amphora sherd is a body fragment from a 'Carrot' amphora, dating to the late 1st century AD but found residually within cleaning layer 1161; a Mediterranean source seems likely for this relatively uncommon type which may have carried dates.

A small quantity of early Romano-British imported mortaria (Table 3.3) was also identified. These include rims from at least two examples of Gillam form 238 (Group II: AD 65–110) from the Oise/Somme area of Northern Gaul (Hartley 1998, 203). All appear to be residual within features of mid- to late Romano-British date. Later imported finewares comprise a Central Gaulish black-slipped ware cup fragment (*c.* AD 150/160–200/250) from late Romano-British pit 1164 and a 3rd century AD Moselkeramik indented beaker body sherd from late Romano-British ditch 1908.

Regional wares

Traded regional wares are moderately well represented (9.0% by sherd count and weight) and include table wares from the Verulamium region, Nene Valley, New Forest and Oxfordshire kilns as well as South-east Dorset Black Burnished wares. By far the most common of these are the South-east Dorset Black Burnished wares which amount to 7.6% by count of the total Romano-British assemblage. These comprise a typical range of vessels, including jars (Seager Smith and Davies 1993, forms WA1–3), shallow straight-sided dishes (*ibid.*, form WA20) and bowls/dishes with flat, grooved or dropped flanges (*ibid.*, forms WA22, 24 and 25). Less common forms include a fish dish (form WA21; unstratified) and a fragment of a previously undocumented wall-sided mortarium with a beaded rim and variable pink, white and clear quartz trituration grits (form WA110; see Fig. 3.11, 113; late Romano-British ditch 1908). Other, mortaria-like bowls are known but none so far have been gritted. In addition to burnishing, surface treatments include coarse wiping which is a characteristic of the later 3rd to 4th centuries AD for this ware. Decoration consists of burnished lattice and overlapping hoop motifs and, in one instance, combed lines in a zig-zag pattern as seen on a jar body from late Romano-British layer 1910 (Fig. 3.11, 123). Chronologically, these span the 2nd to later 3rd–4th centuries AD.

Products of the Oxfordshire industry account for 0.8% of the Romano-British assemblage (Table 3.3), the majority dating from the mid-3rd century AD onwards. The red and brown colour-coated wares include a bead rim from a wall-sided, carinated bowl with rouletted decoration (Young 1977, type C81; 4th century AD) from ditch 1516, and a copy of a samian form 31 bowl (*ibid.*, type C45; AD 270–400) from posthole 1488. Several sherds from colour-coated ware mortaria are also present, although only one rim is identifiable (*ibid.*, type C97; AD 240–400 from ditch 1911). Ditch 1516, however, contained sherds from a red colour-coated ware mortarium, probably also type C97 (*ibid.*,), that appears to have had the rim deliberately removed. Two pieces of white colour-coated ware (a mortaria body sherd, and a rim from a wall-sided, carinated bowl decorated with red paint (*ibid.*, type WC3; AD 240–400) were found in possible well 1936 and ditch 1915. With the exception of three plain body sherds, all of the whitewares are from mortaria. One of these, a bead and roll-rim type (see Fig. 3.10, 101; *ibid.*, type M1; AD 100–150) from mid-Romano-British ditch 1443, is stamped with a rectangular panel with a circle in the centre and a double 'herringbone' style motif either side, comparable to stamps from Littlemore, Ashurst Clinic (*ibid.*, 58, fig. 13, 17). Other whiteware mortaria represented date from the 2nd century AD (type M2), 3rd century (type M18) and later 3rd into the 4th centuries AD (types M17 and M22).

The small quantity of New Forest colour-coated wares all date to the late Romano-British period. The majority are body sherds from beakers, some indented, along with one from a closed form, possibly a flagon (robber trench 1927). Other diagnostic or featured sherds include two beaker rims from natural feature 1583 and ditch 1937, neither of which are identifiable to type, and an indented beaker body with white painted decoration.

Other less well represented regional wares include seven sherds of Verulamium region whiteware, dated to the second half of the 1st through to the mid-2nd century AD. With the exception of one mortaria fragment found in oven 1934, all are undiagnostic body sherds. Fragments from two bead and flanged Nene Valley ware mortaria were found in colluvium 1371 and late Romano-British ditch 1516 (Fig. 3.11, 124). The piece from ditch 1516 is a complete profile and the very smooth/worn trituration grits indicate that it had been well used. These vessels were produced throughout the 2nd to 4th centuries AD (Perrin 1999, 129).

Local wares

A diverse range of local wares dominate the assemblage. These include a small number of fine and specialist wares as well as utilitarian coarsewares predominantly occurring in a variety of sandy fabrics (Table 3.3).

Single sherds of North Wiltshire colour-coated ware (from late Romano-British ditch 1911) and lead glazed ware (pit 1697) are products of the poorly documented Wiltshire industry dating from the late 1st to 2nd century AD (Anderson 1979). The 33 sherds of mica-dusted ware may also belong to this industry, although kilns in Gloucester were also producing such wares between *c.* AD 80–110 (Rawes 1972, 28). The sherds are likely to derive from just three vessels: a possible platter from early Romano-British oven 1563; a flanged bowl from mid-Romano-British feature 1932; and a large globular bodied vessel (probably a beaker) with external rilling found in the terminal of ditch 1907. Small quantities of mica-dusted ware have been found at other sites in the region such as Groundwell Ridge, Swindon (Timby 2012, 52; Timby forthcoming) and Kingscote (Timby 1998, 251, fabric TF3B) in south Gloucestershire. Elsewhere in Britain, mica-dusted wares were widespread during the early 2nd century AD (Marsh 1978, 122). Small quantities of other unsourced but probably local fine wares include undiagnostic sherds of miscellaneous colour-coated ware, fine greyware and fine whiteware.

Local oxidised sandy wares

A large proportion (85.6% by sherd count) of the local oxidised wares are manufactured from relatively coarse, gritty, sandy fabrics characterised by rounded white and pink quartz inclusions combined with iron-rich grains (fabrics Q100–Q104). Although the centre of production is unknown, the distribution suggests a source in north Wiltshire, or possibly in the Avon area and the frequency of and wide range of forms present at Beanacre suggests that it may have been made nearby. Given the large quantity and the absence of a detailed type series, this fabric group was fully recorded.

Vessels are wheelmade and generally hard fired, and although predominantly oxidised are sometimes fired to a dark grey with a distinct speckled orange surface. Although most sherds are in a coarse variant (Q101), a small number (154 sherds) are in a finer fabric containing a smaller proportion of coarse quartz sand (Q100). Both variants can also appear with a white-slip (Q102 and Q103 respectively) of varying thickness. It is highly likely that more of the assemblage originally had a white-slip which has subsequently been lost as a result of post-depositional processes. In addition, the use of this fabric to make white-slipped mortaria (Q104) indicates that this group corresponds to South-West White-slipped ware (SOW WS) in the National Roman Fabric Reference Collection (Tomber and Dore 1998, 192); mortaria fabric 8 at Wanborough, Wiltshire (Hartley 2001, 221); fabrics 15/15a/15v and 90 at Kingscote (Timby 1998, 252–3); fabric 15/A/D and 90 at Atworth (Timby 2008, 107); fabric 13 at Uley, Gloucestershire (Leach 1993, 230) and fabric 88 at Cirencester (Rigby 1982, 119).

Although of slightly different appearance in that it has been fired, fairly consistently, to a more red-brown colour and has a more leathery feel to touch, fabric Q105 has also been considered as part of this group. This is because the quartz sand and iron-rich components within the fabric suggest that it is highly likely to be related to fabrics Q100–Q104. Detailed fabric descriptions are given below and see Appendix 1.

Oxidised sandy ware fabric descriptions

Q100: Fine oxidised sandy ware. A moderately hard sandy fabric containing rare (2–3%), moderately sorted, rounded quartz sand (0.25–1 mm), rare (2%) sub-rounded iron-rich grains up to 1 mm, rare (1%) chalk fragments (1–3 mm) and clay pellets (< 1 mm) in a slightly micaceous clay matrix. This fabric generally has oxidised interior and exterior surfaces with a grey core, although rarely it may be oxidised all the way through (Appendix 1, A1–A2).

Q101: Coarse oxidised sandy ware. A hard sandy fabric with common (20%), moderately sorted, rounded quartz sand (0.25–1 mm), rare to sparse (2–3%) sub-rounded iron-rich grains up to 1 mm and rare clay pellets (< 1 mm). Generally this fabric is oxidised on the surfaces with a grey core but can be fired to a grey colour with a distinctive speckled orange surface (Appendix 1, A3–A4).

Q102: Fine, white-slipped oxidised sandy ware. A moderately hard fabric containing rare (2%), moderately sorted, rounded quartz sand (0.25–0.5 mm, rarely up to 1 mm), rare (2%) sub-rounded iron-rich grains up to 1 mm and rare clay pellets (< 1 mm). This is a variant of fabric Q100 with a white/pale cream slip (Appendix 1, A5).

Q103: Coarse, white-slipped oxidised sandy ware. A hard sandy fabric with common (20%), moderately sorted, rounded quartz sand (0.25–1 mm), rare to sparse (2–3%) sub-rounded iron-rich grains up to 1 mm and rare clay pellets (< 1 mm). A variant of fabric Q101 with a white/pale cream slip (Appendix 1, A6–A7).

Q104: South-West White-slipped ware (Tomber and Dore 1998, 192, NRFRC fabric SOW WS). Coarse, white-slipped oxidised sandy ware. Mortaria fabric. A hard sandy fabric containing very common to abundant (30–40%), moderately sorted, rounded quartz sand (0.25–1 mm), rare to sparse (2–3%) iron-rich grains (< 1 mm) and rare clay pellets (< 1 mm). This is a variant of Q101 that generally contains a higher proportion of quartz sand, surfaces are oxidised (orange) with a grey core, the white/pale cream slip is as seen on Q103. Trituration grits consist of common, well-sorted mono- and polycrystalline white and pink quartz between 1–5 mm (but generally 1–2.5 mm) with iron-rich grains (Appendix 1, A8).

Q105: Red-brown oxidised ware. A soft fabric containing moderate (10–15%) amounts of moderately sorted, rounded quartz sand (< 1 mm), sparse (3–5%) sub-rounded iron-rich grains (< 1 mm), sparse (3%) clay pellets (0.5–1 mm) and very rare white (?chalk) flecks and flint inclusions. This fabric generally has duller red-brown oxidised surfaces and a grey core; it can also have a laminar appearance and feel slightly leathery (Appendix 1, A9).

Forms

Nine major classes of vessel were defined in these wares. They are presented here in the order of closed to open vessel forms: flagons, jars, beakers, tankards, bowls, dishes, mortaria, lids and miscellaneous unknown forms. Each class is subdivided into a number of different types where relevant. Quantification of types is by number of rims (conjoining rim fragments from a single vessel counted as one), with the exception of a single flagon within type 4 where the rim is missing but the defining rings on the neck allowed the vessel to be included within the type 4 category. Bases were also subdivided into nine types as they contribute to illustrating the range of vessel forms present, particularly the open forms. Examples that best illustrate the range of each type including bases have been illustrated (Figs 3.6–3.8). The quantification of vessel forms by type and fabric is presented in Table 3.6. Twelve handles/handle fragments were recorded under a generic code of H100, seven have a single external groove, three have double grooves whilst the remaining two are fragments only. Given their size, it is likely that they come from relatively small vessels such as flagons.

The oxidised sandy ware type series:

Flagons (types 1–7; 14 examples)

Type 1: (Fig. 3.6, 1). Collared flagons with cylindrical neck, concave mouth and undercut collar

Type 2: (Fig. 3.6, 2). Pulley-wheeled flagons with cylindrical neck and slightly cupped mouth

Type 3: (Fig. 3.6, 3). Well-moulded, ring-necked flagons and slightly flaring rim

Type 4: (Fig. 3.6, 4–6). Flagons with cylindrical neck and flaring, triangular rim that can be grooved on the outer edge. Residual ring mouldings on the neck

Type 5: (Fig. 3.6, 7). Flagons with cupped mouth

Type 6: (Fig. 3.6, 8–9). Triangular-rimmed flagons with tapering neck

Type 7: (Fig. 3.6, 10). Flagon with flared mouth and flatter rim

Jars (types 8–14; 56 examples)

Type 8: (Fig. 3.6, 11–12). Necked jars with neck/shoulder junction defined by a groove. Rims generally everted and sometimes thickened or beaded

Type 9: (Fig. 3.6, 13). Small carinated, necked jar

Type 10: (Fig. 3.6, 14). Necked, round shouldered jar

Type 11: (Fig. 3.6, 15). Everted rim jar, miscellaneous category

Type 12: (Fig. 3.6, 16). High shouldered jar with short, everted rim

Type 13: (Fig. 3.6, 17–18). A catch-all group for necked jars (or jar/bowls) broken at the neck. Most are narrow necked and, as with type 8, rims are generally everted and sometimes thickened or beaded

Type 14: Jar rim fragments (not illustrated)

Beakers (types 15–26; 85 examples)

Type 15: (Fig. 3.6, 19–22). Beakers with short, sharply everted, externally grooved rims. These vessels generally have a bag-shaped profile with a low belly/carination and (when present) simple footed bases

Type 16: (Fig. 3.6, 23). Handled beaker with short, sharply everted, externally grooved rim, a slightly rounded shoulder, possible low belly/carination and simple, footed base

Type 17: (Fig. 3.6, 24). Beakers with a high, rounded shoulder and short, externally grooved rim. Rim profile can vary from upright to everted or cupped.

Type 18: (Fig. 3.6, 25). Indented beakers with high rounded shoulder and short, everted rims with external groove

Type 19: (Fig. 3.6, 26). Possible face pot or indented beaker with high rounded shoulder, plain, short, everted rim and other applied decoration

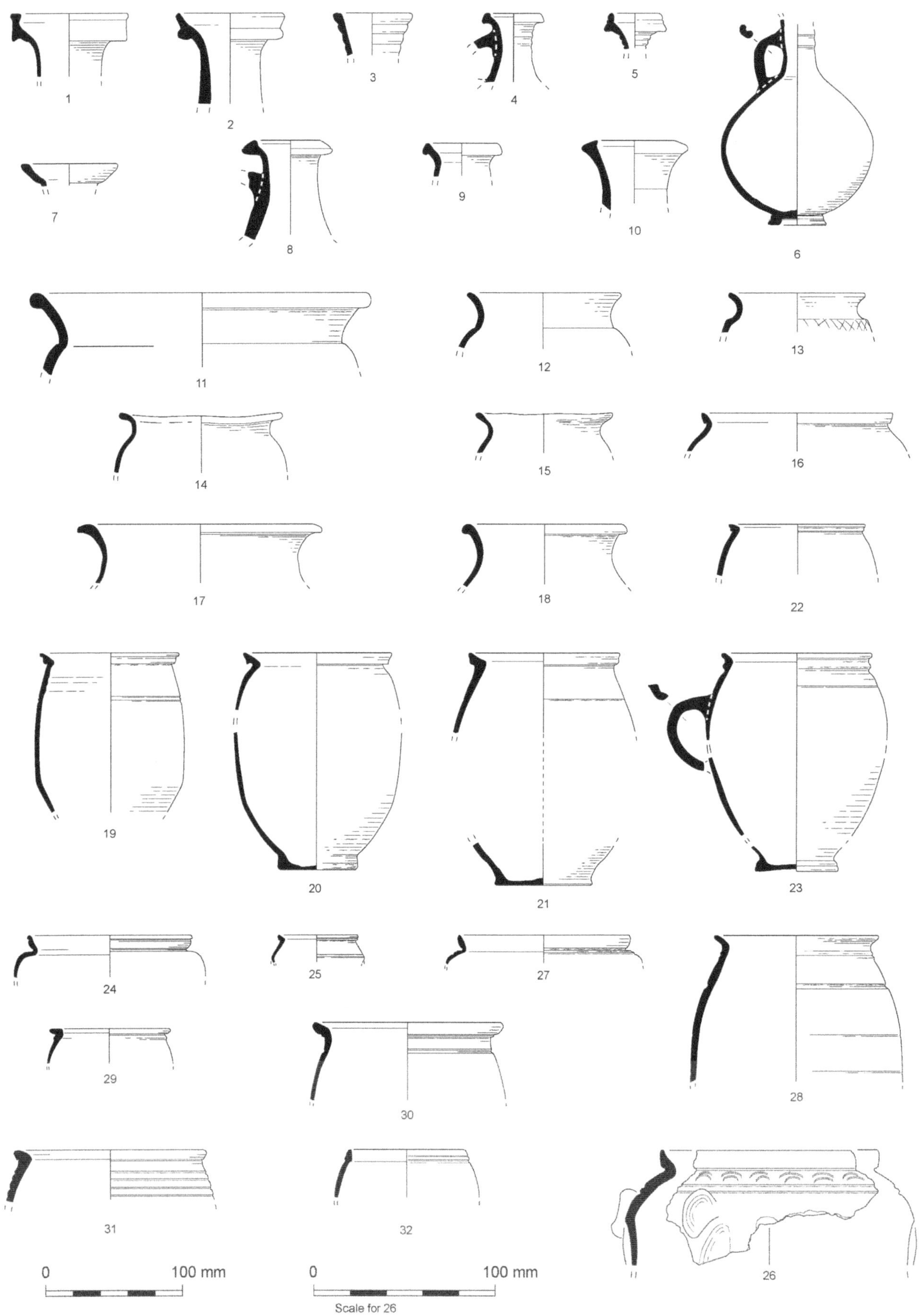

Figure 3.6 Pottery (nos 1–32)

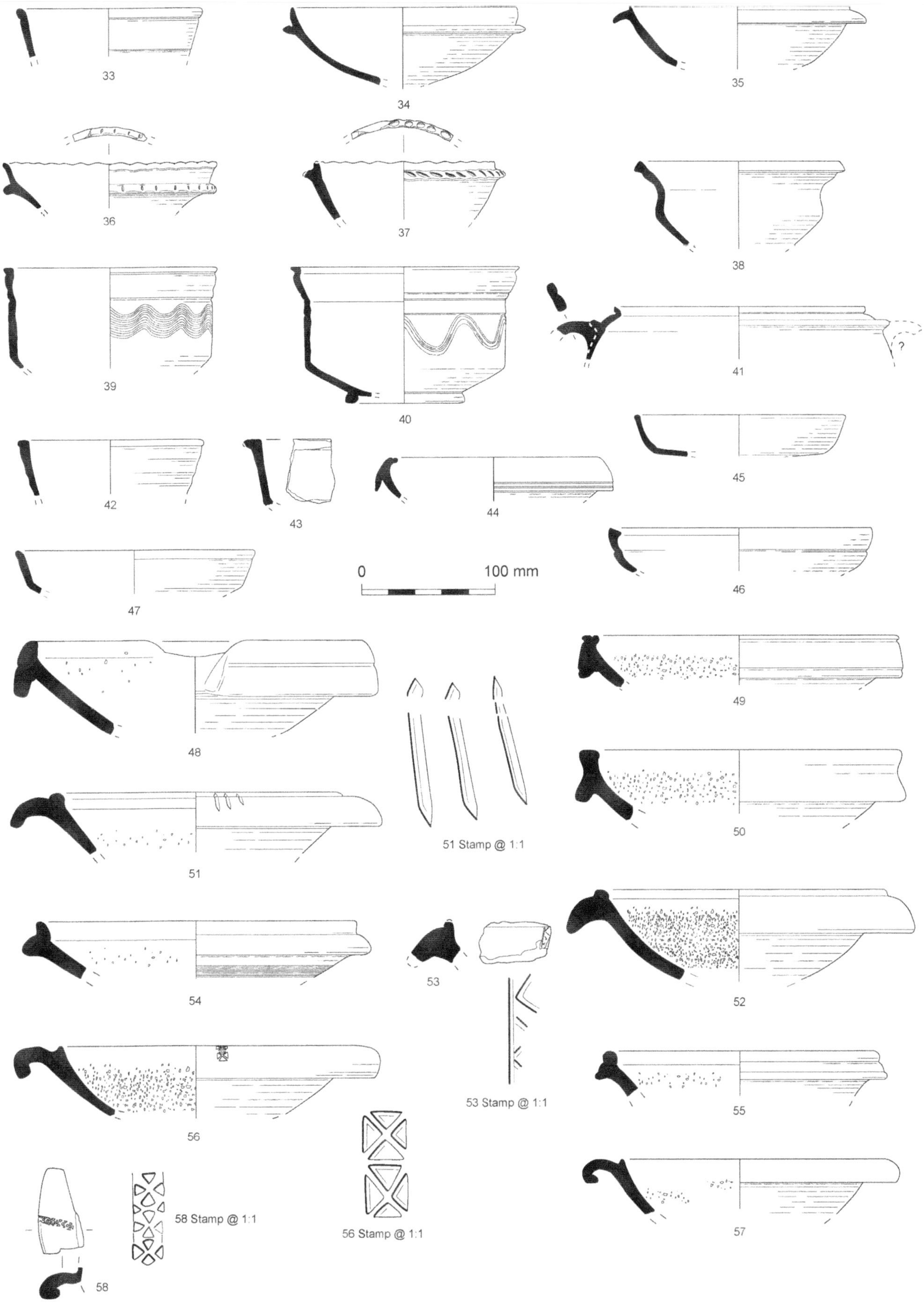

Figure 3.7 Pottery (nos 33–58)

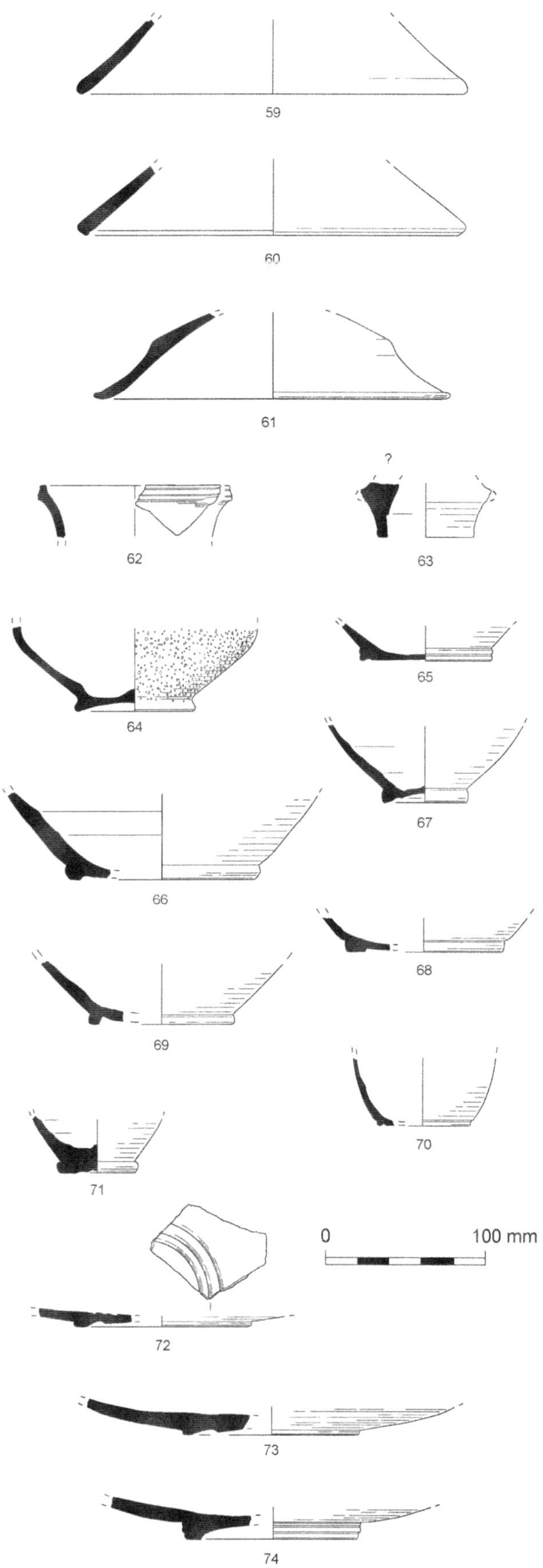

Figure 3.8 Pottery (nos 59–74

Type 20: (Fig. 3.6, 27). Beakers with high rounded shoulder and plain, short, everted rim

Type 21: (Fig. 3.6, 28). Beakers with plain, short, sharply everted rim. As type 15 but with a plain rim

Type 22: (Fig. 3.6, 29). Beakers with very short, sharply everted (almost flat) rims. May have a slight moulding at the rim/body junction

Type 23: (Fig. 3.6, 30). Beakers/Jars with thick, sharply everted rims and gently sloping shoulders

Type 24: (Fig. 3.6, 31). Beakers/Jars with short, out-turned rim and gently sloping shoulder

Type 25: (Fig. 3.6, 32). Beaker with upright, externally grooved rim and gently sloping shoulder

Type 26: Beaker rim fragments, uncertain type (not illustrated)

Tankards (type 27; 6 examples)

Type 27: (Fig. 3.7, 33). A broad category for all tankards, including both straight- and flaring-profiled examples, all have a slightly beaded rim

Bowls (types 28–36 and 52; 32 rims)

Type 28: (Fig. 3.7, 34). Hemispherical bowls copying samian form 38 with a straight flange a short way below the rim

Type 29: (Fig. 3.7, 35). Hemispherical bowl copying samian form 38 with downward curving flange a short way below the rim

Type 30: (Fig. 3.7, 36–37). Hemispherical bowl with straight flange a short way below the rim, both the rim and flange are decorated

Type 31: (Fig. 3.7, 38). Concave-mouthed bowl with curved wall and triangular rim

Type 32: (Fig. 3.7, 39–40). Carinated bowl copying samian form 29; the rim is beaded and there is a cordon a short way below the rim that defines a slight off-set in the vessel wall, the carination is well-defined

Type 33: (Fig. 3.7, 41). Bowl with short, sharply everted rim and small external body flange to which a handle is attached

Type 34: (Fig. 3.7, 42). Bead rim bowl, vessel wall profile is slightly concave

Type 35: Bowl with rounded, thickened rim (not illustrated)

Type 36: (Fig. 3.7, 43). Flat rimmed bowl/dish

Type 52: (Fig. 3.7, 44). Bowl with inturned rim and near vertical flange

Dishes (types 37–39; 6 examples)

Type 37: (Fig. 3.7, 45). Simple dish with plain rim and near upright wall

Type 38: (Fig. 3.7, 46). Dish with groove a short way below the rim creating a double concave profile

Type 39: (Fig. 3.7, 47). Carinated dish with bead rim

Table 3.6 Quantification of local oxidised sandy ware forms by fabric (number of rims)

Form		*Fabric*						*No. of rims*	*% no. of rims*
		Q100	*Q101*	*Q102*	*Q103*	*Q104*	*Q105*		
Flagons	Type 1	–	1	–	–	–	–	1	0.4
	Type 2	–	–	–	1	–	–	1	0.4
	Type 3	1	–	2	–	–	–	3	1.3
	Type 4	–	–	–	4	–	–	4	1.7
	Type 5	–	–	1	–	–	–	1	0.4
	Type 6	–	1		1		–	2	0.9
	Type 7	–	–	–	2	–	–	2	0.9
Sub-total flagons							–	*14*	*6.1*
Jars	Type 8	–	8	–	–	–	–	8	3.5
	Type 9	–	1	–	–	–	–	1	0.4
	Type 10	–	2	–	–	–	–	2	0.9
	Type 11	–	6	–	–	–	–	6	2.6
	Type 12	1	–	–	–	–	–	1	0.4
	Type 13	1	21	–	2	–	1	25	10.9
	Type 14	–	13	–	–	–	–	13	5.7
Sub-total jars								*56*	*24.5*
Beakers	Type 15	1	26	–	1	–	–	28	12.2
	Type 16	1	–	–	–	–	–	1	0.4
	Type 17	–	6	–	–	–	–	6	2.6
	Type 18	–	3	–	–	–	–	3	1.3
	Type 19	–	1	–	–	–	–	1	0.4
	Type 20	–	1	–	–	–	–	1	0.4
	Type 21	1	7	–	2	–	–	10	4.4
	Type 22	–	4	–	1	–	1	6	2.6
	Type 23	–	8	–	9	–	–	17	7.4
	Type 24	–	1	–	1	–	–	2	0.9
	Type 25	–	1	–	–	–	–	1	0.4
	Type 26	–	9	–	–	–	–	9	3.9
Sub-total beakers								*85*	*37.1*
Tankards	Type 27	1	5	–	–	–	–	6	2.6
Bowls	Type 28	–	3	–	–	–	2	5	2.2
	Type 29	–	1	–	–	–	–	1	0.4
	Type 30	–	–	–	2	–	–	2	0.9
	Type 31	–	2	–	–	–	–	2	0.9
	Type 32	4	3	–	–	–	4	11	4.8
	Type 33	–	–	–	1	–	–	1	0.4
	Type 34	2	5	–	–	–	–	7	3.1
	Type 35	–	–	–	1	–	–	1	0.4
	Type 36	–	1	–	–	–	–	1	0.4
	Type 52	–	–	1	–	–	–	1	0.4
Sub-total bowls								*32*	*14.0*
Dishes	Type 37	2	–	–	–	–	–	2	0.9
	Type 38	1	1	–	–	–	–	2	0.9
	Type 39	2	–	–	–	–	–	2	0.9
Sub-total dishes								*6*	*2.6*
Mortaria	Type 40	–	–	–	1	–	–	1	0.4
	Type 41	–	–	–	–	1	–	1	0.4
	Type 42	–	–	–	–	1	–	1	0.4
	Type 43	–	–	–	–	5	–	5	2.2
	Type 44	–	–	–	–	3	–	3	1.3
	Type 45	–	–	–	–	3	–	3	1.3
	Type 46	–	–	–	–	1	–	1	0.4
	Type 47	–	–	–	–	3	–	3	1.3
Sub-total mortaria								*18*	*7.9*
Lids	Type 48	–	2	–	–	–	–	2	0.9
	Type 49	–	1	–	–	–	1	2	0.9
	Type 50	–	–	–	–	–	2	2	0.9
Sub-total lids								*6*	*2.6*
Miscellaneous	Type 51	1	3	–	–	–	2	6	2.6
Total		**19**	**147**	**4**	**29**	**17**	**13**	**229**	

Mortaria (types 40–47; 18 examples)

Type 40: (Fig. 3.7, 48). Wall-sided mortaria with rounded rim and single groove at mid-point of collar, bead is pulled down to form spout

Type 41: (Fig. 3.7, 49). Wall-sided mortaria, top of bead is grooved with additional grooves at top and bottom of collar

Type 42: (Fig. 3.7, 50). Near wall-sided mortaria with expanded bead and plain collar

Type 43: (Fig. 3.7, 51). Bead and flange mortaria with a low bead and fairly wide flange

Type 44: (Fig. 3.7, 52–53). Bead and flange mortaria with a low bead and heavy, slightly downturned flange

Type 45: (Fig. 3.7, 54). Bead and flange mortaria with a high bead and short flange

Type 46: (Fig. 3.7, 55). Mortaria with short, stubby, grooved flange and upstanding thick, rounded bead

Type 47: (Fig. 3.7, 42, 56–58). Mortaria with a low bead and hooked flange

Lids (types 48–50; 6 examples)

Type 48: (Fig. 3.8, 59). Lids with plain, rounded lip

Type 49: (Fig. 3.8, 60). Lids with slightly squared-off lip

Type 50: (Fig. 3.8, 61). Lids with out-turned lip

Miscellaneous (6 examples)

Type 51: (Fig. 3.8, 62–63). Miscellaneous forms

Bases (types 100–108)

Type 100: Mortaria bases, plain, flat (not illustrated)

Type 101: (Fig. 3.8, 64; 49 examples) Simple, footed base

Type 102: (Fig. 3.8, 65–67; 8 examples) Moulded, footed base

Type 103: (Fig. 3.8, 68; 8 examples) Moulded base

Type 104: (Fig. 3.8, 69; 11 examples). Footring base

Type 105: (Fig. 3.8, 70; 1 example). Moulded base with external groove at base of wall

Type 106: (Fig. 3.8, 71; 5 examples). Heavy, footed base

Type 107: (Fig. 3.8, 72–73; 2 examples). Moulded bases from vessels of open form

Type 108: (Fig. 3.8, 74; 2 examples). Footring bases from vessels of open form

Discussion of local oxidised sandy wares (Q100–Q105)

A total of 229 vessels are represented in the local oxidised sandy ware assemblage (Table 3.6), these largely comprise tableware forms including beakers, bowls, dishes, flagons and tankards (62% of total number of vessels in the local oxidised sandy ware group) in addition to the more specialist ware mortaria (7.9%), whilst jars comprise 24.5%.

Beakers are by far the most dominant individual class (37.1%). Most are in fabric Q101 whilst a smaller proportion are white-slipped (Q103); only three beakers are in the finer fabric (Q100). The range of vessel sizes is broad, with rim diameters varying from 60 mm for a miniature indented beaker (Fig. 3.6, 25) to 180 mm for a large beaker/jar. The majority, however, have rim diameters within the range of 100–120 mm. The most common are those with short, sharply everted rims either with or without an external groove (types 15 and 21). The handled beaker (type 16; Fig. 3.6, 23) and a possible face pot (type 19; Fig. 3.6, 26) are of particular note. The handled beaker came from enclosure ditch 1909 and is in a fine fabric (Q100). It shares the short, sharply everted and grooved rim and groove on the shoulder with other beaker types within the series, but the addition of a simple handle makes this vessel distinctive. No local parallels have yet been found but a few handled beakers are known from sites in London dating to the mid–later 2nd century AD, although they are not a common form (Marsh and Tyers 1978, 569, fig. 239, IIIE.2; Davies *et al.* 1994, 83, fig. 70, 422 and 108, fig. 94, 607).

The possible face pot (pit 1302) has a slightly cupped rim and is decorated on the shoulder with a double row of finger-nail impressions below which is an applied semi-circular shaped lug/'ear'. Appearing soon after the Claudian conquest (Braithwaite 1984, 103), and documented across much of Britain, face pots were never common and their function and significance remains uncertain. They have been found on a wide range of settlement sites and one suggestion is that they may have been associated with areas of religious importance, as complete vessels have been found in ritual deposits (*ibid.*, 123). The most local examples include one, probably of early Romano-British date, found in the Fosse Way ditch at Camerton, Somerset and one from Littlecote dated to post AD 360 (*ibid.*, 129). The range of ceramics associated with the Beanacre face pot include three additional beaker rims and a mortarium base, all in the local oxidised sandy ware fabrics, as well as a black/brown sandy ware flat rimmed bowl and Savernake-type ware storage jar body sherds, all dating from the 2nd, possibly into the 3rd century AD.

Bowls and dishes collectively amount to 16% of the identifiable vessel forms. When compared to the beaker class, a higher proportion of these forms, particularly the dishes, are in the finer fabric (Q100). The majority are copies of well-known samian forms; types 28–30 copying form 38 for example, whilst carinated bowl type 32 (Fig. 3.7, 39–40) replicates samian form 29. The wavy line decoration on these vessels shares affinities with products from other north Wiltshire industries, such as the lead glazed wares and colour-coated wares seen at Wanborough (Seager Smith 2001, 295–6, fig. 102, 51 and fig. 103, 58–62) for example. The concave mouthed bowl (type 31) also appears to be a relatively common form locally, with comparable vessels from a number of sites in area (Timby 2008, 105, fig. 30, 14; Seager Smith 2001, 275, fig. 89, 247; Timby 1998, 265, fig. 111, 45). The remaining bowls and dishes include a typical range of simple, almost straight-sided forms with plain, flat or bead rims.

More minor forms comprise flagons (6%), tankards (2.6%) and lids (2.6%), which are generally in the coarse variants of the ware group, although the flagons tend to be white-slipped. Within the miscellaneous category (type 51) is a possible 'coffee pot' lid (Fig. 3.8, 63), although the flange and upper part are missing, and a triangular-rimmed vessel of open form, possibly a small bowl or cup (Fig. 3.8, 62).

Amongst the mortaria, those with a low bead and wide flange (type 43) are the most numerous. Unfortunately, although mortaria in the South-West White slipped ware fabric are relatively well documented, generally there is a lack of published detailed data regarding the range of forms that were produced and so comparisons with other site assemblages have not been possible. One example of a type 43 vessel (cleaning layer 1161) is marked on the flange with three parallel tooled lines (Fig. 3.7, 51), possibly in place of a trademark stamp. Three other more clearly defined stamps were also found (Fig. 3.7, 53, 56 and 58). These comprise a double-cross motif (Fig. 3.7, 56), a smaller, triple-cross motif (Fig. 3.7, 58) and part of a possible illiterate stamp (Fig. 3.7, 53). All of the stamped pieces were found within deposits of late Romano-British date, although all contained residual earlier material as well as late Romano-British ceramics. Examples of stamped South-West White slipped mortaria have been recorded elsewhere (J. Timby pers comm), but currently published examples could not be found for comparison.

Jars make up 24.5% of the local oxidised sandy ware assemblage (Table 3.6). However, of the 56 rims represented there are no complete profiles and the majority (38) are broken at the neck/shoulder junction or immediately below the rim. With the exception of three vessels, all are in the coarse fabric (Q101) whilst just two are white-slipped (Q103). Of the more diagnostic forms, necked jars (types 8–10) with either carinated or rounded shoulders are the most common whilst everted rim jars (type 11) and one high-shouldered jar (type 12) make up the remainder of the assemblage. Six of the jar rims are slightly distorted/uneven resulting from mis-firing in the kiln, but despite this were probably perfectly usable vessels. However, the presence of mis-shapen usable 'seconds' further enhances the possibility that this oxidised sandy ware group were relatively local products.

The overall distribution of these wares at Beanacre and their association with other datable wares (see feature groups and discussion below), suggests that their production was taking place by the earlier to middle part of the 2nd century AD, with a floruit during the mid-/late 2nd–3rd centuries AD. This broadly corresponds with evidence seen elsewhere (eg, Timby 1998 and 2008; Rigby 1982).

Other oxidised wares and whitewares

The other unsourced oxidised ware sherds (Table 3.3) generally occur in far less gritty sandy fabrics than those defined above, although they do vary quite considerably in their coarseness. A small quantity of thin-walled sherds in a fine oxidised, slightly micaceous fabric (Table 3.3) include rims from two campanulate cups, probably imitating samian form 27. Otherwise, the range of forms is similar to those of the local oxidised sandy ware fabrics. Rims from at least two small jars, one decorated with burnished lattice (middle Romano-British rake out pit 1171), a possible tankard, a flanged bowl (middle Romano-British pit 1414) and a carinated bowl copying samian form 18/31 (unstratified) occur among these wares. Nine of the white-slipped redware sherds are from the lower part of a single vessel (Fig. 3.9, 77; Building 1), probably a jar, with a wide footring base. This vessel had been repaired in antiquity with a double pair of lead rivets (see below).

The coarse whitewares (35 sherds, 365 g) are also unsourced and include just two identifiable forms – a wide-mouthed flagon rim (ditch 1443) and a bowl rim with a sharply downturned flange (Fig. 3.9, 87) from Building 1. Other whiteware body sherds indicate the presence of at least three globular-bodied vessels, possibly flagons.

Local unoxidised coarsewares

The unoxidised coarsewares comprise the majority of the Romano-British assemblage, amounting to approximately 58% by sherd count (Table 3.3). The black/brown sandy wares alone account for almost 42% and are used to make jars, bowls, flat rimmed and flanged dishes/bowls, cups, beakers, platters and lids. Where surfaces survive, they are often burnished and some jars or bowls are decorated with burnished lines (eg, Fig. 3.11, 125) or lattice motifs. These forms span the later 1st through to the later 3rd/4th centuries AD. Earlier elements are indicated by imitation Gallo-Belgic platters while wide-mouthed, necked jar/bowls with girth grooves, wide-mouthed carinated jar/bowls (eg, Fig. 3.11, 126) and straight-sided bowls with girth cordons continue through in to the 2nd century AD. The latest forms include dropped flange bowls, typical of the later Romano-British period. Other less well represented sandy wares include a hard-fired blue-grey ware, glauconitic sandy greyware and two very micaceous fabrics. With the exception of the black micaceous ware (see below), the range of forms present in these fabrics is broadly comparable with those of the black/brown sandy ware. The almost complete absence of storage jar forms within these local unoxidised coarseware fabrics is not unexpected given the prevalence of Savernake-type ware in the region which would more than cater for that part of the market. The black micaceous ware may be comparable to fabric 5 at Kingscote dated to the 2nd to 4th centuries AD (Timby 1998, 251); but no diagnostic or featured sherds are present within the Beanacre assemblage.

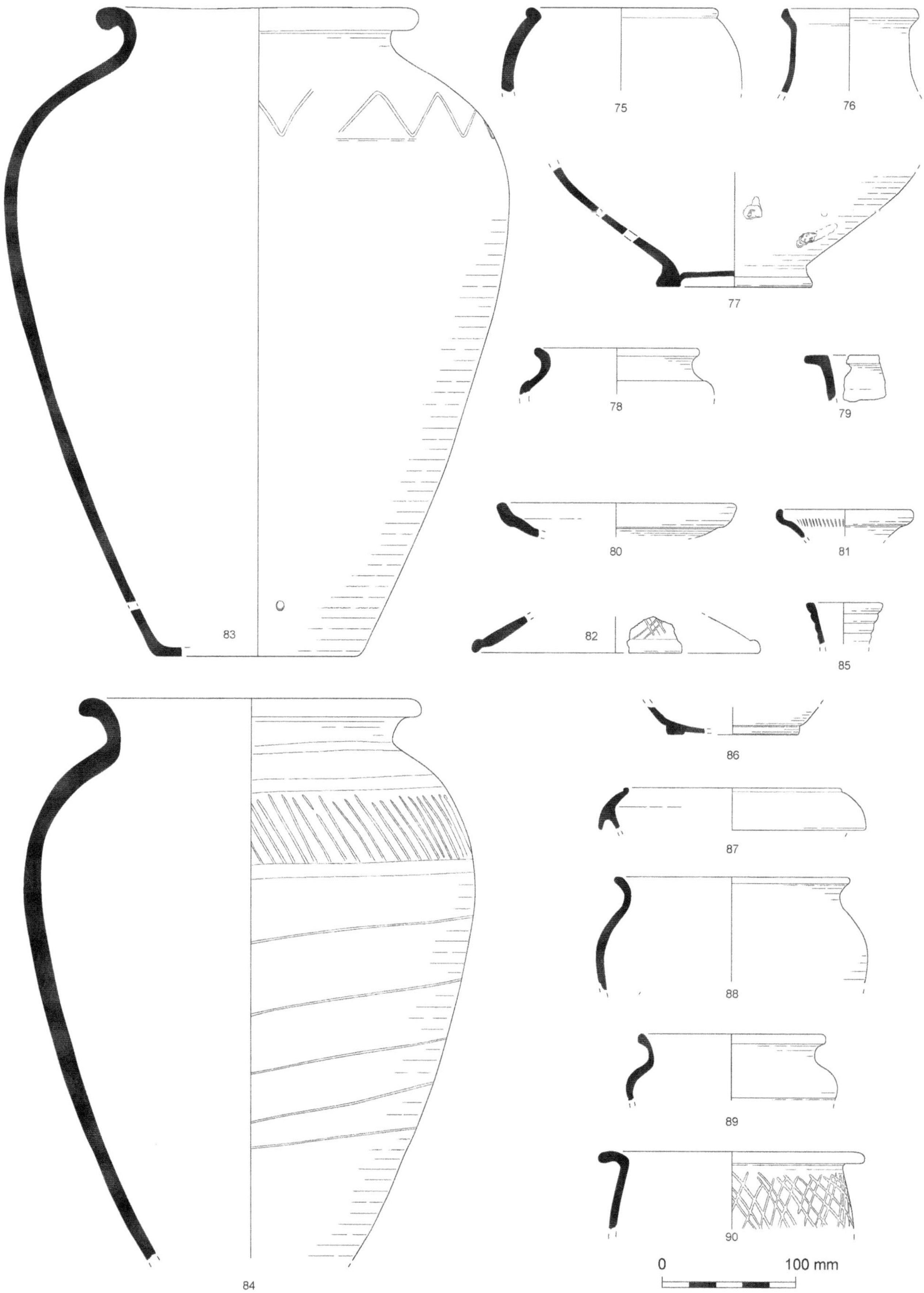

Figure 3.9 Pottery (nos 75–90)

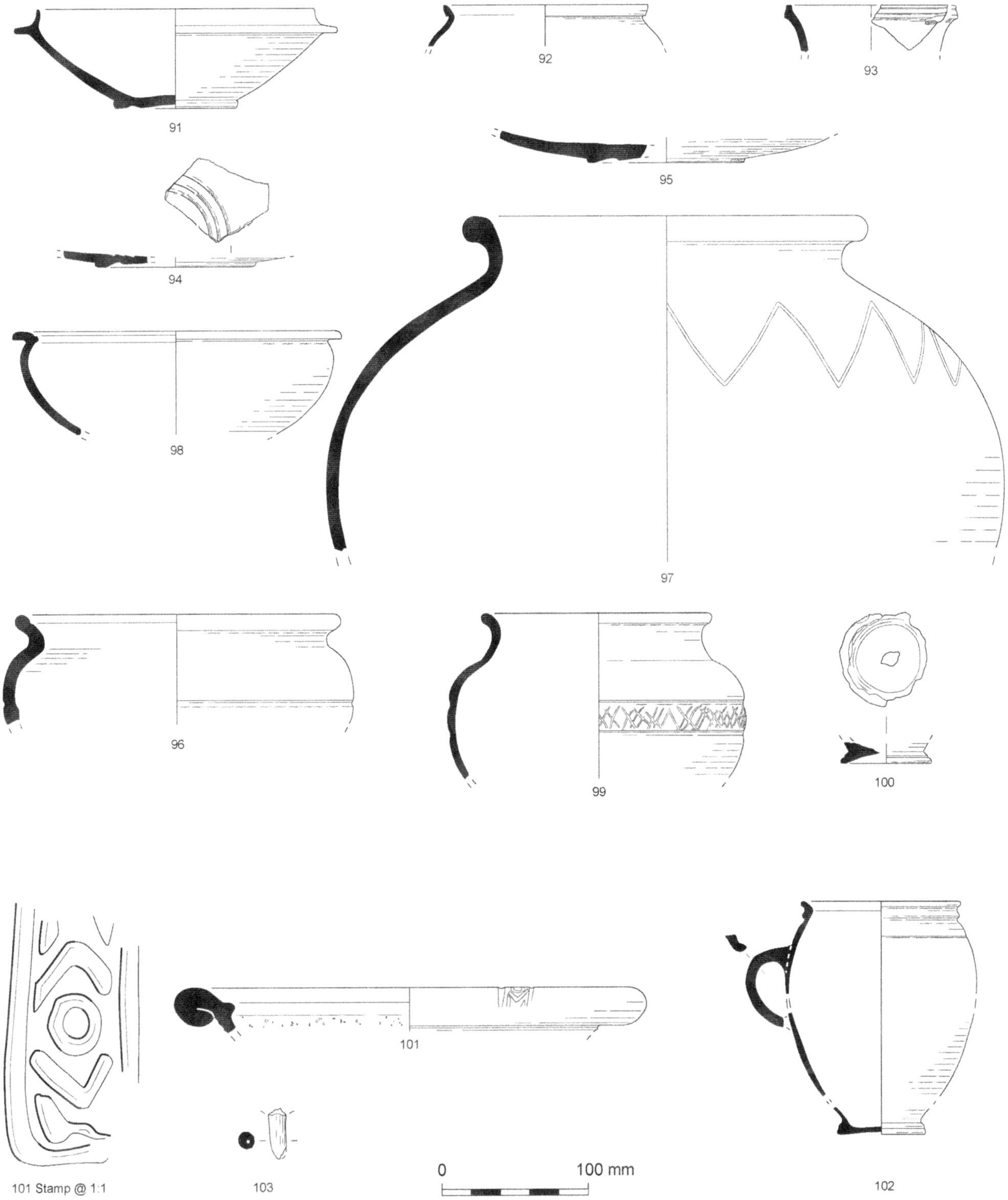

Figure 3.10 Pottery (nos 91–103)

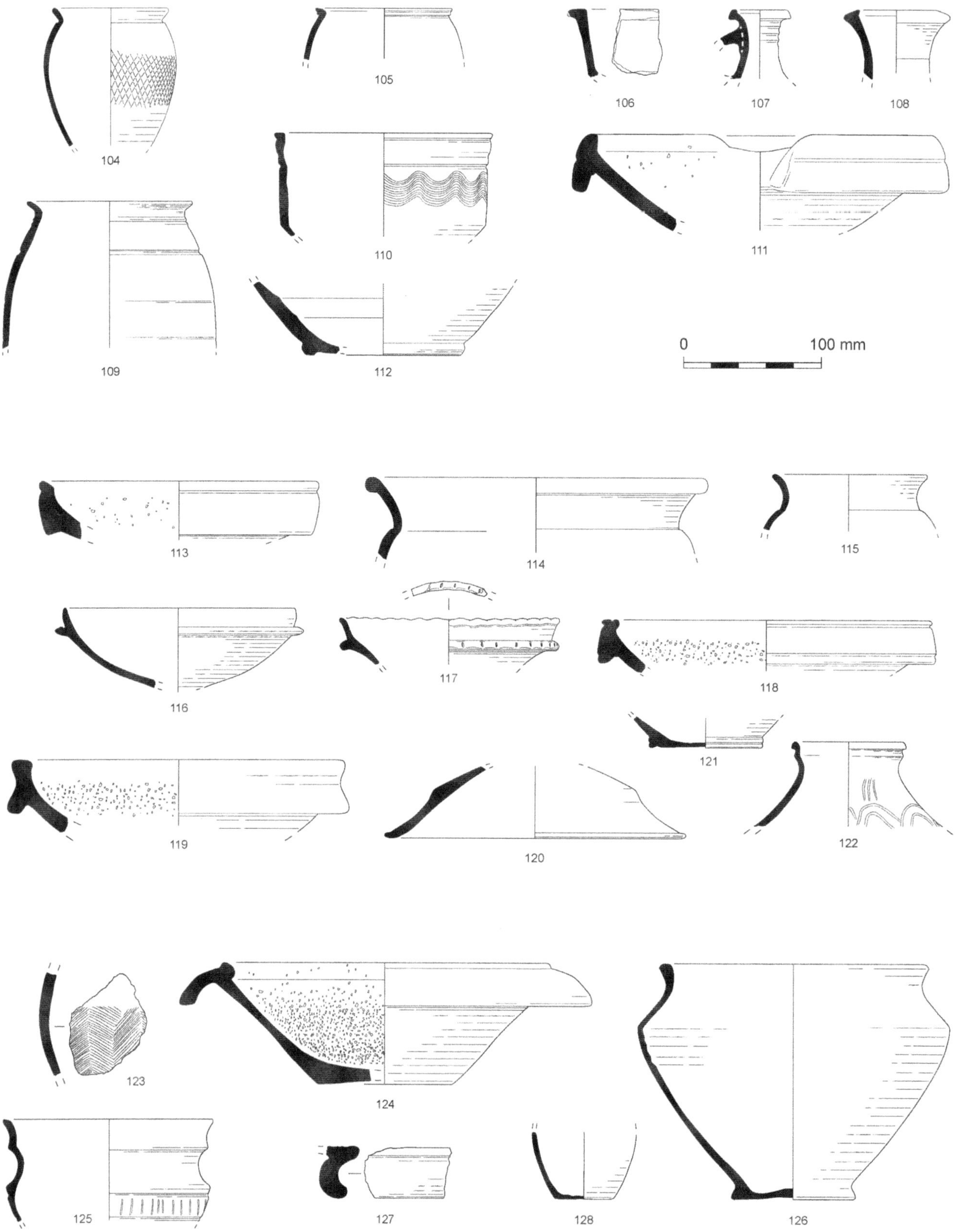

Figure 3.11 Pottery (nos 104–126)

Hard fired, grog-tempered Savernake-type wares amount to 12% of the Romano-British assemblage. These were made in the Savernake Forest (Annable 1962; Swan 1975) and at Purton and other kilns to the west of Swindon (Anderson 1979; 1980). Forms include large storage jars with beaded, necked or everted rims and smaller numbers of narrow-mouthed, necked, cordoned jars and jar/bowls (eg, Fig. 3.10, 96). Vessels can be decorated with tooled lines, often on the shoulders, in zig-zag or diagonal line motifs (eg, Fig. 3.9, 83 and 84), and in one instance with wavy line decoration. One slightly odd fragment, from cleaning layer 1161 (Fig. 3.11, 127), is possibly from a flanged vessel of quite large diameter but too little of the profile is present to further identify the vessel form. With the exception of this piece, the range of forms is typical of Savernake-type ware, dating predominantly to the 1st to 2nd centuries AD, possibly extending into the earlier part of the 3rd century AD.

Minor fabrics within the unoxidised coarseware group include flint-tempered wares as well as those containing varying amounts of sand, flint, grog and calcareous (either fine shell or possibly limestone) inclusions. A similar range of minor fabrics has been found at other Romano-British sites in the locality, at Atworth (Timby 2008, 106), Silbury Hill (Timby 2013a, 132) and in the area of the Winterbourne Romano-British settlement (Seager Smith 1996, 47) for example. Diagnostic forms are limited to a straight-sided dish/bowl with a flat, reeded rim in a sand and calcareous-tempered fabric (middle Romano-British ditch 1909). Elsewhere, similar forms date to the latter 1st through to the 2nd centuries AD (Marsh and Tyers 1978, 571, group IVA; Marsh 1978, 158, type 26).

Use and repair

Evidence for the use and curation of ceramic vessels was noted on both coarse and fine ware vessels. Post-depositional burning was noted on 10 of the samian sherds, some of which are heavily burnt and blackened. Although generally scattered across the site, these include three from mid-Romano-British oven rake out pit 1171 and one from pit 1165 which cut through it; all three were imported between AD 120 and 200. A handful of the coarseware sherds also have sooted residues surviving, either on the interior or exterior surfaces, suggesting their use in the preparation of foodstuffs or other materials.

Few vessels show signs of prolonged use, although some of the mortaria, for example, lack grits and appear internally worn, whilst a small black/brown sandy ware jar or beaker (trackway/quarry 1932) had been so well-used that a hole was worn through the base (Fig. 3.10, 100). On samian vessels, the presence

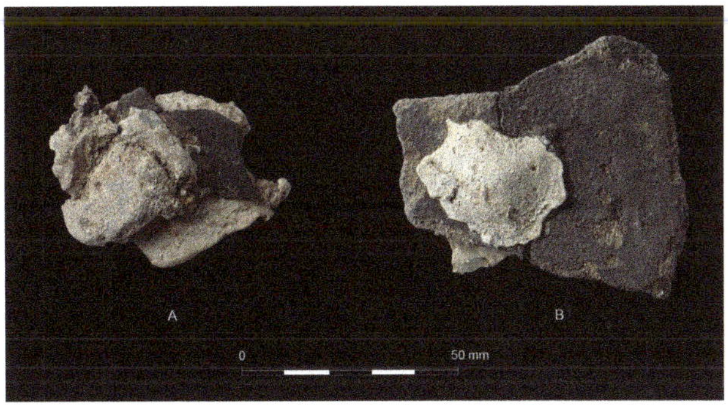

Plate 3.3 Romano-British lead pot-mends (a and b)

of worn areas of slip often gives an indication not only of how certain vessels may have been used, but also of the intensity and duration of that use. Here, just three vessels (<1.5%), all imported between AD 120 and 240, show signs of such use. These include a Central Gaulish form 27 cup from well 1678; sometimes these vessels are sufficiently worn not only to have removed the interior slip but for small dimples or pits to have been ground into the surface. No pits were noted on this cup, but the slip had been removed. Similar internal, abraded use-wear was observed on sherds from a Central Gaulish Curle 21 bowl from calf burial 1158 and a Rheinzarben form 38 flanged bowl from ditch 1908. The Curle 21 form is generally interpreted as a gritless mortaria, and form 38 bowls may also have been used for grinding in this way, so heavy internal wear may be expected on these forms. Little slip remains on either surface of the unstratified Trier form 45 collar/rim, but this cannot be taken as evidence for heavy or prolonged use, as the grinding surface does not survive. It perhaps results from the action of ground water on a thinly-slipped vessel.

Given the low level of use-wear observed, it is perhaps surprising that evidence for repair was noted on six samian and at least three coarseware vessels (eg, Fig. 3.9, 77 and Pl. 3.3). For the samian, this repair rate (2.8% of the assemblage) is largely in line with the mean rate of 2% suggested by Willis (2005, section 11). It is generally accepted that the high cost of samian vessels made repair acceptable and economically viable (Peña 2007, 213–49); the high firing temperatures would have ensured that the vessels were uniform enough and strong enough to allow mends to be effective. The practice is well documented (Seager Smith 2015, 223; Schuster 2011, 249; Redknap 1998, 112, fig. 64, 15.23–4), and two types of lead pot-mends are known (Schuster 2011, 247–8); both are evident here. The repaired white-slipped red ware vessel from Building 1 is likely to be of late 1st or early 2nd century AD date, while four of the repaired samian vessels (a form 33 cup (ditch 1920), an 18/31 or 31 bowl (ditch 1961), a form 42 dish (ditch 1933) and an unassigned body sherd (pit 1121)) are from Lezoux and imported from AD 120–200. A fifth vessel, an unstratified Rheinzarben Walters 81 bowl, extends this range to AD 240.

Recently, evidence of glued repairs using an adhesive derived from birch-bark tar has been recognised (Marter-Brown and Seager Smith, 2012). In this assemblage, a single sherd from a Central Gaulish samian form 31 bowl (soil layer 1308, overlying pit 1302) has traces of a tar-like substance on the break which may well be such an adhesive. This particular sherd also appears to have been smoothed around the edge of the base, perhaps to enable use of the broken vessel as a small dish or lid, but whether this occurred before or after gluing cannot be discerned.

Unusually amongst the samian, this is the only vessel that may have been cut down after breakage to make it suitable for reuse as most sites produce examples of cut-down bases and more might have been expected in this group. However, at least two black/brown sandy ware vessels also appear to have been trimmed in order to extend their useful life. These comprise a flat jar-type base (ditch 1914), perhaps deliberately smoothed off to make a small palette or lid, and the lower part of a jar (Fig. 3.11, 128) neatly trimmed for reuse as a small bowl/dish. An Oxfordshire red colour-coated ware mortarium (Young 1977, 173, fig. 67, type C97; AD 240–400; ditch 1516) also appears to have had its rim removed to the level of the external offset, perhaps also to extend the life of the vessel.

Two Savernake-type ware vessels also carry signs of deliberate modification. Both have a single post-firing perforation (5 mm in diameter) drilled through the wall. In the case of a large storage jar found within Building 1 (Fig. 3.9, 83), the perforation is located in the lower part of the wall close to the base. The positioning of the perforation is unclear in the case of the second example, a body sherd from trackway/quarry 1932. Both could be examples of holes made for repair, but equally, they may evidence a deliberate change in the use of these vessels. This type of modification is widespread across southern Britain during the late Iron Age and Roman periods (Seager Smith 2015, 223), with local examples including a large Savernake-type ware jar, very similar to the Beanacre vessel, from Uley (Leach 1993, 224, fig. 165, 73).

Even once broken, pottery continued to be a useful resource for the manufacture of other objects. Two Dressel 20 amphora handle fragments (cleaning layer 1161 and tree-throw hole 1357) appear to have been purposely removed from their parent vessel(s). Once empty, amphora were routinely traded as empty containers, and to facilitate easier access into the narrow-necked, globular-bodied Dressel 20 form, the rim/neck/handle zone was often removed to create a new, wider 'rim' at the former shoulder level. These handles were probably removed in just such an operation, and may have been intended for reuse themselves as, on other sites (eg, Brook and Seager Smith 2017, 35), examples have been found with their broken ends worn or rubbed smooth, suggesting use as pestles or grinders.

Similarly, rough discs cut from sherds are not uncommon finds on Romano-British sites at all levels of the social scale. In this assemblage, five sherds of various ware types had been treated in this way (Pl. 3.2), with diameters measuring between 28–37 mm. The two perforated examples (Savernake-type ware, ditch 1061 and brown/black sandy ware, cleaning layer 1161) may have been used as spindlewhorls, but the rough edges of the Savernake-type ware example may indicate that it was abandoned before completion. Of the three unperforated examples two are made from coarseware sherds (Savernake-type ware, ditch 1147 and oxidised sandy ware, ditch 1933), and may also represent unfinished spindlewhorls, although they could also have been used as gaming counters, while a more recent interpretation suggests that they may have been an early form of toilet paper (Charlier *et al.* 2012; Papadopoulos 2002).

The final ceramic disc was found in the backfill of calf burial 1158 and had been quite roughly cut or chipped from a Central Gaulish samian form 37 decorated bowl (Fig. 3.4, 7; Dec. Cat. No. 24, Pl. 3.2). The two edges of this curving sherd which rest flat when the decoration is uppermost are worn smooth, suggesting that it was used that way up and in contact with a flat surface, probably as some kind of gaming counter. The decoration, however, does not seem to have had any great importance, as the disc cuts across the motifs, with only part of a medallion border and most of a panther surviving. If these images had been of any relevance, one might expect that the disc would have been cut to encompass the complete animal which would have fitted onto a disc of this size.

Distribution

The pottery was recovered from 322 contexts in 175 features/feature groups. The majority of sherds came from the fills of ditches (34% by sherd count, 29% by weight), with 13% (15% by weight) from pits and a similar proportion (14%/16%) from layers. Pottery found within ovens/crop driers amounts to 8% (5% by weight) of the total assemblage, whilst approximately 7% came from trackways/hollow-ways. The remainder was found in a range of feature types including postholes (6%), two wells, robber trenches, a hearth, natural features, and residually within inhumation grave 1440 and animal burial 1537, while a further 7% was unstratified.

Most features/feature groups contained only small quantities (40% of the assemblage by sherd count (45% by weight) occurred in just 14 groups) and/or too few diagnostic sherds to merit description or precise dating. However, the material from 10 groups has been selected to chart the changing nature of the assemblage through time; these are described below.

Building 1

The earliest chronological group (387 sherds, 12,896 g) came from features associated with Building 1 (Fig. 3.9, 75–90). Overall, imports are limited to four body flakes of Dressel 20 amphora, as well as La Graufesenque and Lezoux samian, the latter source including one piece of the 1st century, micaceous fabric. Even taking into account the fact that 83 sherds (7611 g) of Savernake-type ware derive from just two large storage jars (post-pit 1299), this fabric and the local black/brown sandy ware dominate this assemblage (82% by sherd count, 92% by weight). Other minor fabric groups include the fine grey- and fine oxidised wares, as well as blue-greyware and unsourced oxidised wares, but no featured sherds are present amongst them.

Pottery from deposits associated with the initial phase of the building (group 1924) is limited to just 28 sherds (532 g). These include the 1st century Lezoux samian form 29 bowl (Fig. 3.4, 4), as well as sherds from a Savernake-type ware bead rim jar (Fig. 3.9, 75), a long-necked vessel in black/brown sandy ware (Fig. 3.9, 76) and the base of the repaired white-slipped redware vessel (Fig. 3.9, 77), all from the basal fill (layer 1296). The three coarseware vessels are likely to be of late 1st or early 2nd century AD date, while the samian sherd is dated to AD 50–85 AD. However, additional rejoining sherds from both the long-necked and white-slipped redware vessels also occur in contexts 1295 and 1236, both stratigraphically later than 1296.

Sherds from features associated with the second phase of the building include four flakes of Dressel 20 amphora and three La Graufesenque samian sherds, although all these pieces are small, abraded and could be residual. One of the samian sherds, a Ritt 8 cup base, came from beamslot 1270. Ritt 8's are a pre-Flavian form, and this is probably the earliest piece in the whole samian collection. The others, a decorated body from a form 29 bowl (Dec. Cat. No. 2), and a form 18R rim, both came from floor layer 1295.

Other identifiable vessels from these levels include a necked jar/bowl (Fig. 3.9, 78) and a flat rimmed bowl/dish (Fig. 3.9, 79) in the local black/brown sandy ware, as well as rejoining fragments of the long necked vessel (Fig. 3.9, 76) found within the phase one deposits (see above). Post-pit 1299 located on the northern corner of the structure contained almost half of the pottery from Building 1 (173 sherds, 8438 g). Early forms comprise fragments from two imitation Gallo-Belgic platters (Fig. 3.9, 80 and 81), both in black/brown sandy ware and likely to belong within the second half of the 1st century AD. Other featured sherds include a decorated lid (Fig. 3.9, 82) and a body sherd with a post-firing perforation, both in black/brown sandy fabrics, along with the remnants of two large Savernake-type ware storage jars (Fig. 3.9, 83 and 84). Both are necked forms and decorated on the shoulder. The rim of the more complete vessel (Fig. 3.9, 83) is very slightly distorted in one area, coinciding with a patch of darker firing extending onto the shoulder. The lower wall of this vessel is also very thin for its size and at some point post-firing, a perforation has been made just above the base. It is uncertain whether this was to facilitate repair or for some other purpose. The decoration on the second jar (Fig. 3.9, 84) is very similar to that seen on a late 1st or early 2nd century AD vessel from Uley (Leach 1993, 224, fig. 165, 73).

A comparable range of 1st to early/mid-2nd century AD material (129 sherds, 3381 g) came from post-abandonment deposits within Building 1 (group 1916, layers 1178, 1236 and 1294). The nine (59 g) sherds of La Graufesenque samian span the period from AD 45–110 and include pieces from at least one form 29 bowl (AD 45–75), two form 18 plates and a stamped base (Stamp Cat S3) from a possible third, as well as cup forms 27 and 27g. A rim from a small, South Gaulish form 37 decorated bowl (Fig. 3.4, 2; Dec. Cat. No. 5) was also found in these levels (post-abandonment layer 1178). This form is a Flavian introduction, and the vessel can therefore be dated to AD 75–100.

The remaining sherds are from more local sources and include vessels in the coarse oxidised sandy fabrics Q100 and Q101 (eg, Fig. 3.9, 85 and 86), further sherds from the repaired white-slipped redware vessel (Fig. 3.9, 77) and a whiteware flanged bowl or mortaria rim (Fig. 3.9, 87) from an uncertain source. Local unoxidised coarsewares are also well represented, particularly black/brown sandy ware jars (Fig. 3.9, 88 and 89) and bowls (Fig. 3.9, 90), as well as rim fragments from at least four Savernake-type ware jars or storage jars.

Although clearly early Roman, the comparable nature and date range of the ceramic assemblages from all three phases of this structure make it difficult to establish a more precise range for its use and abandonment. However, it is perhaps noteworthy that the two rejoining vessels (Fig. 3.9, 76 and 77) exhibit only ancient breaks (ie, they were not broken during excavation), perhaps suggesting that much of the material may originally have been deposited elsewhere, such as on a midden, prior to its redeposition here during relatively rapid, post-abandonment backfilling of the structure.

Trackway/quarry 1932

The largest group of pottery from a feature assigned to the mid-Romano-British period came from trackway/quarry 1932 (414 sherds, 8595 g) (Fig. 3.10, 91–100). In comparison with Building 1, there is a broader range of ware types represented. Continental imports include small quantities of mid-1st–2nd century AD samian from La Graufesenque, Montans, Les Martres and Lezoux, Dressel 20 amphora and fragments of mortaria from the Oise/Somme area of Northern Gaul, datable to the second half of the 1st century AD into the mid-2nd century AD. Although limited in number, British regional imports include a single plain body sherd of Verulamium region whiteware and two South-east Dorset Black Burnished ware jar rims (Seager Smith and Davies 1993, WA types 1 and 2), also of late 1st or 2nd century AD date.

Among the local wares, the finer components include a mica-dusted flanged bowl (Fig. 3.10, 91) dating to the early part of the 2nd century AD. The local oxidised sandy wares are represented by the finer (Q100), coarse (Q101), coarse white-slipped (Q103) and red/brown variants (Q105), although not in any large quantities (7.7% of the feature group by sherd count). Forms are limited to a high shouldered jar (Fig. 3.10, 92), a possible small bowl or cup (Fig. 3.10, 93) and moulded bases from two dishes/platters (Fig. 3.10, 94 and 95). The presence of flagons is indicated by body sherds from globular-bodied vessels in both unsourced whiteware and oxidised ware fabrics.

As with Building 1, the unoxidised coarsewares (black/brown sandy ware and Savernake-type ware) dominate the assemblage, amounting to 320 sherds (6747 g). The broad range of forms includes sherds from an imitation Gallo-Belgic platter (context 1798), flagons, necked, everted rim and wide-mouthed jars (eg, Fig. 3.10, 96), storage jars (eg, Fig. 3.10, 97), carinated and flat-rimmed bowls (eg, Fig. 3.10, 98, ctx 1873) and straight-sided dishes. A wide-mouthed, necked jar with girth grooves and burnished lattice decoration (eg, Fig. 3.10, 99) is comparable to a number of late 1st- to early 2nd-century AD vessels from Wanborough (Seager Smith 2001, 265, figs 82 and 83, eg, 66, 70 and 87). Two rejoining sherds of black/brown sandy ware from context 1756 are possibly from an unguent jar, although they are too small to be illustrated, while the holed base of a small black/brown sandy ware jar or beaker (Fig. 3.10, 100) highlights the presence of extensively used vessels among this group.

Chronologically, the pottery from trackway/quarry 1932 spans a wide date range. This is particularly clear from the samian, with the earliest, La Graufesenque fragments (from a Drag form 15/17 dish and a rim chip possibly from a form 29 decorated bowl) dating from AD 45–85, while the latest sherd is perhaps a rim from a bowl or dish of Drag form 31R (context 1886), from Lezoux, dated to *c.* AD 165–200. This extensive date range is reflected by the coarse wares too, but unfortunately, it cannot be clearly defined in relation to the stratigraphy as the material from all the deposits is quite mixed.

Enclosures

In the southern area of activity, ditch 1907 contained a total of 227 sherds (3522 g). Continental imports comprise four sherds of Gallic (Pelichet 47) wine amphorae dating to the 1st to 3rd centuries AD (Peacock and Williams 1986, 143) and two sherds of Central Gaulish samian, both base angles, one from a form 31 bowl (AD 140–200) and the other of uncertain form (AD 100–160). Regionally traded wares comprise small quantities of South-east Dorset Black Burnished ware and an Oxfordshire whiteware mortaria flange fragment, but none are particularly datable. Body sherds (18 pieces, 463 g) from a relatively large, mica-dusted ware beaker or jar with external rilling were found in the lowest deposit, along with three sherds of South-West White-slipped ware (fabric Q104) mortaria (eg, Fig. 3.7, 52). Proportionally, there is an increase in the frequency of these local oxidised sandy coarsewares (12% of the group by sherd count) compared with the material recovered from Building 1 and trackway/quarry 1932. Forms include flagon types 1 and 6 (Fig. 3.6, 1 and 9), a beaker rim (type 15) and a necked jar rim (Fig. 3.6, 18). The black/brown sandy wares from this ditch also include a straight-sided bowl with a girth cordon comparable to vessels from Wanborough (eg, Seager Smith 2001, 267, fig. 84, 120), and similar to the Class 5 ‘Atrebatic bowls’ manufactured by the Alice Holt/Farnham industry in Surrey during the late first to mid-2nd century AD (Lyne and Jefferies 1979, 31).

A similar range of 2nd-century AD material was recovered from ditches 1443 (233 sherds, 2794 g) and 1909 (119 sherds, 1247 g). Samian from ditch 1443 (5 sherds, 31 g) includes both Southern and Central Gaulish pieces, the earliest being a rim from a La Graufesenque form 27 cup (AD 45–60), while the latest pieces are both body sherds from Lezoux dated to AD 120–200. Other 2nd century AD material from this feature includes a stamped Oxfordshire whiteware mortaria fragment (Fig. 3.10, 101; Young 1977, type M1), which can be dated to AD 100–150, and a hemispherical flanged bowl (Fig. 3.7, 35). No imports occurred within ditch 1909, although a straight-sided dish/bowl with a flat, reeded rim in a sand and calcareous-tempered fabric, the unusual handled beaker (Fig. 3.10, 102) in local oxidised ware and a possible *tetina* spout or tripod foot fragment (Fig. 3.10, 103) in a black/brown sandy ware all suggest that this feature filled during the 2nd century AD.

Layers 1590 and 1602

In Area 1B, a finds-rich, dark soil deposit, comprising layers 1590 and 1602, contained 313 sherds (5344 g) of pottery (Fig. 3.11, 104–112). The date range of this material spans the period from the later 1st century AD through to the mid-/late 3rd century AD, although the degree to which some of this material is residual or indeed, intrusive, is uncertain. The earlier, possibly residual, components include South Gaulish samian (5 sherds, 42 g; forms 15/17 or 18, 27 and 37), dated from AD 50–100, from layer 1590, and fragments from at least two imitation Gallo-Belgic platters in black/brown sandy fabrics, one from each layer.

The bulk of the assemblage from these layers is more clearly of 2nd-century AD date. Two further South Gaulish samian sherds (layer 1602; forms 18/31 and 33) are likely to be of late Flavian-Trajanic date, while the 11 Central Gaulish samian sherds, including a stamped cup base (form 33 or 46; Stamp Cat S5), and pieces from forms 31, 33, 36 and in the 18/31 series, span the period from AD 120–200 AD. Within this range, two pieces can be more precisely dated – a fragment from a decorated bowl (Fig. 3.6, 6) attributed to Austrus (AD 125–150), from layer 1602, and a form 31R bowl rim (AD 165–200), from layer 1590.

Regional imports are limited to three undiagnostic pieces of Verulamium region whiteware and 17 sherds of South-east Dorset Black Burnished ware, including everted rim jars, a shallow, plain-rimmed dish and a flat-rimmed dish/bowl (Seager Smith and Davies 1993, WA types 2, 20 and 24), all of *c.* AD 120 into the early decades of the 3rd-century AD date. One jar body sherd carries the coarse wipe marks typical of vessels from this region after the middle of the 3rd century AD, but in the absence of any other obviously late indicators (such as Oxfordshire or New Forest products) within the group, this piece is considered likely to be intrusive. The local black/brown sandy wares include a small beaker/jar with burnished lattice decoration (Fig. 3.11, 104). These wares still dominate the group (42% by sherd count), but the quantity of Savernake-type wares has diminished, amounting to just 11% by sherd count. Conversely, however, the local oxidised sandy wares represent almost 30% of the sherds from these deposits and include a broad range of flagon (Fig. 3.11, 107 and 108), jar, beaker (Fig. 3.11, 105 and 109) and bowl (Fig. 3.11, 106 and 110) forms as well as a wall-sided mortarium (Fig. 3.11, 111).

Ditches

A large group of material (254 sherds, 5422 g) spanning the period from the mid-2nd century to at least the late 3rd century AD, if not beyond, was recovered from ditch 1908 (Fig. 3.11, 113–121). Continental imports include a small body sherd (2 g) from a Moselkeramik indented beaker (3rd century AD) and five sherds of Central Gaulish samian. Four of these, from forms 18/31 or 31, 31 and 33, date from AD 120–200 AD, but a single, internally worn body sherd from a Rheinzarben bowl extends the range to at least AD 240. Other 3rd century AD indicators comprise an Oxfordshire whiteware mortaria (Young 1977, type M17, AD 240–300) and a South-east Dorset Black Burnished ware dropped flange bowl (Seager Smith and Davies 1993, type WA25), a type introduced into the repertoire of the Wareham/Poole Harbour potters after AD 250/270 AD. Overall, sherds from this region represent 12% of the group by sherd count and include body sherds displaying the coarse wiping typical of this ware post-240 AD. The wall-sided mortaria (Fig. 3.11, 113) also came from this feature, but the form remains undated given the broad span of this group. The black/brown sandy wares (75 sherds, 748 g) account for approximately 30% of the sherds from this feature, while together the local oxidised sandy wares (91 sherds, 1590 g) represent 36% by sherd count. These include a wide range of forms with jars (Fig. 3.11, 114 and 115), bowls (Fig. 3.11, 116 and 117) and mortaria (Fig. 3.11, 118 and 119) the most common. Other more minor wares include a blue/grey sandy ware jar with a projecting shoulder similar to a vessel from Kingscote (Timby 1998, 249, fig. 114.139).

Ditches 1920 and 1933 also contained considerable quantities of sherds (240 sherds, 3494 g and 211 sherds, 2115 g respectively). Typically for ditch deposits, both groups contained sherds spanning a wide date range, the earliest being a South Gaulish samian form 27 cup rim (AD 50–100; ditch 1933) and a North Gaulish mortaria rim (ditch 1920). Both groups are dominated by black/brown sandy wares (36% and 27% by sherd count), which include a narrow-mouthed jar decorated with a double arc motif on the neck (Fig. 3.11, 122), while the local oxidised sandy wares account for 19% and 25% of the sherds respectively. However, the presence of South-east Dorset Black Burnished wares, which include sherds from the three most widely traded late Roman forms (Seager Smith and Davies 1993, types WA3, WA20 and WA25), and body sherds from Oxfordshire and New Forest colour-coated ware vessels, confirm that these features were filling during the late 3rd or 4th century AD.

Discussion

The range of fabrics and forms represented within the Beanacre assemblage is comparable to that seen on a number of other sites in the area (Powell in press; Timby 2008 and 2013a and b). The continental imports (the samian, the Baetican and Gallic amphorae, as well as the North Gaulish mortaria) indicate that the Beanacre settlement was well-served and had access to a wide range of vessels and perhaps exotic commodities from other parts of the Empire. This may at least in part be due to the settlement's proximity to *Aquae Sulis* and the road serving it from the east. The wide range of samian forms and fabrics extend from the pre-Flavian period through to the mid-3rd century AD, when the supply of samian to Britain ceased. At Beanacre, some deposits also appear to contain a higher proportion of sherds from decorated forms than might be expected for a small town. This is often viewed as an indicator of wealth and status (Willis 2005, section 7.3), but the size of this assemblage is too small to produce statistically robust observations on the full implications of this. In comparison to other rural settlements, there is a slightly higher incidence of samian at Beanacre (3.4% by sherd count, 2.5% by weight) than that seen at other rural settlements. At Blacklands, Staverton, for example, samian comprised 2.2% of sherds (Timby 2013b, 29, table 2) whilst at Mill Lane and Groundwell in Swindon it comprises 1.1% and 1.9% respectively (Timby 2012, 52, table 3). The Beanacre assemblage is more akin to that from Atworth villa (3%; Timby 2008, 106, table 5), although both are far from the quantities seen within urban settlement assemblages such as Cirencester (Cooper 1998) or the small town at Wanborough (Pengelly *et al.* 2001). Other imported fine table wares are rare but are complemented by a range of local finewares including lead glazed ware, colour-coated ware and mica-dusted wares probably from north Wiltshire sources.

Throughout the 2nd century and into the 3rd century AD regional imports increase in number, particularly the South-east Dorset Black Burnished wares, along with smaller quantities of specialist wares, most commonly mortaria, from Oxfordshire and the Lower Nene Valley. By the late 3rd century AD colour-coated wares from both the Oxfordshire and New Forest industries are present, although not in any large numbers. Compared to the nearest sites of Atworth and Blacklands, Staverton, there are several differences in the relative quantities of, for example, South-east Dorset Black Burnished ware which are far fewer at Beanacre, amounting to 7.6% (by sherd count) in comparison to 13% at Atworth and 16% at Blacklands. The same is true for the quantities of material from the Oxfordshire region that comprises 0.8% sherds from Beanacre, but 2.9% at Atworth and 2.2% at Blacklands. It is possible that these may be more of a chronological indicator with increased activity at both Atworth and Blacklands continuing well into the late 4th century AD. In comparison to sites in southern Gloucestershire, such as Kingscote and Uley, the complete absence of Severn Valley wares and the low incidence of micaceous greywares, particularly the black micaceous greyware (fabric 5 at Kingscote) at Beanacre, is not unexpected and supports the theory that the area lies beyond the limits of distribution for these two industries. A similar pattern was noted at Atworth (Timby 2008, 103) which is situated approximately 6 km to the west.

By far the greatest part of the assemblage comprises the products of a series of local industries providing utilitarian everyday wares for cooking and storage as well as oxidised table wares. Storage jars are predominantly from the Savernake production centres which is entirely to be expected, given their proximity to the site. Unfortunately, given the absence of large, stratigraphically secure feature groups and the mixed nature of many groups, particularly those that are from ditch deposits and surface layers, it has not been possible to tie down the chronological development of the local oxidised sandy ware fabrics as much as was initially hoped. However, some comments can be made that complement observations made elsewhere (eg, Timby 1998 and 2008). The low proportion (approximately 3.0% by sherd count) of these fabrics amongst the assemblage from Building 1 indicates that the industry may have been producing small quantities of material, including flagons and jars, by the early/mid-2nd century AD. Beakers and mortaria then begin to appear in groups dating to the mid-/late 2nd century, such as ditch 1907 where the local oxidised sandy wares amount to 12% of the feature group. However, the greatest quantities of these wares appear within groups spanning the mid-/late 2nd through to at least the late 3rd centuries AD (eg, layers 1590 and 1602 and ditch group 1908 for example). In ditch 1908, for example, the local oxidised sandy wares formed 32% of the sherds, and out-numbered even the local black/brown sandy ware component. Whether this truly reflects the chronological development of the fabric, or just spatial deposition within the site, is uncertain, but the pattern seems to broadly correspond with the situation at Atworth (Timby 2008) for example, whilst at Cirencester the mortaria fabric largely dates from the Antonine period to mid-/late 3rd century AD (Rigby 1982, 119). The quantities of this group of wares at Beanacre which includes a small proportion of mis-fired vessels that could be classed as usable seconds (eg, jars, see above), provides further evidence for a production source within the immediate north Wiltshire area.

Overall, the composition of the Beanacre assemblage is typically that of a roadside settlement with good access to imported goods but with an abundance of locally available, often high quality, products that meant that it was not necessary to rely on the importation of large quantities of regional goods. However, it is difficult to determine what this may say with regards to the status of the site. Much of the material is of the everyday and mundane, but amongst the detail are elements that are not so common, such as the unusual handled beaker and the possible face pot. As noted above, it is possible that face pots could be associated with areas of religious importance and when considered with other artefactual evidence, in particular the two small stone altars, further credence can be given to this suggestion.

Catalogue of illustrated sherds

Illustrated type series (Figs 3.6–3.8, 1–74)

Fig. 3.6

1. Collared flagon (type 1); coarse oxidised sandy ware (Q101); context 1083, ditch 1907, PRN 1
2. Pulley-wheeled flagon (type 2); coarse, white-slipped oxidised sandy ware (Q103); unstratified, PRN 2
3. Ring-necked flagon (type 3); fine oxidised sandy ware (Q100); layer 1294, group 1916 (building 1), PRN 3
4. Flagon (type 4); coarse, white-slipped oxidised sandy ware (Q103); layer 1602, PRN 6
5. Flagon (type 4); coarse, white-slipped oxidised sandy ware (Q103); unstratified, PRN 7
6. Flagon (type 4); coarse, white-slipped oxidised sandy ware (Q103); subsoil 1002, PRN 10
7. Flagon (type 5); fine, white-slipped oxidised sandy ware (Q102); context 1538, animal burial 1537, PRN 11
8. Triangular-rimmed flagon (type 6); coarse oxidised sandy ware (Q101); layer 1736, PRN 12
9. Triangular-rimmed flagon (type 6); coarse, white-slipped oxidised sandy ware (Q103); context 1083, ditch 1907, PRN 13
10. Flagon (type 7); coarse, white-slipped oxidised sandy ware (Q103); layer 1602, PRN 14
11. Necked jar (type 8), coarse oxidised sandy ware (Q101), context 1231, ditch 1908, PRN 19
12. Necked jar (type 8), coarse oxidised sandy ware (Q101), context 1073, ditch 1908, PRN 20
13. Small, carinated necked jar/bowl (type 9); coarse oxidised sandy ware (Q101); context 1359, tree-throw hole 1357, PRN 28
14. Necked, round shouldered jar (type 10); coarse oxidised sandy ware (Q101); context 1629, robber trench 1927, PRN 29
15. Everted rim jar (type 11); coarse oxidised sandy ware (Q101); context 1359, tree-throw hole 1357, PRN 31
16. High shouldered jar with short, everted rim (type 12); fine oxidised sandy ware (Q100); context 1799, trackway/quarry 1932, PRN 32
17. Necked jar (type 13); coarse oxidised sandy ware (Q101); context 1162, pit 1164, PRN 36
18. Necked jar (type 13); coarse oxidised sandy ware (Q101); context 1082, ditch 1907, PRN 40
19. Beaker (type 15); coarse oxidised sandy ware (Q101); context 1228, oven 1227, PRN 101
20. Beaker (type 15); coarse oxidised sandy ware (Q101); context 1085, wall 1922, PRN 102
21. Beaker (type 15); coarse oxidised sandy ware (Q101); context 1172, pit 1171, PRN 104
22. Beaker (type 15); coarse oxidised sandy ware (Q101); layer 1590, PRN 100
23. Handled beaker (type 16); fine oxidised sandy ware (Q100); context 1208, ditch 1909, PRN 151
24. Beaker (type 17); coarse oxidised sandy ware (Q101); context 1156, oven 1157, PRN 106
25. Indented beaker (type 18); coarse oxidised sandy ware (Q101); context 1156, oven 1157, PRN 111
26. Possible face pot (type 19); coarse oxidised sandy ware (Q101); context 1306, pit 1302, PRN 113
27. Beaker (type 20); coarse oxidised sandy ware (Q101); context 1783, gully 1782, PRN 114
28. Beaker (type 21); white-slipped oxidised sandy ware (Q103); layer 1602, PRN 122
29. Beaker (type 22); coarse oxidised sandy ware (Q101); context 1156, oven 1157, PRN 128
30. Beaker/jar (type 23); white-slipped oxidised sandy ware (Q103); context 1096, robber trench 1923, PRN 134
31. Beaker/jar (type 24); white-slipped oxidised sandy ware (Q103); context 1461, ditch 1933, PRN 146
32. Beaker (type 25); coarse oxidised sandy ware (Q101); context 1774, ditch 1773, PRN 148

Fig. 3.7

33. Tankard (type 27); coarse oxidised sandy ware (Q101); context 1145, pit 1146, PRN 154
34. Hemispherical bowl with straight flange (type 28); red-brown oxidised ware (Q105); context 1072, ditch 1908, PRN 360
35. Hemispherical bowl with downward curving flange (type 29); coarse oxidised sandy ware (Q101); context 1446, ditch 1443, PRN 162
36. Hemispherical bowl decorated on rim and flange (type 30); white-slipped oxidised sandy ware (Q103); context 1073, ditch 1908, PRN 163
37. Hemispherical bowl decorated on rim and flange (type 30); white-slipped oxidised sandy ware (Q103); context 1162, pit 1164, PRN 164
38. Concave mouthed bowl (type 31); coarse oxidised sandy ware (Q101); context 1423, ditch 1422, PRN 165
39. Carinated bowl (type 32); fine oxidised sandy ware (Q100); layer 1602, PRN 167

40. Carinated bowl (type 32); red-brown oxidised ware (Q105); context 1592, pit 1591, PRN 376
41. Bowl (type 33); white-slipped oxidised sandy ware (Q103); context 1768, pit 1767, PRN 174
42. Bead rim bowl (type 34); coarse oxidised sandy ware (Q101); context 1461, ditch 1933, PRN 180
43. Flat rimmed bowl (type 36); coarse oxidised sandy ware (Q101); layer 1590, PRN 183
44. Bowl with near vertical flange (type 52); fine, white-slipped oxidised sandy ware (Q102), layer 1161, PRN 377
45. Simple dish with plain rim (type 37); fine oxidised sandy ware (Q100); context 1416, pit 1414, PRN 375
46. Dish (type 38); coarse oxidised sandy ware (Q101); context 1199, pit 1387, PRN 185
47. Carinated dish with beaded rim (type 39); fine oxidised sandy ware (Q100); layer 1161, PRN 187
48. Wall-sided mortaria (type 40); coarse, white-slipped oxidised sandy ware (Q104); layer 1602, PRN 189
49. Wall-sided mortaria (type 41); coarse, white-slipped oxidised sandy ware (Q104); context 1073, ditch 1908, PRN 193
50. Near wall-sided mortaria (type 42); coarse, white-slipped oxidised sandy ware (Q104); context 1232, ditch 1908, PRN 194
51. Bead and flange mortaria (type 43); coarse, white-slipped oxidised sandy ware (Q104); layer 1161, PRN 199
52. Bead and flange mortaria (type 44); coarse, white-slipped oxidised sandy ware (Q104); context 1068, ditch 1907, PRN 206
53. Bead and flange mortaria (type 44); white-slipped oxidised sandy ware (Q104); context 1209, ditch 1204, PRN 203
54. Bead and flange mortaria (type 45); white-slipped oxidised sandy ware (Q104); layer 1741, PRN 207
55. Mortaria with short, stubby grooved flange (type 46); white-slipped oxidised sandy ware (Q104); unstratified, PRN 211
56. Mortaria with low bead and hooked flange (type 47); white-slipped oxidised sandy ware (Q104); context 1090, wall 1922, PRN 215
57. Mortaria with low bead and hooked flange (type 47); white-slipped oxidised sandy ware (Q104); layer 1308, PRN 213
58. Stamped mortarium flange, probably a type 47; white-slipped oxidised sandy ware (Q104); context 1363, rubble surface 1910, PRN 212

Fig. 3.8

59. Lid with plain, rounded lip (type 48); coarse oxidised sandy ware (Q101); unstratified, PRN 230
60. Lid with squared-off lip (type 49); red-brown oxidised ware (Q105); context 1096, robber trench 1923, PRN 344
61. Lid with out-turned lip (type 50); red-brown oxidised ware (Q105); context 1072, ditch 1908, PRN 345
62. Possible bowl (type 51); coarse oxidised sandy ware (Q101); context 1755, trackway/quarry 1932, PRN 363
63. Possible coffee pot lid (type 51); coarse oxidised sandy ware (Q101); context 1109, pit/well 1936, PRN 367
64. Simple, footed base (type 101); coarse oxidised sandy ware (Q101); context 1038, ditch 1920, PRN 329
65. Moulded, footed base (type 102); coarse oxidised sandy ware (Q101); context 1072, ditch 1908, PRN 331
66. Moulded, footed base (type 102); white-slipped oxidised sandy ware (Q103); layer 1602, PRN 332
67. Moulded, footed base (type 102); white-slipped oxidised sandy ware (Q103); context 1757, trackway/quarry 1932, PRN 330
68. Moulded base (type 103); white-slipped oxidised sandy ware (Q103); context 1236, layer group 1916, Building 1, PRN 333
69. Footring base (type 104); white-slipped oxidised sandy ware (Q103); unstratified, PRN 334
70. Moulded base (type 105); white-slipped oxidised sandy ware (Q103); context 1606, hollow-way 1603, PRN 335
71. Heavy, footed base (type 106); red-brown oxidised ware (Q105); context 1518, ditch 1516, PRN 358
72. Moulded base, open form vessel (type 107); fine, oxidised sandy ware (Q100); context 1873, trackway/quarry 1932, PRN 338
73. Moulded base, open form vessel (type 107); coarse oxidised sandy ware (Q101); context 1886, trackway/quarry 1932, PRN 339
74. Footring base, open form vessel (type 108); coarse oxidised sandy ware (Q101); layer 1161, PRN 340

Illustrated sherds from feature groups (Figs 3.9–3.10, 75–122)

Building 1

Fig. 3.9

75. Bead rim jar; Savernake-type ware; layer 1296, group 1924
76. Long necked vessel rim; black/brown sandy ware; context 1295/1296, structure 1328
77. Footring base with lead rivet repair; white-slipped redware; layer 1236/1296, group 1916, ON 30
78. Necked jar/bowl rim; black/brown sandy ware; context 1295, structure 1328
79. Flat rimmed bowl/dish; black/brown sandy ware; context 1319, intervention 1320
80. Imitation Gallo-Belgic platter; black/brown sandy ware; context 1300, post-pit 1299
81. Imitation Gallo-Belgic platter decorated on the interior with narrow band of vertical burnished lines; black/brown sandy ware; context 1301, post-pit 1299
82. Lid with burnished lattice decoration; black/brown sandy ware; context 1301, post-pit 1299

83. Storage jar with zig-zag line decoration on the shoulder; Savernake-type ware; context 1330, post-pit 1299
84. Storage jar with tooled diagonal line decoration on the shoulder; Savernake-type ware; context 1330, post-pit 1299
85. Ring-necked flagon (type 3); fine oxidised sandy ware (Q100); layer 1294, group 1916, PRN 3
86. Moulded base (type 103); white-slipped oxidised sandy ware (Q103); context 1236, group 1916, PRN 333
87. Flanged bowl/mortaria rim; whiteware; layer 1236, group 1916
88. Round shouldered jar; black/brown sandy ware; layer 1236, group 1916
89. Wide mouthed jar/bowl; black/brown sandy ware; layer 1297, group 1916
90. Flat rimmed bowl with burnished lattice decoration; black/brown sandy ware; layer 1294, group 1916

Trackway/quarry 1932

Fig. 3.10

91. Hemispherical flanged bowl; mica-dusted ware; context 1887, intervention 1888
92. High shouldered jar with short, everted rim (type 12); fine oxidised sandy ware (Q100); context 1799, intervention 1794, PRN 32
93. Possible bowl (type 51); coarse oxidised sandy ware (Q101); context 1755, intervention 1794, PRN 363
94. Moulded base, open form vessel (type 107); fine, oxidised sandy ware (Q100); context 1873, intervention 1870, PRN 338
95. Moulded base, open form vessel (type 107); coarse oxidised sandy ware (Q101); context 1886, intervention 1888, PRN 339
96. Jar/bowl with girth groove; Savernake-type ware; context 1872, intervention 1870
97. Storage jar; Savernake-type ware; context 1873, intervention 1870
98. Flat rimmed bowl; black/brown sandy ware; context 1873, intervention 1870
99. Wide mouthed, necked jar with girth grooves; black/brown sandy ware; context 1757, intervention 1757
100. Footring base with hole through centre; black/brown sandy ware; context 1885, intervention 1888

Enclosures

Fig. 3.10

101. Bead and flange mortaria with herringbone stamp (Young 1977, 68, fig. 18, type M1); Oxfordshire whiteware; context 1446, ditch 1443
102. Handled beaker (type 16); fine oxidised sandy ware (Q100); context 1208, ditch 1909, PRN 151
103. Possible *tetina* spout or tripod foot fragment; black/brown sandy ware; context 1208, intervention 1207, ditch 1909

Layers 1590 and 1602

Fig. 3.11

104. Small jar/beaker with burnished lattice decoration; black/brown sandy ware; layer 1590
105. Beaker (type 15); coarse oxidised sandy ware (Q101); layer 1590, PRN 100
106. Flat rimmed bowl (type 36); coarse oxidised sandy ware (Q101); layer 1590, PRN 183
107. Flagon (type 4); coarse, white-slipped oxidised sandy ware (Q103); layer 1602, PRN 6
108. Flagon (type 7); coarse, white-slipped oxidised sandy ware (Q103); layer 1602, PRN 14
109. Beaker (type 21); white-slipped oxidised sandy ware (Q103); layer 1602, PRN 122
110. Carinated bowl (type 32); fine oxidised sandy ware (Q100); layer 1602, PRN 167
111. Wall-sided mortaria (type 40); coarse, white-slipped oxidised sandy ware (Q104); layer 1602, PRN 189
112. Moulded, footed base (type 102); white-slipped oxidised sandy ware (Q103); layer 1602, PRN 332

Ditches

Fig. 3.11

113. Wall-sided mortaria with groove at top of collar; South-east Dorset Black Burnished ware; context 1231, intervention 1235, ditch 1908
114. Necked jar (type 8); coarse oxidised sandy ware (Q101); context 1231, ditch 1908, PRN 19
115. Necked jar (type 8); coarse oxidised sandy ware (Q101); context 1073, ditch 1908, PRN 20
116. Hemispherical bowl with straight flange (type 28); red-brown oxidised ware (Q105); context 1072, ditch 1908, PRN 360
117. Hemispherical bowl decorated on rim and flange (type 30); white-slipped oxidised sandy ware (Q103); context 1073, ditch 1908, PRN 163
118. Wall-sided mortaria (type 41); coarse, white-slipped oxidised sandy ware (Q104); context 1073, ditch 1908, PRN 193
119. Near wall-sided mortaria (type 42); coarse, white-slipped oxidised sandy ware (Q104); context 1232, ditch 1908, PRN 194
120. Lid with out-turned lip (type 50); red-brown oxidised ware (Q105); context 1072, ditch 1908, PRN 345
121. Moulded, footed base (type 102); coarse oxidised sandy ware (Q101); context 1072, ditch 1908, PRN 331
122. Narrow mouthed jar, decorated on the shoulder; black/brown sandy ware; context 1038, intervention 1039, ditch 1920

Other illustrated sherds

Fig. 3.11, 123–128

123. Decorated body sherd; South-east Dorset Black Burnished ware; context 1363, layer group 1910

124. Bead and flange mortaria; Nene Valley ware; context 1518, ditch 1516
125. Necked, carinated bowl with burnished line decoration; black/brown sandy ware; context 1345, intervention 1344, ditch 1921
126. Wide mouthed, carinated jar; black/brown sandy ware; context 1103, pit 1102
127. Possible flanged rim; Savernake-type ware; cleaning layer 1161
128. Lower part of vessel, possibly deliberately trimmed; black/brown sandy ware; context 1594, oven 1593

Other Finds

by Elina Brook

With the exception of the worked flint, coins and pottery (see above) all other material categories have been grouped and are presented here according to functional categories following Crummy (1983, 5–6).

Personal Adornment or Dress

Brooches

Seven copper alloy brooches or brooch-related objects were found. Bow brooches include the upper part of a small hinged strip-bow brooch (Fig. 3.12, 1) possibly of 1st-century AD date, a possible Polden Hill type brooch (Fig. 3.12, 2) from pit 1697, and a South-western T-shaped brooch (Fig. 3.12, 3) from posthole 1739, similar to one from Uley (Butcher 1993, 152, fig. 124, 5). Both the Polden Hill and South-western T-shaped brooches are datable to the second half of the 1st century into the first half of the 2nd century AD. Pit 1527 contained an almost complete, small, enamelled rectangular plate brooch (Fig. 3.12, 4, and back cover), along with the remains of food debris including pig bones. An almost identical brooch was found at Old Sarum, Wiltshire and dated to the 2nd century AD (Hattatt 2000, 349, fig. 208, 586), whilst a further, very similar item was found at Broughton, Hampshire (Shoemark 2014, PAS WILT-596884). The bow and partial catchplate of a small brooch of unidentifiable type was found unstratified, whilst brooch-related items consist of one sprung brooch pin (layer 1308) and one hinged brooch pin (oven 1157).

Hairpins

Two hairpins were found (Fig. 3.12, 5 and 6), one of copper alloy and one of bone. The copper alloy example has a spherical decorated head (Fig. 3.12, 5) and falls within Cool's group 13 (Cool 1990, 164), possibly dating to the 2nd century AD. The group 13 types typically have a distribution centred on the West Country, but more local examples include a similar object from Kingscote, Gloucestershire (Redknap 1998, 93, fig. 54, 1.5). The bone hairpin (Fig. 3.12, 6) is of Crummy type 6 (1983, 24), dated from the 2nd century AD onwards. Both came from late Romano-British deposits (ditch 1915 and layer 1161 respectively).

Beads

Two small glass beads were recovered. Layer 1161 contained a complete blue-green cylinder bead (Fig. 3.12, 7; 18 mm long, 6 mm diameter). Clear striations are visible along its length, indicating that it may be of late Romano-British date (Guido 1978, 94, fig. 37.4). The second bead (ON 38; late Romano-British robber trench 1923) is incomplete; it is dark blue in colour, teardrop-shaped and broken at the narrower end.

A possible copper alloy *bullae* pendant (Fig. 3.12, 8) was found in the phase 2 deposits of early Romano-British Building 1. These items were worn like a locket around the necks of male children to protect against evil spirits and forces.

Bracelets

One fragment from a plain, lathe-turned shale bracelet came from late Romano-British ditch 1933. The internal edge is slightly chamfered, with a diameter of approximately 50 mm. Such objects were in use from at least the late 1st century to the end of the Roman period (Lawson 1976, 248–50). A tapering strip of copper alloy (pit 1802) may also be from a bracelet.

Other items of personal adornment/dress

Other objects likely to be associated with personal adornment include several links from a very fine chain (ditch 1909), possibly from an item of jewellery, and a worked bone toggle (Fig. 3.12, 9) made from a shaft fragment of a sheep metacarpal (pit 1164). The latter may have been used to fasten clothing or a bag.

Twenty-four iron hobnails were found in grave 1440, around the feet of an adult female, suggesting that she had been buried wearing nailed boots/shoes and is, therefore, likely to have been buried fully clothed (Phillpot 1991, 147). One fragment from a probable cleat (late Romano-British ditch 1937) is also likely to have come from the sole or heel of a boot (Manning 1985, 131).

Toilet Equipment

Four almost complete copper alloy toilet implements were found. They comprise two nail cleaners (Fig.

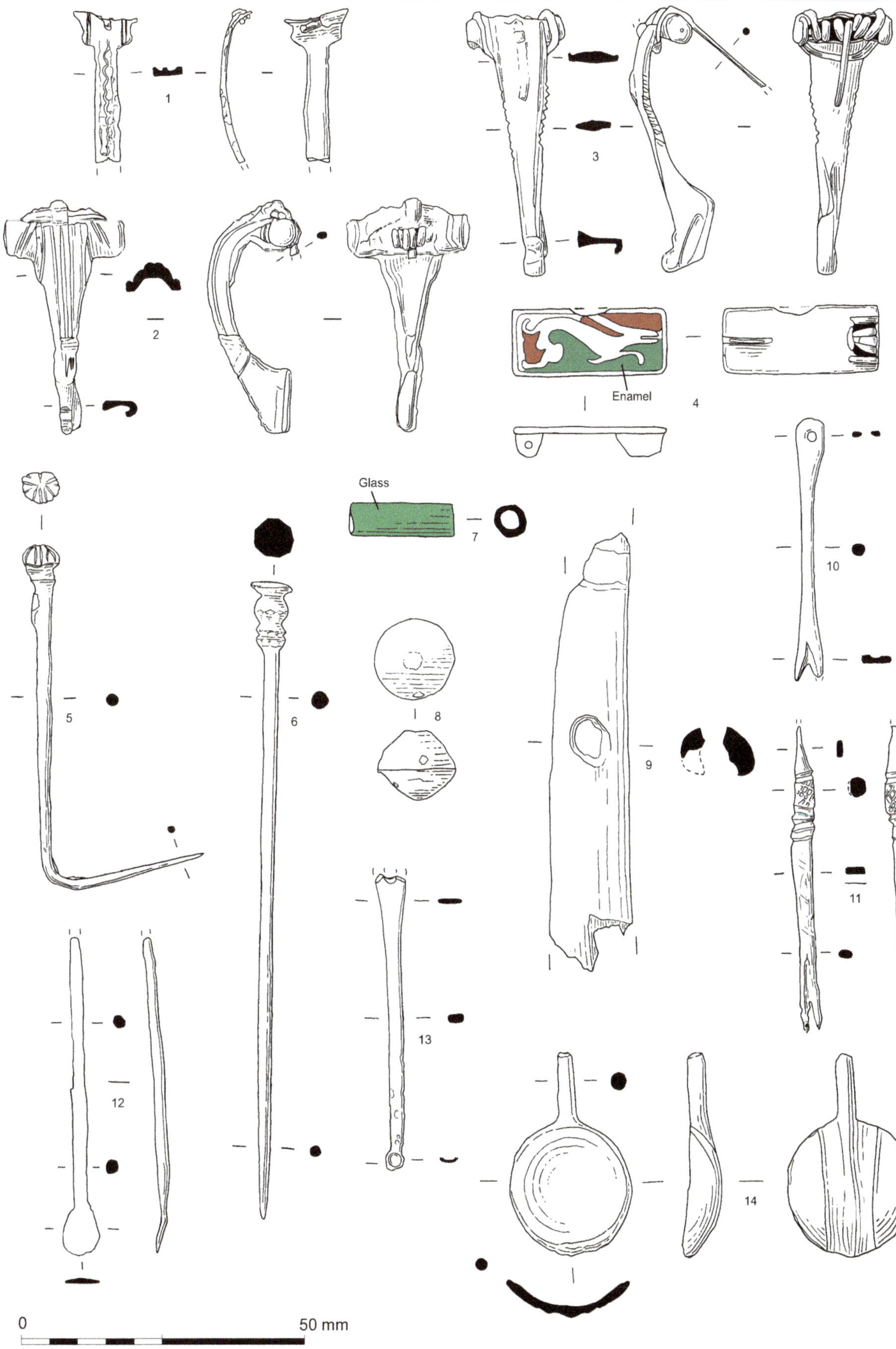

Figure 3.12 Other finds: copper alloy (nos 1–5, 8, 10–14); worked bone (nos 6 and 9); glass (no 7)

3.12, 10 and 11) from the phase 2 deposits of early Romano-British Building 1 and mid-Romano-British pit 1302, and two ear scoops (Fig. 3.12, 12 and 13) from Romano-British oven 1200 and late Romano-British layer 1161. Along with tweezers, such items often formed parts of a set, and were manufactured throughout the entire Roman period (Crummy and Eckardt 2003, 51).

Objects Used in the Manufacture or Working of Textiles

Five well-polished, tapering, shank fragments from worked bone pins or needles were also recovered. Three have surviving points (pit 1164; robber trench 1923; layer 1602), whilst the other two (ditch 1920; pit 1352) are broken at both ends. With the exception of the shank fragment from mid-Romano-British layer 1602, all came from features of late Romano-British date. Two possible spindlewhorls made from sherds of coarse pottery were also recovered (Pl. 3.2, see Brook and Seager Smith above for further discussion).

Household Utensils

Part of a round-bowled copper alloy spoon (Fig. 3.12, 14) dated to the second half of the 1st to 2nd century AD (Crummy 1983, 69, type 1, fig. 73, 2008) was found in pit 1165. The reverse of the bowl has a broad rib extending down the centre from the handle.

Non-ceramic vessels are represented by a small, shale fragment/flake from a possible tray or platter and 12 pieces from others made of glass. The surface of the shale tray or platter fragment (late Romano-British rubble surface 1910) is decorated with two shallow, slightly curving, parallel grooved lines with multiple diagonal lines in between. Shale vessels are not uncommon on Romano-British sites and elsewhere, particularly in south-western Britain, and platters were in use from the late 1st to 2nd century continuing through into the 3rd century AD (Cool 2008, 97). Local examples include one from Atworth villa (*ibid.*, 97, object 49). The majority of the glass pieces are from vessels in a range of blue-green colours. One unstratified fragment was pale yellow. No rims are present and featured sherds are limited. They include two base fragments, one from a square bottle with a concentric circle visible on the underside (ON 5; mid-Romano-British pit 1152). Elsewhere in Britain, most square bottles date to the late 1st to 2nd centuries AD (Monk 2001, 165). A pale blue-green body fragment (ON 69), from late Romano-British ditch 1913, has part of a pinched handle trail surviving – a characteristic feature of 1st and 2nd century AD ribbon handles (Price and Cottam 1998, 25), commonly found on jugs.

Pieces from three possible querns were also recovered. A fragment of sandy limestone found in early Romano-British post-pit 1299 (within Building 1) has one very smooth/worn flattish surface and may be from a saddle quern. Romano-British pit 1879 contained six very worn and abraded fragments of Mayen lava from the Middle Rhine, a type commonly imported during the Roman period onwards (Shaffrey 2015a–b), although its survival can be poor on many sites. The pieces are probably from a rotary quern. Part of a possible upper stone from a rotary quern came from late Romano-British ditch 1933; it is made from a fine-grained, slightly micaceous reddish-brown sandstone, probably Old Red Sandstone.

Other household items include seven irregularly shaped lead rivets/pot-mends. Four are comparable to Schuster type 1 (2011, 247). Two still contain traces of ceramics; one (Pl. 3.3a; rubble surface 1910) had been used on a thin-walled vessel in a black/brown sandy ware, whilst the other (Pl. 3.3b; ditch 1933) had been used to repair a South-east Dorset Black Burnished ware jar. These items were recovered from features of late Romano-British date (hollow-way 1404; rubble surface 1910; ditch 1933), a post-medieval hollow-way (1603) and unstratified.

Weighing and Measuring

A rectangular copper alloy fragment (unstratified) has been tentatively identified as part of an arm from a steelyard. It is comparable to an example from Colchester of 1st century AD date (Crummy 1983, 100, fig. 104, 2508), although steelyards dating throughout the Roman period have been found in Britain.

Writing and Written Communication

An iron stylus (Fig. 3.13, 15), in very poor condition, came from late Romano-British layer 1741. It is similar to an example from London of 1st- or 2nd-century AD date (Manning 1985, 86, pl. 35, N20, type 2a), although the eraser end is slightly narrower.

Transport

One item associated with transportation is represented – occupation layer 1891 contained an iron ring with an additional loop attached that is part of a snaffle bit.

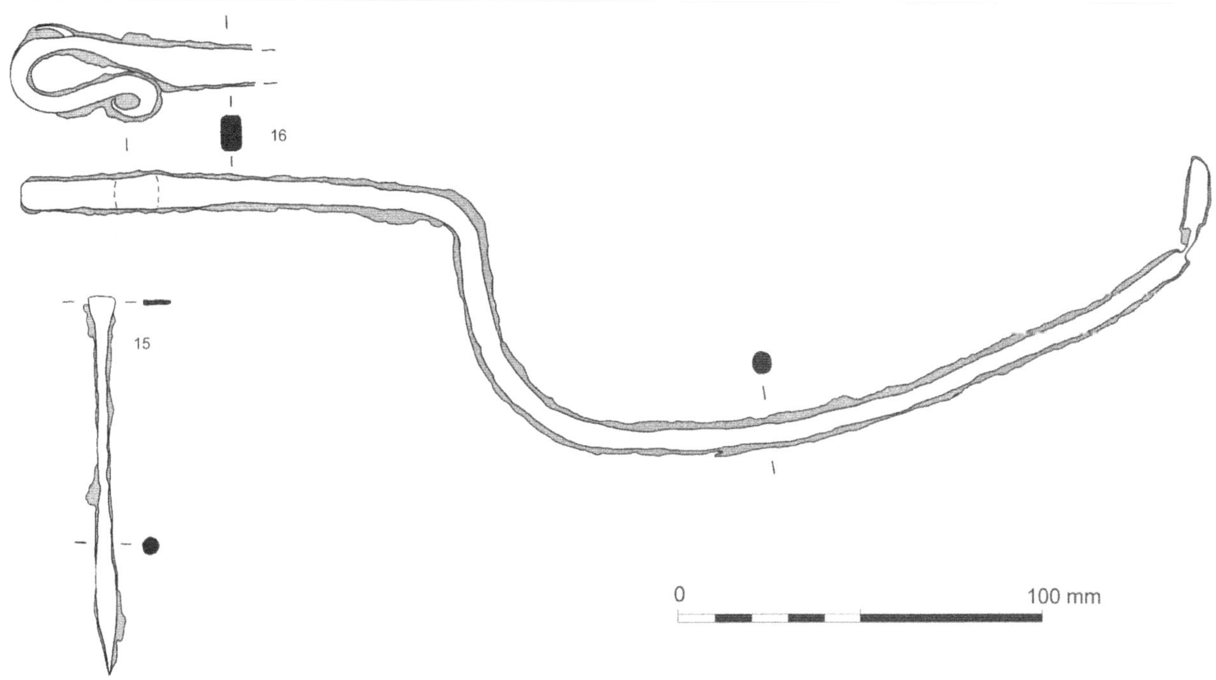

Figure 3.13 Other finds: iron (nos 15–16)

Fasteners and Fittings

Nails

The majority (133) are flat, round-headed iron nails with square-sectioned tapering shanks or nail shank fragments. Although not closely datable, it is likely that most are Romano-British. Of the 13 complete examples, all correspond to Manning's type 1B (1985, 134), which are by far the most common form to be found on most Roman sites. In addition to the 24 hobnails found in grave 1440 (see above), a total of 15 hobnails/tacks may derive from other boots/shoes, or perhaps furniture as similar dome-headed tacks were used in upholstery and to decorate woodwork.

Other fittings

Two copper alloy studs were found (late Romano-British wall 1922; unstratified), both are dome-headed with square-sectioned tapering shanks; one has a rivet still in place. A small number of other structural fittings include fragments from two T-clamps (Manning 1985, 132, pl. 62, R66–72) from pits 1936 and 1697 (ON 162), an L-clamp (*ibid.*, 132, R73) also from pit 1697 (ON 31) and two loop-headed spikes (*ibid.*, 130, pl. 59, R31) found in late Romano-British ditch 1516 and layer 1161 (ON 45). An iron holdfast with a flat, round head and sub-circular rove at the opposing end (ON 168; posthole 1833) may possibly have been used to join two pieces of wood together. A copper alloy cylindrical object attached to a loop/ring (ON 35) from hollow-way 1925 is also probably a fitting of some sort.

Latchlifter

An almost complete latchlifter (Fig. 3.13, 16) was found in occupation layer 1582 – these were the simplest form of key and were widely used in Britain from the late Iron Age continuing throughout the Roman period.

Building Materials

Stone

Stone was commonly used as a building material on the site, as evidenced by surviving foundations consisting of predominantly unshaped lumps of local limestone. However, no deliberately shaped blocks from the walling survived *in situ* and, therefore, no quantification or detailed record of such material is available. Of the building stone that was collected, the majority (15 pieces, 20.7 kg) are fragments of roof tiles. Most of the stone roofing is of fine-grained, slightly micaceous reddish-brown sandstone, probably Old Red Sandstone. Two of the more complete tiles (layer 1763) are in a fine-grained limestone, possibly from a local, Jurassic source. Where enough of the tile is present to record shape, all are polygonal. Three have sub-circular nail holes, two of which are off-centre. This characteristic was also noted amongst the stone roof tiles from the

Figure 3.14 Architectural fragments (nos 17–18)

Roman buildings at Truckle Hill, North Wraxall in north-west Wiltshire (Andrews and Little 2016). The piece from occupation layer 1582 still has part of a flat headed iron nail present in the nail hole.

The remaining stone building materials include two architectural fragments. One piece (Fig. 3.14, 17) of shelly limestone came from pit 1387; it has two parallel surfaces, one of which has a slightly moulded recess. The other is a large fragment of oolitic limestone (Fig. 3.14, 18) found within the backfill of well 1678. This piece is curved with an approximate internal diameter of 450 mm (external 600 mm). The interior edge is slightly chamfered and there is a slight lip on the outer edge; the underside/reverse face is unworked indicating this has broken away from a larger block of stone that probably formed a curved or arched structure of some description. Given its stratigraphic position, it is possible that this fragment formed part of a stone superstructure surrounding the top of the well, but given the known presence of several other stone-built structures on the site (all evidenced by stone footings), this cannot be certain.

Ceramic building material

Ceramic building material (CBM) was collected in its entirety but was notably scarce on this site, the assemblage comprising just 56 fragments (5247 g) recovered from 28 contexts in a range of feature types (ditches, a hollow-way, pits, one posthole and one oven). All pieces are relatively small (average weight 93 g), worn and abraded. With the exception of two undatable fragments, all the material is of Romano-British date and includes fragments of *tegula*, *imbrex*, brick and one fragment of probable box flue/*voussoir*. The majority consist of flat or featureless fragments; no complete dimensions are measurable. One fragment from a *tegula* (layer 1602) has part of a double, curved, finger signature. Based on thickness (between 30–40 mm), the two brick fragments may derive from one of the smaller brick types, *bessalis*, *pedalis* or *lydion*.

Fired clay

The fired clay (199 fragments, 3176 g) derived from 47 contexts, but only 10 contexts contained more than 100 g. The majority are small, abraded, featureless fragments made in slightly sandy, predominantly oxidised fabrics with some pieces containing rare flint or calcareous inclusions. The dating of all pieces relies on associated material. Bronze Age posthole 1521 and pit 1525 each contained a single undiagnostic fragment (3 g and 1 g respectively). The remainder came from contexts spanning the 1st to 4th centuries AD.

Several pieces have flattish surfaces or angled edges which suggest they derive from the linings of ovens, kilns or hearths, and indeed 47% (by weight) of the fired clay assemblage came from the ovens. Fragments from at least two perforated triangular objects were found in mid-Romano-British oven 1225 and late Romano-British ditch 1908. Although traditionally interpreted as loomweights, there is now increasing evidence to suggest that these items may have been used as oven/hearth furniture (Lowther 1935; Poole 1995; 2015), from the Iron Age well into at least the 2nd century AD (Wild 2002, 10).

Other pieces of note include a fragment from a perforated object of uncertain function found in mid-Romano-British oven 1792.

Tools

Eight objects have been tentatively identified as tools, four are of metal, whilst four are of stone. The metal tools comprise a possible awl with a square cross section and tapering ends from late Romano-British robber trench 1923, a fragment from a knife blade with part of the tang still present (ditch 1499) and pieces from two socketed tools of uncertain type from mid- Romano-British hollow-way 1932.

The stone tool fragments consist of pieces from four whetstones, all from features of Romano-British date. Two are from bar-shaped items (hearth 1775; undated tree-throw hole 1357), both of fine-grained, micaceous limestone. Two irregularly-shaped pebbles with oval cross-sections (mid-Romano-British ditch 1921 and Romano-British oven 1934) had been utilised as whetstones/polishing stones. The piece from ditch 1921 has elongated shallow grooves on both flat surfaces indicating that it had been used on both sides. Such objects could have been utilised for sharpening household utensils, as well as other tools.

Objects Associated with Religious Beliefs and Practices

Two small altars (Fig. 3.15, 19 (ON 39) and 20 (ON 40)), made from locally sourced oolitic limestone, were recovered from the subsoil (1002) immediately to the north of the Roman road. The objects are almost identical in size and shape (ON 39 320 mm high, 127 mm wide and 125 mm deep; ON 40 310 mm high, 134 mm wide and 120 mm deep). The body of both altars consists of a block of stone with a projecting capital and base, both of which are simply moulded and decorated with single horizontal lines. One face of the capital of ON 40 has two diagonal grooved lines visible, indicating additional decoration. Both altars have a lozenge shaped *focus* (80 mm by 50 mm with a depth of approximately 20 mm) flanked by stylised bolsters carved into their upper surfaces. The *focus* is where offerings could

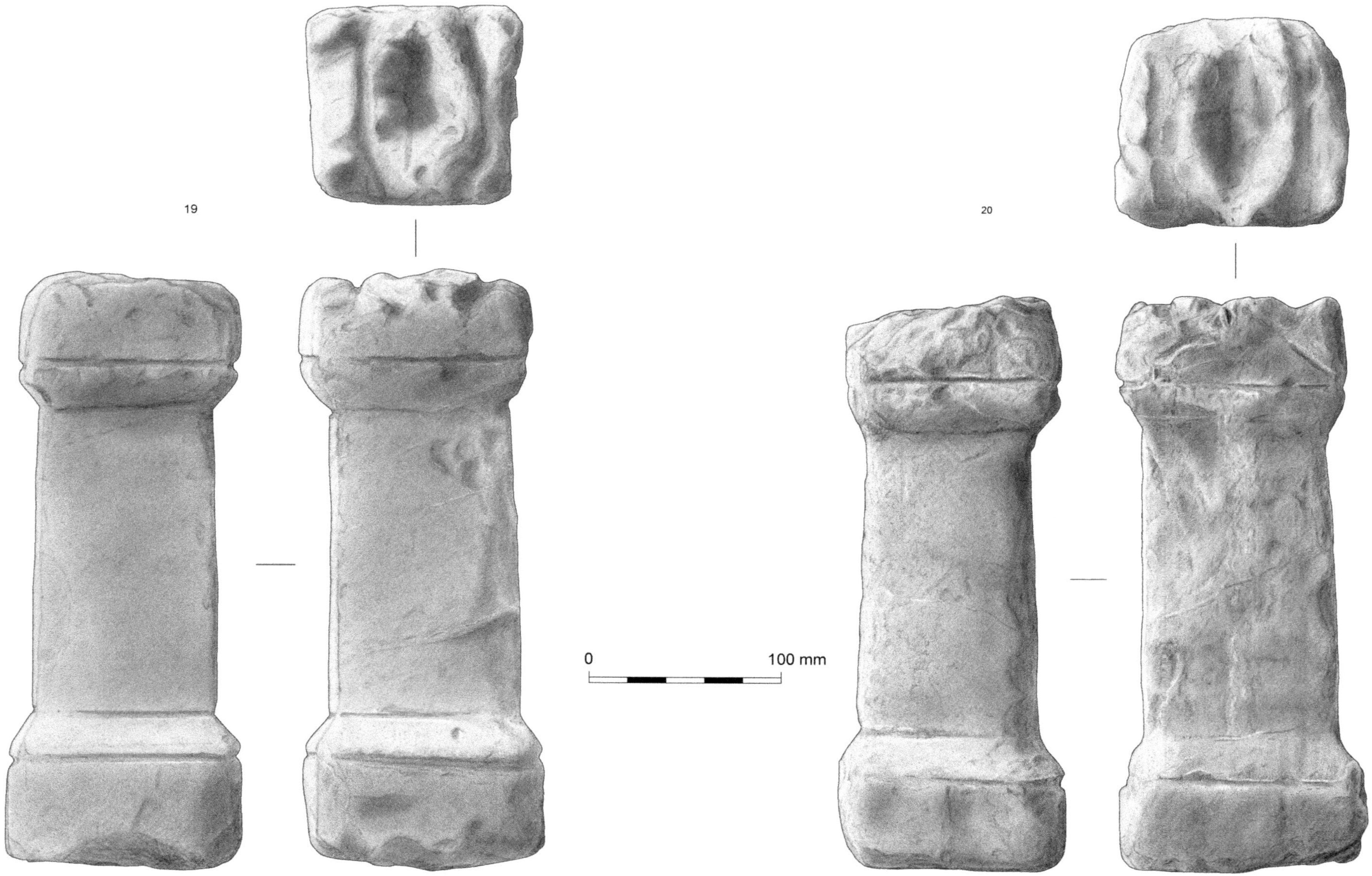

Figure 3.15 Stone altars (nos 19–20)

have been placed or burnt, but microscopic examination (x10 magnification) of the surfaces of these cavities has established that no traces of residues survive. Both stones are moderately weathered and no inscriptions are visible, even with the enhanced views provided by Reflectance Transformation Imaging. Although such stones are normally inscribed with the names of the donor(s) and the deity to whom the altar was dedicated, this was not inevitably the case. A similar, small, uninscribed altar was found redeposited in the squatter level from within the east side of the octagonal shrine (post AD 249) at Nettleton, Wiltshire (Wedlake 1982, 198, fig. 80, 69) for example, and even 'uninscribed' stones may have originally carried a painted inscription. Stone altars were the primary site for making sacrifices and offerings to the gods during the Roman period and although they are commonly associated with sites of religious significance, such as temples, they could also be placed in household, workplace (Allason-Jones 2011, 273) or even roadside shrines. Elsewhere in the region, fragments from at least three larger altars were found within the ritual complex at Uley, Gloucestershire. These were also redeposited, within phase 7 deposits dating to the mid- 5th to 7th centuries AD (Henig 1993, 94, fig. 78 and 79).

Illustrated objects

Fig. 3.12

1. Copper alloy strip-bow brooch, punched dot decoration down length of bow, possibly tinned; unstratified, ON 17
2. Copper alloy possible Polden Hill type brooch, notched decoration; context 1696, pit 1697, ON 96
3. Copper alloy South-western T-shaped brooch; context 1740, posthole 1739, ON 100
4. Copper alloy zoomorphic enamelled plate brooch, with hound (or hare) running right with areas above head/behind tail red/orange, remainder pale green; context 1528, pit 1527, ON 70; see back cover
5. Copper alloy hairpin, spherical head; layer 1161, ON 11
6. Worked bone hairpin, bead and reel-shaped head, slightly swollen, well-polished shank, Crummy type 6 (1983, 24); context 1409, ditch 1915, ON 53
7. Glass bead, blue-green cylinder type; cleaning layer 1161, ON 46
8. Copper alloy biconical pendant; context 1239, sunken-featured building 1328, ON 175
9. Worked bone toggle; context 1162, pit 1164, ON 22
10. Copper alloy nail cleaner; context 1250, sunken-featured building 1328, ON 34
11. Copper alloy nail cleaner; context 1307, pit 1302, ON 41
12. Copper alloy earscoop; context 1203, oven 1200, ON 21
13. Copper alloy earscoop; layer 1161, ON 72
14. Copper alloy spoon; context 1169, pit 1165, ON 18

Fig. 3.13

15. Iron stylus; layer 1741, ON 105
16. Iron latchlifter; occupation layer 1582, ON 90

Fig. 3.14

17. Architectural fragment, shelly limestone; pit 1387
18. Architectural fragment, oolitic limestone; well 1678, ON 97

Fig. 3.15

19. Stone altar, oolitic limestone; subsoil 1002, ON 39
20. Stone altar, oolitic limestone; subsoil 1002, ON 40

Material Associated with Metalworking

by Phil Andrews

Virtually all the slag (77.2 kg) came from 80 contexts of Romano-British date, with just a very small amount being unstratified. All derives from ironworking.

Smelting slag

The vast majority (approximately 72 kg) of the assemblage comprises fragmentary smelting slag, which is generally in fresh condition, with very little abraded material that might be indicative of a high level of residuality. The smelting slag is characteristically dense and relatively flat, with a ropey flow structure on the upper surface resulting from it having been tapped from a furnace.

However, no furnace remains were found within the excavation area, geophysical survey in the vicinity showed no anomalies that might certainly indicate furnaces, no iron ore was present and furnace lining was absent. On this basis, while it is possible that smelting furnaces did lie within or just outside the roadside settlement, it must also be considered that the slag was brought to the site from furnaces located further away, for use as hardcore or similar. One source might be at Seend, just over 5 km to the south-east, where ferruginous sands exploited during the 19th century occur, or else one or more of the small ironstone deposits which may have provided sources of ore since at least the Roman period.

The smelting slag occurred widely across the site within a variety of features, though none was incorporated in any of the surviving metalled surfaces, including the Roman road itself. Fourteen contexts produced more than 1 kg of slag, but only one had over 3 kg (animal burial 1538; 3.015 kg) and one over 4 kg (posthole 1295, within Building 1; 4.014 kg). However, 1680, the backfill of the construction cut

Table 3.7 Smithing hearth bottoms

Context	*Feature*	*Type*	*No*	*Wt (g)*	*Size (mm)*
1236	1177	SFB	1	555	115 x 95 x 65
1592	1591	Pit	2	512	100 x 90 x 50
				107	80 x 55 x 20
1622	1621	Pit	1	789	120 x 110 x 60
1654	1653	Hearth	3	425	120 x 95 x 40
				290	110 x 75 x 30
				179	75 x 60 x 30

for well 1678, contained 37.4 kg. This represents more than half of the smelting slag recovered, and perhaps only 25% of the context was excavated.

Smithing slag

The relatively small (approximately 5 kg) but significant group of debris deriving from iron smithing comprises 1.562 kg from late Romano-British pit 1591, 1.485 kg from mid-Romano-British hearth 1653, 0.868 kg from pit 1622 (associated with oven 1935), 0.642 kg from hollow-way 1932 (layer 1873) and 0.555 kg from Building 1.

This material mainly comprises smithing hearth bottoms (SHB), the (commonly) hemispherical buns of slag that formed in the base of smithing hearths. There were seven examples of these (Table 3.7), in addition to a number of fragments.

The single SHB from Building 1 occurred along with smelting slag, but the other four contexts contained only smithing debris. In addition to the SHBs, there was some hearth lining, principally from 1873, a layer in hollow-way 1932, and hammerscale, which occurred in particular abundance in hearth 1653, along with some hearth lining and smithing slag. This concentration of hammerscale is indicative of iron smithing having taken place in the immediate vicinity.

Hearth 1653, which comprised a small, sub-rectangular, flat-bottomed pit, showed some evidence for *in situ* burning but was otherwise unremarkable. It lay in close proximity to the road and other features/deposits containing smithing debris, and it is therefore likely that hearth 1653 was the focus of this activity. Furthermore, all of these contexts appear to belong to the earlier part of the sequence, pre-dating the building(s) with stone foundations, and can be broadly assigned to the 2nd–3rd century AD.

Overall, this evidence might suggest small-scale, possibly relatively short-lived iron smithing activity rather than a permanent, long-established smithy adjacent to the Roman road. Such an occurrence would not be unusual in a settlement of this type.

Non-ferrous metalworking

Evidence for this type of activity was limited to just three possible crucible sherds from oven 1054. In addition, 37 fragments of lead comprising 21 irregularly-shaped, melted waste fragments and 16 flattish scrap/sheet off-cuts indicate the use of this metal on the site. Of these, 21 were unstratified while eight came from the subsoil. Stratified pieces came from Romano-British pit 1934, mid-Romano-British oven 1173, hollow-way 1925 and late Romano-British ditches 1147, 1516, 1519 and 1937. There are also several miscellaneous sheet/strip fragments of copper alloy and iron that could also be related to the manufacture and/or repair of metal items.

Miscellaneous Items or those of Uncertain or Unknown Function

Thirty-four fragments of copper alloy and iron comprising miscellaneous pieces from rods, bars and rings, as well as pieces too corroded to identify, were also recovered. The dating of these pieces relies on associated material. A flat, facetted, possible bolt head is of uncertain date despite coming from Romano-British layer 1602 – it is possibly of much later date and therefore intrusive. A single fragment of melted blue-green glass came from robber trench 1923.

A total of 52 oyster shell fragments, from 26 contexts, were collected. Both left and right valves were identified, indicating that the shells are likely to represent food remains. The pieces are mostly small and fragmentary, appearing in small groups – the greatest quantity came from ditch 1925 (six pieces, 49 g).

Artefacts Recorded by the Portable Antiquities Scheme

by Richard Henry

Eight pieces of Roman metalwork have been recorded onto the Portable Antiquities Scheme (PAS) database from the vicinity of the site. These comprise four brooches, two finger-rings and two furniture fittings. The copper alloy brooches consist of one plate brooch (AD 100–200) and three bow brooches, including an enamelled Polden Hill type dating to AD 75–175. The two silver finger-rings consist of one Henig type VIII (2007) finger-ring dating from AD 200–400 acquired by the Wiltshire Museum (WILT-6D7DE7) and a Henig type XI dating to AD 200–300 (WILT-6DF737). One furniture fitting recorded as WILT-EF2E7D is of particular note; similar examples included in the Corbridge hoard (Allason-Jones and Bishop 1988, fig. 95, nos 238–240) are likely to be from a folding stool.

Table 3.8 Human bone: summary of results

Context	*Feature*	*Date*	*Deposit type*	*Quantity*	*Age/sex*	*Pathology/indices*
1281	1280 (posthole)	ERB	R	*c.* 10 frags a.u.	neonate *c.* 2–6 wk	generalised porosity
1286	1367 (burrow)	ERB	R = 1365	*c.* 10 frags s.u.	neonate *c.* birth	
1297	1177 (SFB)	ERB	R = 1324	1 bone u.	neonate *c.* birth	
1324	1323 (?hearth)	ERB	inh. burial	*c.* 15% s.a.u.	neonate *c.* birth	poor mineralisation – skull, pelvis, upper limbs; flared rib end
1351	1364	ERB	R = 1324	6 frags s.a.u.	neonate *c.* birth	
1365	1364	ERB	inh. burial	*c.* 20 frags s.u.	neonate *c.* birth	poor mineralisation – petrous temporal
1442	1440	LRB	inh. burial	*c.* 80%	adult >60 yr female	amtl; apical voids; *hyperostosis frontalis interna* (with assoc. endocranial impressions); *cribra orbitalia*; *osteochondritis dissecans* – left olecranon; ?solitary bone cysts – right lunate; sinusitis; ddd – C3–S1; oa – C2–T1, 2T, 4L, S1 ap, Ls, S1, left temporo-mandibular, 4 right, 2 left ribs, 1st MtC-Ps, 1st proximal IPs & 3 right, 3 left distal IP (fingers); op – C2 as, T1, 3, 5, 8 c-v, acetabulae, right glenoid, proximal left radius, proximal radii, distal right radius, left lunate, 1st proximal IPs & 3 right distal IPs (fingers), 2 left proximal IPs (toes); pitting – right temporo-mandibular, right sacro-iliac, right acetabulum, right acromio-clavicular, sterno-claviculars, left proximal ulna, right scaphoid; rotator cuff degeneration – right humerus; enth – innominates, right acetabulum, upper limbs, hands, left patella; cortical defects – 1st MtTs & 1st proximal phalanx; exostoses – left 5th MtC; plastic change – left scapula; ossified cartilage – rib; ?hydatid cyst; MV – mylohyoid bridge, C2 foramen, septal aperture
1587	1586	RB	inh. burial	*c* 90%	neonate *c* birth –2 wk	extensive endo- & exocranial new bone, incl. orbits, mandible (?scurvy); pnb – limbs, rib necks, pelvis; striated surfaces – ribs; sharp blade cut – left 5th proximal phalanx (toe)

KEY: R – redeposited; s.a.u.l. – skull, axial, upper limb, lower limb (where not all skeletal regions are represented); amtl – *ante mortem* tooth loss; pnb – periosteal new bone; ddd – degenerative disc disease; C, T, L, S – cervical, thoracic, lumbar, sacral vertebrae; oa – osteoarthritis; op – osteophytes; enth – enthesophytes; IP – inter-phalangeal; MtC – metacarpal

Human bone

by Kirsten Egging Dinwiddy

The remains of four *in situ* Romano-British inhumation burials were analysed along with redeposited bone from four other similarly dated contexts (Table 3.8). One of the burials was made next to a field boundary ditch towards the northern end of the site, while the remainder of the assemblage was from features closely associated with Buildings 1 and 3.

The condition of the bone was recorded according to McKinley (2004, fig. 6), and age and sex was estimated using standard methodologies (Bass 1987; Beek 1983; Buikstra and Ubelaker 1994; Scheuer and Black 2000). Various metric and non-metric data were recorded (Berry and Berry 1967; Brothwell and Zakrzewski 2004; Finnegan 1978), and pathological lesions were described in text, photographed and x-radiographed as appropriate.

Results

The results are summarised in Table 3.8. Due to the small sample size, no attempt has been made to calculate rates or undertake detailed comparative analysis.

Burial remains were encountered at between 0.06 m and 0.15 m below the stripped level. Graves 1324 and 1365 (both possibly associated with the use of Building 1) were disturbed by animal burrowing, as was the upper fill of posthole 1280. Redeposited bone probably deriving from the two aforementioned graves was locally dispersed as a result of bioturbation (including animal burrowing) (contexts 1286, 1297 and 1351). A small quantity of redeposited bone was also found within the undisturbed lower fill of posthole 1280, which pre-dated grave 1365.

The condition of the bone is generally good to excellent (grades 0–2) with only slight root etching and/or erosion of the ends. The degree of fragmentation varied. Recovery of the skeletal material from the remains of two undisturbed burials was excellent, whilst a large proportion of bone had been lost from the two that had been heavily disturbed and truncated.

The assemblage represents a minimum (MNI) of five individuals comprising an elderly female and four neonates. As is often the case during the Romano-British period, all of the neonatal remains were associated with domestic settings rather than an area put aside for burial – motivations for which have been discussed at length elsewhere (Philpott 1991, 97–102; Struck 1993; Scott 1999, 115; McKinley 2011, 5–9). The more distant location of the adult burial – beside a field boundary some 95 m to the NNE of the main settlement area – is also fairly commonplace.

Limited calculable indices demonstrate the femora to be platymeric, ie, flattened – the left (75.8) more so than the right (84.6). The right tibia is within the eurycnemic (broad) range (78.7). All are within the general norms. A few morphological variations were noted in the adult remains, including a fairly uncommon mylohyoid bridge and a perforation through one of the articular surfaces of the axis.

The woman had lost all of her teeth some time prior to death, the mandibular anterior teeth evidently the last to be shed. Reduction in the height of the mandibular body was extreme – it being no higher than the mental foramen on the left side. It is likely that there was at least some dental pathology, possibly contributing to the signs of sinusitis within the frontal and maxillary sinuses. *Cribra orbitalia* in both of the adult orbits indicate either iron or vitamin B12 deficiency, which may be associated with dietary lack, certain diseases and conditions (particularly gastrointestinal), blood loss and heavy parasitic load (Lewis 2010, 408; Molleson 1993; Roberts and Manchester 1997, 163–9; Walker *et al* 2009). Pieces of osseous material from the woman's thorax may be remnants of hydatid cysts – associated with the parasitic infection by a tapeworm of the *Echinococcus* genus (Manchester 1983, 49; Aufderheide and Rodríguez-Martín 1998, 240–4).

The haemorrhagic nature of new bone deposits on the mandible and in the orbits of neonate 1587 are characteristic of scurvy (a lack of vitamin C), which is further corroborated by generalised poor mineralisation and 'puffiness' of other elements. Similar poor/abnormal formation of the most recently laid bone deposits of neonates 1324 and 1365 suggest that they, too, had been nutrient deficient. The condition of these very young individuals suggests problems *in utero*, potentially due to poor maternal health or obstetric issues such as placental insufficiency. Similar cases have been observed by the writer; research into potential causes is still somewhat limited (eg, Egging Dinwiddy 2011, 129–30; Lewis and Roberts 1997; Lewis 2007; 2010).

Hyperostosis frontalis interna (an asymptomatic condition characterised by the accumulation of endocranial new bone, usually affecting older women) was observed in the skull of the elderly female. Further indicators of her advanced age include ossified rib cartilage and possible thoracic soft tissue.

Traumatic injuries comprise a lesion consistent with partially healed *osteochondritis dissecans* – where a small piece of articular surface is traumatically dislodged or necrotises due to an interrupted nutrient supply – within the left olecranon of the adult. Such lesions in the elbow are usually caused by repetitive overhead and upper limb weight-bearing activities such as gymnastics and throwing (Iwasaki and Minami 2008). Exostoses (an overgrowth of bone in response to injury) on the latero-palmar aspect of her fifth metacarpal may have been associated with the injury.

Though very small, it was possible to identify an oblique, peri-mortem sharp blade cut to the tip of a proximal phalanx of neonate 1587, implying the deliberate removal of the end of the left fifth toe. This may represent *os resectum* – part of a rite associated with commemoration and the purification of the household after a death (Graham 2011), though it was more typically carried out on adults prior to cremation. Alternatively, the toe may have been kept as a *memento mori* – though surely it was very small, or perhaps the action served to confirm the infant's demise. Accidental loss is also a possibility.

Joint diseases are commonly observed in archaeological assemblages, and are usually associated with age-related wear-and-tear, however, certain disease processes can also produce similar lesions. Degenerative disc disease – pitting of the vertebral body surfaces due to the breakdown of the intervertebral disc, often associated with marginal osteophyte growth – was evident in 23 of the 25 adult vertebrae (Table 3.8). Lesions consistent with osteoarthritis (Rogers and Waldron 1995, 43–4) are manifest on the articular process joints of seven vertebrae. Of the 109 extra-spinal joints, 17 are affected, including the mandible, ribs, thumbs and distal interphalangeal joints of the fingers. Lone osteophytes are present on the articular process joints of four vertebrae and 16 extra-spinal joints (upper limbs, hips and toes). Pitting was seen on the articular process joints of five vertebrae and eight extra-spinal joints.

Plastic changes to the adult left scapula indicate an increased strengthening of the coracohumeral ligament, which prevents the anterior/posterior dislocation of the shoulder, and there are signs of degeneration of the right rotator cuff. Rather marked muscle attachment sites and enthesophytes on the upper limb and hand bones (though not exclusively), together with the joint degeneration pattern, imply the use of the upper limbs for tasks involving strength and repetition. However, enthesophyte formation commonly increases with age and can be stimulated by certain diseases and conditions, whilst some individuals may have a natural predisposition ie, 'bone-formers'.

In conclusion, the assemblage is small and demographically biased, precluding in-depth discussion. Overall the burial circumstances are typical of the period. Notable observations include the apparent poor health of the neonates, and the intriguing possible peri-mortem toe amputation. The adult female had evidently led an active life, and she had endured some of the conditions typical of her advanced age and of the period.

Table 3.9 Animal bone: number of identified specimens present (or NISP) by phase

Species	*early Romano-British*	*middle Romano-British*	*late Romano-British*	*Romano-British*	*Post-medieval*	*Total*
cattle	16	75	115	30	3	239
sheep/goat	22	159	99	32	3	315
pig	8	36	31	13	1	89
horse	4	23	5	3	1	36
dog	1	5	5	1	–	12
cat	–	–	1	–	–	1
red deer	–	1	–	–	–	1
fox	–	–	2	–	–	2
hedgehog	–	–	–	–	1	1
mole	–	1	–	–	–	1
domestic fowl	–	–	2	–	–	2
goose	–	–	1	–	–	1
duck	–	1	–	–	–	1
white-tailed eagle	–	–	2	–	–	2
passerine	–	1	–	–	–	1
Total identified	*51*	*302*	*263*	*79*	*9*	*704*
large mammal	17	179	158	26	7	387
medium mammal	5	94	83	23	–	205
small mammal	–	229	1	–	–	230
mammal	12	6	67	33	3	121
Total unidentified	*34*	*508*	*309*	*82*	*10*	*943*
Overall total	**85**	**810**	**572**	**161**	**19**	**1647**

Animal bone

by L. Higbee

A total of 2395 fragments (39.632 kg) of animal bone was recovered. The majority was collected by hand during the normal course of excavation and an additional quantity retrieved from the sieved residues of 70 bulk soil samples. Once conjoins and associated bone groups (or ABGs) are taken into account this total falls to 1647 fragments (Table 3.9).

Most of the animal bones came from middle and late Romano-British contexts including ditches, pits, ovens and buildings. The rest came from a small number of early Romano-British features, including a sunken-featured building (or SFB), and from a post-medieval hollow-way and ditch.

Methods

The following information was recorded for each identifiable fragment: species, element, anatomical zone (after Serjeantson 1996, 195–200; Cohen and Serjeantson 1996, 110–12), anatomical position, fusion state (after O'Connor 1989; Silver 1969), tooth eruption/wear (after Grant 1982; Halstead 1985; Hambleton 1999; Payne 1973), butchery marks (after Lauwerier 1988; Sykes 2007), metrical data (after von den Driesch 1976; Payne and Bull 1988), gnawing, burning, surface condition, pathology (after Vann and Thomas 2006) and non-metric traits. This information was directly recorded into a relational database (in MS Access) and cross-referenced with relevant contextual information.

Quantification methods applied to the assemblage include the number of identified specimens (NISP) and the minimum number of individuals (MNI). The NISP figures have been adjusted to take account of ABGs (after Grant 1984, 533; Morris 2008, 34–5; 2010, 12; 2011).

Caprines (sheep and goat) were differentiated based on the morphological criteria of Boessneck (1969), Payne (1985) and Halstead *et al.* (2002). The majority of the positively differentiated caprine bones belong to sheep; this term will therefore be used throughout the report to refer to all undifferentiated caprine bones.

Results

Preservation, fragmentation and provenance

Gnaw marks were recorded on 8% of fragments; this is a relatively low incidence and suggests that the assemblage has not been significantly biased by the bone chewing habit of scavenging carnivores. Bone preservation is generally good, cortical surfaces are intact and surface details such as fine knife cuts are clear and easily observed. Inconsistences in preservation were noted for a small number of contexts and this is a general indication that these contexts include residual fragments that have been reworked from earlier contexts. These findings are generally consistent with the evidence for residuality provided by some early Roman sherds within the mid- to late Roman ceramic assemblage (see Brook and Seager Smith, above).

The mean fragment weight is less than 1 g, however this figure is skewed by a number of large deposits of highly fragmented burnt pig bones from several pits. These deposits account for 21% of fragments. The fragments had been either partially or

Table 3.10 Associated bone groups (or ABGs)

Area	*Period*	*Cut*	*ABG*	*Feature*	*Comments*
A	middle Romano-British	1158	1160	pit	complete skeleton 8-18 month old calf
A	Romano-British	1180	1179	pit	partial dog skeleton
A	Romano-British	1245	1219	ditch	partial calf skeleton
B	Romano-British	1641	1918	pit	partial sheep/goat skeleton
B	middle Romano-British	1725	1919	pit	near complete sheep/goat skeleton & partial remains of a juvenile sheep/goat plus remains of a neonatal dog
C	late Romano-British	1537	1535 & 1536	pit	complete dog skeleton & partial remains of another smaller dog

completely burnt at temperatures high enough to calcine or char bones. It is likely that the remains of pig carcasses roasted in the multipurpose ovens had been left to incinerate and the remnants raked out and dumped into nearby pits.

The majority of bone fragments came from Areas 1A (36%) and 1B (43%), and the rest (21%) from Area 1C. Sheep/goat bones dominate the assemblages from Areas 1A and 1B, while cattle bones dominate the assemblage from Area 1C. Most of the assemblage came from cut features including ditches, pits and ovens.

Species represented

Approximately 43% of the assemblage can be identified to species (Table 3.9). Bones from livestock dominate the assemblage, accounting for 91% NISP. Sheep/goat is the most common species overall, followed by cattle and then pig. Modest numbers of horse and dog bones were also identified. The rarer components of the assemblage are only represented by one or two bones each and include cat, red deer, fox, hedgehog, mole, domestic fowl, goose, duck, white-tailed eagle and a small species of garden bird from the *passerine* family. The hedgehog and mole bones are probably intrusive and are not included in the following discussion. The fox bones could also be intrusive, however the preservation condition was consistent with the other bones from the same contexts, indicating that they had been subjected to the same taphonomic processes and likely, therefore, to have been deposited at the same time.

Early Romano-British

As indicated above, most (89%) of the early Romano-British assemblage came from features and deposits associated with Building 1 in Area 1B. The deposits used to backfill the SFB once it had gone out of use probably originate from surface middens (see Tipper 2004, 157–9). The other bone fragments from Building 1 came from postholes 1249, 1257, 1259 and 1284, and from post-pit 1299. Posthole 1259 contained a small quantity (42 g) of burnt pig bones similar to the larger deposits recorded from a number of mid- and late Romano-British oven rake-out pits. A small number of unidentifiable bone fragments were recovered from pit 1385 in Area 1C.

Only 51 bone fragments could be identified from the small early Romano-British assemblage and most belong to sheep/goat and cattle. The sheep/goat assemblage includes long bones from both the fore- and hindquarters, and a mandible from a 2–3 year old animal. One of the long bones, a radius from backfill deposit 1297 in Building 1, is from a neonatal lamb and this evidence implies that pregnant ewes were kept close to the building over the winter and into the spring lambing season. Most of the cattle bones recovered from early Romano-British deposits are waste elements such as the skull, mandibles, and limb extremities that are usually discarded at the primary butchery stage. One of the mandibles is from a senile animal, which suggests that cattle were maintained for secondary products and traction.

Less common species include pig, horse and dog. Burnt pig bones, including part of a pelvis, were recovered from posthole 1259, part of Building 1. Pig bones were also recovered from layers associated with the building and include the mandible from a 21–27 month old animal (mandible wear stage (or MWS) E, after Hambleton 1999). Fragments of horse scapula, calcaneus and two lumbar vertebrae were also recovered from the building together with the mandible from a dog.

Mid-Romano-British

Most of the mid-Romano-British assemblage came from Areas 1A (44%) and 1B (45%), with only a small amount retrieved from Area 1C. Relatively large groups of material were recovered from layers and ditches associated with hollow-ways 1925 and 1932 in Area 1B. Other notable components of the mid-Romano-British assemblage include ABGs from pits 1158 in Area 1A and 1725 in Area 1B (Table 3.10), and the burnt remains of pigs from pits 1011 in Area 1A and 1527 in Area 1C (Table 3.11).

Of the 810 fragments of animal bone recovered from middle Romano-British contexts, 37% can be identified to species. Sheep/goat bones dominate and account for 53% NISP (Table 3.9) or 59% of bones from livestock species. Cattle bones are also relatively common and account for a further 25% NISP followed by pig at 12% and then horse at 8%. Rarer components include dog, red deer, duck and passerine.

Table 3.11 Features containing burnt pig bones

Area	*Period*	*Cut*	*Feature*	*Weight in grams*
A	middle Romano-British	1011	pit	369
A	Romano-British	1017	pit	204
A	Romano-British	1049	pit	315
A	Romano-British	1119	pit	161
A	late Romano-British	1352	pit	141
A	late Romano-British	1357	pit	239
B	early Romano-British	1259	posthole Building 1	42
C	Romano British	1434	pit	541
C	middle Romano-British	1527	pit	2006

Most parts of the mutton and beef carcass are present in the assemblage and this indicates that livestock were brought to the site to be slaughtered and butchered for local consumption. The sheep/goat bone assemblage includes elements from at least 19 animals, the majority of which are adults. Mandible tooth wear analysis indicates a range of ages from 1–2 years to 4–6 years (MWS D to G, after Payne 1973). Almost half (45%) were slaughtered between the ages of 2–3 years, the optimum age for prime mutton. The semi-articulated remains of an adult and juvenile sheep/goat (ABG 1919) were recovered from pit 1725 in Area 1B together with the partial remains of a neonatal dog. The adult sheep/goat remains comprise the vertebral column and appendicular parts of the skeleton, and the juvenile is represented by bones from the right forequarter and lower right hindquarter. Butchery marks were evident on the left pelvis and femur, and a thoracic vertebra from the adult animal. The marks relate to dismemberment of the carcass and indicate that the remains probably represent meat joints from a single consumption event.

The cattle bone assemblage includes the disarticulated remains from at least six adults and a complete skeleton of an 8–18-month-old calf (ABG 1160) from pit 1158 in Area 1A. There were no obvious signs of trauma or disease on the calf skeleton, although faint cut marks across the frontal bones indicate that the hide was removed from the animal prior to burial. Mandibles were also recovered from older cattle aged between 30–36 months and senile (MWS C to I, after Halstead 1985), however the peak in slaughter was amongst adult animals (MWS G) and this suggests that secondary products and traction were more important than the production of prime beef. Butchery marks recorded on several scapulae and long bones are indicative of specialist processing techniques (see Dobney *et al.* 1996, 24–8; Dobney 2001, 39–41). The distinct pattern of marks noted on scapulae indicates that shoulder joints of beef were often cured for longer-term storage, while long bones were frequently split along their length in order to access the marrow fat within. The evidence implies that cattle carcasses were extensively exploited.

The pig bone assemblage also includes a range of skeletal elements and this suggests that like other livestock, whole pig carcasses were processed on site. The majority of pig bones have unfused epiphyses and are from immature animals. Only two complete mandibles were recovered and these are from animals aged between 14–21 months (MWS D). Burnt (calcined) pig bones were recovered from pits 1011 in Area 1A and 1527 in 1C (Table 3.11). The remains from pit 1011 are from a single animal aged less than one year, while those from pit 1527 are from two animals of slightly different ages. One is less than one year and the other is around 13–16 months of age. Although only a fraction of the burnt bones could be identified to skeletal element, the range of body parts suggests that whole carcasses were burnt. Cut marks were noted on the articular process of the mandible from pit 1527, the marks are consistent with disarticulation of the lower jaw. Further burnt pig bones comprising a mandible from rake out pit 1171 associated with ovens 1217, 1223, 1225 and 1293 in Area 1A, and a metapodia from oven 1715 in 1B, provide direct evidence that the burnt pig bones originate from the multi-purpose ovens. On this basis it can be stated that pig carcasses were roasted in the ovens and the remnants left to be incinerated before being raked out and disposed of in a nearby pit.

A small number of horse bones and teeth were recovered, the majority from ditches, in particular ditch 1907 in Area 1A, and hollow-ways 1925 and 1932 in Area 1B. The bones are all from adult animals and measurements taken on a tibia from hollow-way 1932 indicates that these were pony-sized animals of about 13.2 hands.

The other identified species are all represented by just one bone each. They include a red deer metacarpal from ditch 1457 in Area 1C, a tarsometatarsus from a teal-sized duck from hollow-way 1925 in Area 1B, and a tibiotarsus from the passerine family of birds. A scorched patch on the broken shaft of the red deer metacarpal indicates that fire branding might have been used to weaken the bone prior to breakage.

Late Romano-British

The late Romano-British assemblage is spread fairly evenly across all three areas of the site. Large groups of material were noted from ditch 1908 located at the north end of Area 1C. Also of note are the remains of two dogs (ABGs 1535 and 1536) from grave-like pit 1537 (Pl. 2.20) and a deposit of burnt pig bones from pit 1357, both located in Area 1A.

Of the 572 fragments of animal bone recovered from late Romano-British contexts approximately 46% can be identified to species. Cattle account for 47% of bones from livestock species and sheep/goat a further 40%, while pigs continued to be of minor importance. Other identified species include horse, dog, cat, fox, domestic fowl, goose and white-tailed eagle.

The range of body parts indicates that all three livestock species were slaughtered and butchered on site for local consumption. The sheep/goat bone assemblage includes elements from at least 13 animals, the majority of which are adults. A small number of bones from neonatal lambs were recovered from ditches in Area 1A, the evidence indicating that pregnant ewes were kept close to the site during the spring lambing season. Mandible tooth wear analysis indicates a range of ages from 2–3 years to 4–6 years (MWS E to G), although the majority were slaughtered at the higher end of this range. This suggests that while some animals were slaughtered at the optimum age for prime mutton, the majority were maintained as breeding stock and for wool.

The cattle bone assemblage includes elements from at least eight animals, the majority of which have fused epiphyses and are therefore from adult animals. Two bones from neonatal calves were also recorded from Areas 1B and 1C, indicating that pregnant cows are likely to have been kept close to the site. Mandible tooth wear shows that the age of cattle ranges from 30–36 months to senile (MWS E, and H to I), although the majority were slaughtered as senile animals. This suggests that cattle were managed for secondary products, as breeding stock and, given the general expansion and intensification of arable cultivation at this time, as traction animals (see Thomas and Stallibrass 2008, 10). The butchery evidence seen on cattle bones is identical to that described above for the middle Romano-British period and includes evidence for specialist processes. Marks consistent with trimming and filleting cured shoulder joints were observed on 15 out of 19 late Romano-British cattle scapulae, and evidence for marrow extraction was also relatively common.

The pig bone assemblage includes elements from at least three animals, a sow and two males. Age information is scarce but mandible tooth wear indicates the presence of two animals aged between 14–21 months. Pits 1352 and 1357 in Area 1A each contained burnt pig bones from a single animal aged less than one year. The similarity of these deposits indicates continuity in the types of processes and activities taking place in this part of the roadside settlement.

Most of the horse bones are from ditches in Area 1C. The post-cranial bones are all from adult animals. Butchery marks were noted on a femur from ditch 1462 and this evidence indicates that horse carcasses were processed for meat.

Disarticulated dog bones were recovered from several ditches in Area 1C and a pit in Area 1A. A grave-shaped pit, 1537, in Area 1C to the north of the road in the area of the possible roadside shrine contained the complete skeleton of a male dog and the partial skeleton of a smaller dog (ABGs 1535 and 1536) (Pl. 2.20). The male dog had an estimated shoulder height of 0.55 m and was placed on its left side on the base of the grave, while the other dog is much smaller at just 0.36 m.

The other identified species are represented by one or two bones each. They include cat, fox, domestic fowl, goose and white-tailed eagle (*Haliaeetus albicilla*). Cat is represented by a tibia from pit 1601 associated with Building 2 in Area 1B. The fox bones, a mandible and canine tooth, came from trackway 1920 and construction cut 1089 for wall 1922 in Area 1A. The domestic fowl bones came from the construction cut for well 1678 in Area 1B and from pit 1537 in Area 1C. The white-tailed eagle bones, part of the left wing comprising the ulna and carpometacarpus, came from ditch 1908 in Area 1A. These magnificent birds were once common scavengers around settlement sites in Britain (Mulkeen and O'Connor 1997), however the wing from a dead or injured bird might have been kept in order to make use of the flight feathers.

Romano-British (unphased)

Bones were also recovered from a number of broadly dated Romano-British features and deposits in all three areas. Of note are ABGs from two pits and a ditch in Areas 1A and 1B, and burnt pig bone deposits from pits 1017, 1049 and 1119 in Area 1A, and 1434 in Area 1C.

The ABG from pit 1641 is that of an adult sheep/goat (ABG 1918), the recovered bones comprising the forequarters, left upper hindquarter, ribs and vertebrae. The remains from pit 1180 comprise the hindquarters of a dog (ABG 1179); the animal shows signs of osteoarthritis affecting the right hip joint, possibly the result of dislocation or trauma. The skeleton of a neonatal calf (ABG 1219) was recovered from ditch 1245 and butchery marks consistent with disarticulation were noted on bones of the lower forequarters and left mandible.

The deposits of burnt pig bones are similar to those described above and each comprises the calcined remains of a single animal aged less than one year. Isolated burnt pig bones were also noted from three other pits (1019, 1060 and 1146), a ditch (1245) and colluvial layer 1246 in Area 1A, and pit 1892, and layers 1590 and 1891 in Area 1B.

Post-medieval

A small number of cattle, sheep/goat, pig and horse bones were recovered from hollow-way 1603 and ditch 1610 in Area 1B. A few of the bones are poorly preserved and eroded, which suggests that some of this material could have been reworked from earlier deposits.

Discussion

Sheep/goat and cattle were clearly important to the local rural economy and diet, followed by pig. The relative importance for livestock generally agrees with previous surveys (King 1978; 1984; 1999) and more recent research (Allen 2011), which generally indicates that sheep/goat and cattle were the mainstay of the livestock economy, and that sheep-farming dominated on a local level at sites such as Silbury Hill (Baker 2013), Whitewalls (Hammon 2006) and Chapperton Down (Ingram 2007). The dominance of sheep/goat probably reflects the suitability of local environmental conditions for sheep-farming and cultural or social traditions. The relative importance of cattle is slightly below the expected range for a roadside settlement, however it is clear that by virtue of their greater size, cattle provided the bulk of the meat consumed at the settlement during the Romano-British period. Sheep/goat and cattle were managed for a range of purposes including meat, dairying, wool (in the case of sheep/goat) and traction (in the case of cattle).

The proportion of pig bones is relatively high for a roadside settlement, but this reflects the number of burnt pig bone deposits recovered from pits associated with the numerous multi-purpose ovens located in this part of the settlement. The evidence suggests that the carcasses of young succulent pigs were roasted in the ovens, presumably to satisfy the demand for pork from local and passing trade. Once the meat had been stripped from the carcass, the remains were left to incinerate inside the oven before being raked out and disposed of in an adjacent pit.

The evidence indicates that livestock were raised nearby and brought to the site to be slaughtered and butchered for local consumption. The pattern of butchery is generally consistent with Roman approaches to carcass processing (Seetah 2006) and includes evidence for specialist processes such as curing and marrow extraction. These types of evidence have been noted at other roadside settlements in the region including Silbury Hill (Baker 2013, 137, and 140, figs 15–16) and Shepton Mallet (Higbee 2007). There were, however, no obvious concentrations of waste material from different stages in the carcass reduction sequence, or from any craft/industrial processes (eg, bone-working, tanning etc.) to indicate spatially distinct activity zones within this part of the settlement.

While most of the animal bones recovered from the settlement derive from normal domestic or commercial activities relating to processing, cooking and consuming meat, the two dogs buried in pit 1537 appear to represent activities outside the normal sphere of the everyday, particularly given the grave-like shape of the pit and its location adjacent to a possible roadside shrine and well. In Roman religion, dogs were associated with healing, death and hunting, and in Roman Britain they were commonly sacrificed and deposited in pits as propitiatory offerings (see Fulford 2001).

Chapter 4
Environmental Evidence

Charred Plant Remains

by Inés López-Dóriga

Introduction

A total of 127 bulk samples were taken from a series of Romano-British features across the site. Sample volumes ranged between 1.5 and 33 litres and on average were around 10 litres. The features sampled included mostly ovens (61 samples), but also hearths, ditches, pits, wells and postholes.

The samples were processed by mechanical flotation for the recovery and assessment of charred plant remains and charcoal. The light fraction was retained in a mesh of 0.5 mm and the heavy fraction in 1 mm meshes. The residues were further fractionated into 5.6 mm, 2 mm and 1 mm fractions and dried. The coarse fractions (>5.6 mm) were sorted, weighed and discarded.

Assessment of 103 selected flots was conducted by Sarah Wyles (2015), and recommendations for analysis were made based on abundance and diversity of plant macrofossils and their archaeological context. A total of nine representative assemblages were analysed. Soil volumes of the analysed samples were between 8 and 20 litres, and on average around 15 litres.

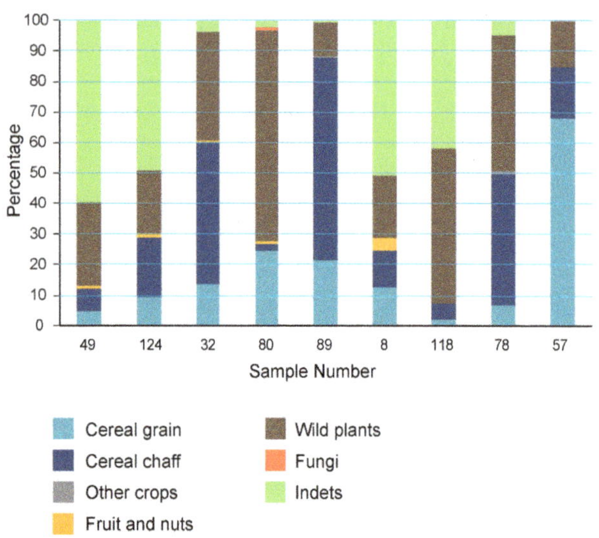

Figure 4.1 Categories of plant taxa per sample

All identifiable charred plant macrofossils were extracted from the flot and the 2 and 1 mm residue fractions using stereo incident light microscopy at magnifications of up to x40. Identifications follow the nomenclature of Stace (1997) for wild plants, and traditional nomenclature, as provided by Zohary *et al.* (2012), for cereals, and with reference to specialised atlases and modern reference collections where appropriate. Quantifications are given as MNI (minimum number of individuals) and are based on anatomy (whole items or the highest type of anatomical fragments; cereals, based on Antolín and Buxó 2011; legume cotyledons divided by two), or size (hazelnut pericarp fragments, based on Antolín and Jacomet 2015). Exempt from quantification are highly fragmented remains from some taxa (eg, Poaceae grain fragments which are not identifiable to anatomical parts) and non-identified (indeterminate) taxa, but they are included in the table as NR.

Results

The charred plant macro-remains assemblages are generally abundant and diverse in taxa, including domestic crops, such as cereals, legumes and flax, fruits or nuts and wild plants, and derive from a range of potential plant processing activities (Fig. 4.1 and Table 4.1; see full table of results in the archive). All taxa noted during the assessment have been recorded in the analysis, with the exception of *Pisum sativum* (garden pea) and tubers of possible *Ranunculus ficaria* (lesser celandine) (see Table 4.2, adapted from Wyles 2015) which were not present in the analysed samples.

The density of plant remains within the samples was varied but generally high, with an average of 75 remains per litre (see Table 4.1). The assemblages were variable in terms of bioturbation (as indicated by the presence of modern seeds and roots) and states of preservation, the latter probably due to different uses and treatment, resulting in different charring conditions and routes of deposition. The differences are, however, consistent across assemblages (grains poorly preserved and chaff well preserved), suggesting similar formation processes. There seems to be a high degree of cereal grain germination in several of the assemblages, most likely underestimated due to

Table 4.1 Taxonomic summary list of charred plant remains from the analysed samples (= subsample; see archive for full list)*

Feature Type		*Ovens*				*Crop-dryer*	*Pits*		*Hollow*	*SFB*	*Total*
Feature		1223	1640	1136	1419	1474	1019	1601	1387	1177	
Context		1269	1668	1138	1420	1475	1020	1600	1373	1296	
Sample		49	124	32	80	89	8	118	78	57	
Vol (L)		18	17	18	14.5	12	19	20	10	8	
Flot size		100	30	100	60	30	160	60	120	225	
Subsample									Yes		
Density (NMI/l.)		23.57	2.47	15.21	87.24	83.67	4.18	23.43	385.40*	53.50	
Cereals											
Avena sativa floret base	Oats	–	–	3	3	7	–	–	–	–	13
Hordeum vulgare grain MNI	Barley	7	–	11	27	8	–	2	–	–	55
Hordeum vulgare spikelet fork	Barley	–	–	–	–	–	–	–	2	–	2
Hordeum vulgare var. *vulgare* grain	Hulled barley	3	–	–	–	–	–	–	–	18	21
Triticum aestivum/turgidum rachis internode	Naked wheat (bread/rivet wheat)	–	–	–	–	–	–	–	1	–	1
Triticum spelta grain MNI (including germinated)	Spelt	–	2 (1 g)	–	–	–	2 (1 g)	–	72 (61 g)	131 (125 g)	207
Triticum spelta spikelet MNI	Spelt	8	1	11	2	106	3	1	226	23	381
Triticum dicoccum grain	Emmer	3	–	–	22	1	1	–	–	–	27
Triticum sp. grain MNI (including germinated)	Wheat	8	3	11 (1 g)	258	165	6	6	57	24 (6 g)	538
Triticum sp. spikelet MNI	Wheat	44	11	74	20	478	11	34	1034	42	1748
Triticeae grain MNI	Large seeded cereal (Wheat/Barley)	16	1	12	–	42	6	5	70	94	246
Triticeae chaff	Large seeded cereal (Wheat/Barley)	4	–	30	3	69	–	–	4	–	110
Other crops											
Vicia faba seed	Broad bean	1	–	–	–	3	–	–	–	–	4
Linum usitatissimum seed	Flax	–	–	–	3	–	–	–	–	–	3
Linum usitatissimum capsule fragment	Flax	–	–	–	–	–	–	–	36	–	36
Fruits and nuts											
Corylus avellana fruit MNI	Hazel nut	–	–	1	–	1	1	1	1	–	5
Prunus spinosa fruit MNI	Sloe	–	1	–	6	–	–	–	–	–	7
Crataegus monogyna fruit MNI	Hawthorn	9	–	0	5	–	4	–	–	–	18
Wild herbaceous plants											
Ranunculus sp. seed	Buttercup	4	1	–	4	–	–	10	–	–	19
Atriplex sp. achene	Orache	–	–	1	–	–	–	–	–	–	1
Chenopodium sp. fruit MNI	Goosefoot	14	–	–	3	–	2	9	2	–	29
Chenopodiaceae fruit MNI	Goosefoots	2	–	1	–	–	–	3	–	–	6
Agrostemma githago fruit MNI	Corncockle	–	–	–	–	–	–	–	5	–	5
Caryophyllaceae fruit MNI	Pink family	8	–	1	–	–	–	–	4	–	13
Persicaria lapathifolia achene	Pale persicaria	1	–	–	–	–	–	–	–	–	1
Rumex sp. fruit MNI	Docks	51	1	–	376	3	7	4	15	1	458
Viola sp. seed	Violet	–	–	–	–	–	–	1	–	–	1
Lepideae seed	Crucifers	–	–	–	–	–	–	2	–	–	2
Brassica/Sinapis seed	Crucifers	2	–	–	–	–	–	–	–	–	2
Raphanus raphanistrum 1/2 capsule	Wild radish	–	1	–	–	–	–	–	–	–	1
Primulaceae seed	Primrose family	1	–	–	–	–	–	–	–	–	1
Trifoliae seed MNI	Trefoil/Clover	33	2	5	1	3	1	149	7	–	201
Lathyrus aphaca seed	Yellow vetchling	1	–	–	–	–	–	–	–	–	1
Lathyrus cf. *aphaca* seed MNI	Yellow vetchling	–	–	–	70	–	–	4	–	–	74
Vicieae seed MNI	Vetches	8	1	6	94	19	–	10	16	3	157
Fabaceae seed fragment	Legumes	–	–	1	10	–	–	–	–	–	11
Apiaceae seed	Umbellifers	3	–	–	–	–	–	–	–	–	3
Lamiaceae seed	Minth family	1	–	–	–	–	–	–	–	–	1
Plantago lanceolata seed	Ribwort plantain	2	3	–	1	–	–	7	1	–	14
Veronica hederifolia seed	Ivy-leaved speedwell	–	–	–	–	–	2	–	–	–	2
Odontites vernus seed	Red Bartsia	2	–	–	5	–	–	–	–	–	7
Galium sp. seed	Bedstraw	1	1	–	–	–	1	–	–	–	3
Sherardia arvensis seed	Field madder	–	–	1	1	–	–	1	–	–	3
Rubiaceae seed	Bedstraw family	–	–	–	–	–	–	–	2	–	2
Asteraceae seed tp. *Anthemis cotula* MNI	Composites	–	–	–	–	1	–	1	–	–	2
Asteraceae seed tp. *Leucanthemum vulgare*	Composites	–	–	–	–	–	–	3	–	–	3
Asteraceae seed MNI	Composites	5	–	–	–	–	–	4	2	–	11
Juncus sp. seed	Rush	–	1	–	–	–	–	–	–	–	1
Carex tp. *acuta* achene	Sedges	–	–	–	1	–	–	–	–	–	1
Carex sp. fruit MNI	Sedges	3	–	2	5	–	6	–	–	–	16
Cyperaceae seed	Sedges	11	–	1	2	1	–	1	1	–	17
Lolium/Festuca grain MNI	Ryegrass/Fescue	2	–	9	195	18	–	28	11	–	263
Poa/Phleum grain MNI	Meadow-grass/Cat-tail's	18	1	16	51	1	1	69	13	–	170
Arrhenatherum elatius var. *bulbosum* bulb	False oat-grass	–	–	–	1	–	–	–	–	–	1
Avena fatua floret base	Oat-grass	–	–	–	–	–	–	–	4	–	4
Avena sp. grain MNI (including germinated)	Oat-grass	–	–	1	4	2	–	–	9 (1 g)	6	22
Avena sp. awn fragment NR	Oat-grass	1	–	3	3	22	–	3	110	5	147
Bromus sp. grain MNI (including germinated)	Brome	10	1	5	–		3	1	1073 (135 g)	32	1123
Avena/Bromus grain MNI	Oat-grass/Brome	2	–		–	6	–	–	11	2	21
Poaceae grain MNI	Grasses	28	–	36	43	33	1	17	27	12	197
Poaceae detached embryo NR	Grasses	3	2	5	2	6	–	4	36	–	58
Poaceae detached sprouted embryo NR	Grasses	–	–	–	–	–	–	–	134	1	135
Poaceae coleoptile NR	Grasses	48	–	7	8	8	3	14	549	2	639

Table 4.1 continued

Feature Type		*Ovens*				*Crop-dryer*	*Pits*		*Hollow*	*SFB*	*Total*
Poaceae spikelet base with rachilla NR	Grasses	–	–	–	–	–	–	–	51	–	51
Poaceae spikelet base NR	Grasses	–	–	–	–	–	–	–	111	–	111
Poaceae rachis segment NR	Grasses	–	–	–	–	–	–	–	2	–	2
Poaceae glume fragment NR	Grasses	–	–	–	–	–	–	2	47	–	49
Poaceae awn fragment NR	Grasses	–	–	–	–	–	1	–	–	–	1
Poaceae culm fragments NR	Grasses	15	7	15	21	–	2	73	1	–	134
Tamus communis seed	Black Bryony	–	–	–	–	–	1	–	–	–	1
		–									
Fungi											
Cenococcum geophilum sclerotium	Mycorrhyzal fungi	–	–	1	4	1	–	–	–	–	6
Claviceps purpurea sclerotium	Ergot	–	–	–	4	–	–	–	–	–	4
Plant remains from indeterminate taxa		–									
Indet fragment NR		337	19	–	–	–	39	111	68	–	574
Indet bud NR		20	1	2	4	–	3	2	17	–	49
Indet seed NR		72	7	7	17	7	15	157	33	–	315
Indet stalk NR		–	2	–	–	–	–	–	5	–	7
Indet stem NR		7	2	–	7	–	1	–	13	–	30
Indet tuber NR		2	–	–	–	–	2	–	–	–	4
Indet gall NR		26	–	–	2	–	–	–	–	–	28
cf. grub NR		–	–	–	–	–	–	1	–	–	1
NR		**1178**	**137**	**480**	**1884**	**2103**	**222**	**1019**	**6207***	**689**	**13919**
NMI		**382**	**41**	**269**	**1249**	**1003**	**65**	**469**	**3746***	**396**	**7619**

bad preservation of the grains, probably damaged during germination (eg, grains with the embryonal part missing).

All assemblages are very similar in their composition. Most of them are dominated by cereal chaff, the good preservation of which contrasts with the much less abundant and poorly preserved cereal grains. However, some post-depositional damage of chaff was evident, presumably the result of sample processing. The contrasting preservation of grains and chaff is indicative of multiple origins for the charred plant remains in the assemblage (Fuller *et al.* 2014), as charring should favour the survival of grain rather than chaff (Boardman and Jones 1990), as would normally have been the result of a single assemblage being charred in a single event. Unfortunately, this mixing reduces the possibilities of finding a functional link between the types of assemblages and the structures from which they were recovered. It is also possible that different oven types were used for a diverse range of purposes and morphological variation does not, therefore, reflect a specific function, or that the original functions for which they were used did not produce any recognisable plant macroremains (van der Veen 1989). The assessment report (Wyles 2015) did not find any relationship between oven form and charred plant assemblages.

The most likely explanation for the over-abundance of chaff in comparison to grains is that spelt processing by-products, in which chaff would have been predominant, were used as fuel to dry grain (for a range of possible purposes). Hulled wheat chaff would have been a readily available fuel source at crop-processing sites, and particularly suitable for roasting grain, as the fuel source can affect the flavour of the grain (Fenton 1978). The two assemblages (remnants of fuel and grain accidentally charred) could have become mixed during or after use, as is also suggested at Catsgore, Gloucestershire (Hillman 1982), or even that grain accidentally charred in previous processing events could have been used as fuel, as suggested for Poundbury, Dorset (Pelling 2011b).

Unfortunately, the preservation of cereal grains is generally so poor that it is difficult to establish the ratio of germinated to un-germinated grain and the uniformity of the germination. Uniform sprouts the same length as the grains would suggest successful malting, whilst heterogeneous lengths suggest accidental sprouting (Monckton 1999, Pelling 2013). As a consequence, it is difficult to ascertain the possibility of malting having taken place (see van der Veen 1989; Carruthers 2011; Stevens 2011). Only one grain of spelt was found still within the spikelet, and spelt wheat for malt must be germinated un-threshed (Stevens 2011; Carruthers 2011).

The enormous quantity of brome grains recovered in one of the assemblages, of which approximately 50% were germinated, suggests that most of the detached embryos and coleoptiles belonged to them, rather than to the much less abundant spelt grains.

Discussion

The assemblage of plant remains identified at Beanacre is characteristic of Romano-British rural settlements (Campbell 2016; Stevens 2006), in which several crop-processing activities took place. Although archaeobotanical data for the Romano-British period is relatively abundant, some biases

Table 4.2 Results of the charred plant remains assessment (adapted from Wyles 2015)

Feature	*Context*	*Sample*	*Vol (L)*	*Flot (ml)*	*Abundance*	*Taxa*
Burnt animal bone deposits						
1323	1350–1351	66	15	160	B	*Triticum* sp.
1352	1353	70	10	60	B	*Avena/Bromus*, Triticeae
	1354	71	5	40	B	*Avena/Bromus, Triticum* sp.
	1353–1356	72–74	10	140	B	*Triticum* sp.
1434	1428	81	2	80	B	*Avena/Bromus, Triticum* sp.
	1429	82	3	175	C	*Vicia/Lathyrus*
	1431–1433	83–86	4	80	–	–
1527	1528–1529	96-103	81.5	1.9	C	*Triticum* sp., *Vicia/Lathyrus, Prunus spinosa, Crataegus* sp., *Avena/Bromus*
Ditches						
1004	1006	1	9	10	A	*Vicia/Lathyrus, Rumex, Triticum* sp.
	1006	16	5	10	B	*Avena/Bromus, Vicia/Lathyrus, Triticum* sp.
1014	1015	7	8	90	–	–
1025	1027	3, 10	3.5	35	B	*Rumex* sp., *Poa/Phleum, Triticum* sp.
1028	1029	17–18	5	180	A	*Vicia/Lathyrus, Chenopodium* sp., *Rumex* sp., *Trifolium/Medicago, Avena/Bromus, Triticum* sp., *Hordeum vulgare*
1054	1056	12	3	60	–	–
1097	1098	5	20	130	A*	*Avena/Bromus, Rumex* sp., *Lolium/Festuca, Vicia/Lathyrus, Triticum* sp.
1099	1100	6	19	100	A	*Avena/Bromus, Brassica* sp., *Vicia/Lathyrus, Rumex* sp., *Chenopodium* sp., *Corylus avellana, Triticum* sp.
1113	1112	22	19	100	B	*Avena/Bromus, Triticum* sp.
1116	1117	19	7	60	A	*Avena/Bromus, Poa/Phleum, Triticum* sp.
1125	1126	23	15	30	A	*Corylus avellana, Avena/Bromus*, Polygonaceae, *Vicia/Lathyrus, Triticum* sp.
	1127	24	20	30	B	*Pisum sativum, Vicia/Lathyrus, Rumex* sp., Triticeae
1128	1129	30	2	30	A	*Vicia/Lathyrus, Avena/Bromus, Rumex* sp., *Polygonum* sp., *Corylus avellana*, Triticeae
	1130	29	6	60	A	*Vicia/Lathyrus, Avena/Bromus, Brassica* sp., *Rumex* sp., *Polygonum* sp., *Triticum* sp.
	1131	27	20	130	B	*Vicia/Lathyrus, Avena/Bromus, Galium, Corylus avellana, Triticum* sp.
1136	1137	31	19	140	A	*Avena/Bromus, Vicia/Lathyrus, Triticum* sp., *Hordeum vulgare*
1157	1153	62	8	90	C	*Avena/Bromus, Triticum* sp., *Hordeum vulgare*
	1156	33	6	25	A*	*Avena/Bromus, Vicia/Lathyrus, Brassica* sp., *Triticum* sp., *Hordeum vulgare*
	1156	63	8	50	A*	*Avena/Bromus, Vicia/Lathyrus, Brassica* sp., *Rumex* sp., *Triticum* sp., *Hordeum vulgare*
1173	1174	36	7	40	B	*Avena/Bromus, Vicia/Lathyrus, Corylus avellana, Triticum* sp.
	1175	25	8	60	B	*Vicia/Lathyrus, Rumex* sp., *Triticum* sp.
	1175	26	5	40	A	*Corylus avellana, Odontites* sp., *Avena/Bromus, Vicia/Lathyrus, Linum ussitatissimum, Triticum sp.*
1200	1201	34	10	25	C	*Avena/Bromus, Triticum* sp.
	1202	38	10	25	–	Triticeae
	1203	35	6	25	C	*Rumex* sp.
1217	1218	37	20	80	A	*Galium sp., Avena/Bromus, Vicia/Lathyrus, Rumex* sp., *Lolium/Festuca, Crataegus* sp., *Triticum* sp.
1223	1224	47	19	60	A	*Avena/Bromus, Plantago* sp., *Vicia/Lathyrus, Chenopodium* sp., *Rumex sp., Trifolium/Medicago, Triticum* sp., *Hordeum vulgare*
	1224	48	17	60	B	*Vicia/Lathyrus, Linum ussitatissimum, Avena/Bromus, Triticum* sp.
	1269	50	18	100	A	*Avena/Bromus, Rumex* sp., *Brassica* sp., *Vicia/Lathyrus, Trifolium/Medicago, Triticum* sp., *Hordeum vulgare*
1225	1226/1309	56	5	25	C	*Avena/Bromus, Triticum* sp.
	1312	59	6	150	A	*Rumex* sp., *Vicia/Lathyrus, Trifolium/Medicago, Triticum* sp
1227	1228	51	16	60	A	*Avena/Bromus, Rumex* sp., *Polygonum* sp., *Galium* sp., *Triticum* sp.
	1287	52	5	10	B	*Avena/Bromus, Vicia/Lathyrus, Triticum* sp.
	1288	53	10	60	A	*Avena/Bromus, Vicia/Lathyrus, Rumex* sp., *Triticum* sp.
1293	1291	54	19	50	A	*Avena/Bromus, Vicia/Lathyrus, Lolium/Festuca, Rumex* sp., *Triticum* sp., *Hordeum vulgare*
	1292	55	19	150	A	*Corylus avellana, Vicia/Lathyrus, Triticum* sp.
1245	1246	44	8	30	A	*Vicia/Lathyrus, Rumex* sp., *Poa/Phleum, Triticum* sp.
1443	1445	87	10	125	C	*Lolium/Festuca*
1516	1518	107	20	80	A	*Corylus avellana, Avena/Bromus, Rumex* sp., *Triticum* sp., *Hordeum vulgare*
Ovens						
1494	1496	90	3	60	B	*Vicia/Lathyrus, Avena/Bromus, Trifolium/Medicago, Triticum* sp.
1561	1562	105	9	15	B	*Rumex* sp., *Galium* sp., *Triticum* sp.
1563	1564	106	3	25	A	*Vicia/Lathyrus, Poa/Phleum, Rumex* sp., *Trifolium/Medicago, Triticum* sp., *Hordeum vulgare*
1581	1579	129	5	10	C	*Vicia/Lathyrus*
1593	1594	117	8	40	B	*Avena/Bromus, Vicia/Lathyrus, Trifolium/Medicago, Rumex* sp., *Triticum* sp.
	1670	125	17	90	B	*Crataegus* sp., *Chenopodium* sp., *Plantago* sp., *Trifolium/Medicago, Triticum* sp.
1647	1707	130	19	50	A*	*Avena/Bromus, Triticum* sp.
	1708	131	19	100	A	*Avena/Bromus, Vicia/Lathyrus, Rumex* sp., *Brassica* sp., *Triticum* sp.
1676	1677	126	9	40	B	*Brassica* sp., *Avena/Bromus, Hordeum vulgare*
1704	1706	132	16	15	C	*Vicia/Lathyrus*
1715	1784	137	8	50	B	*Avena/Bromus, Triticum* sp.
	1716, 1720	138–139	16	80	–	–
1747	1748	135	2.5	40	–	–
1792	1905	144	18	80	A*	*Lolium/Festuca, Trifolium/Medicago, Triticum* sp.
1806	1808	140	12	125	B	*Vicia/Lathyrus*, Triticeae

Table 4.2 continued

Feature	*Context*	*Sample*	*Vol (L)*	*Flot (ml)*	*Abundance*	*Taxa*
1835	1836	142	9	35	A	*Avena/Bromus, Bromus* sp., *Triticum* sp.
1930	1828	141	18	425	–	–
1935	1620	120	12	5	–	–
	1622	121	16	75	B	*Avena/Bromus, Vicia/Lathyrus, Trifolium/Medicago,* Heather type stem, *Triticum* sp.
1732	1733	134	19	275	C	*Triticum* sp.
Hearth						
1653	1654–1655	122–123	33	380	–	–
Pits						
1011	1012	2	20	325	C	Triticeae
	1012	20	10	250	C	*Triticum* sp.
1017	1018	4	10	90	C	*Hordeum vulgare*
1049	1050	11	20	150	C	*Vicia/Lathyrus, Crataegus/Prunus, Triticum* sp.
1060	1059	9	18	150	B	*Avena/Bromus, Triticum* sp.
1119	1120	21	20	100	C	*Ranunculus ficaria?, Triticum* sp.
1934	1133	28	10	100	A	*Avena/Bromus, Sherardia arvensis, Vicia/Lathyrus, Rumex* sp., *Triticum* sp.
1152	1327	58	8	40	B	*Avena/Bromus, Triticum* sp.
1171	1172	60	8	25	A	*Avena/Bromus, Trifolium/Medicago, Rumex* sp., *Brassica* sp., *Poa/Phleum, Triticum* sp., *Hordeum vulgare*
1387	1372	77	10	35	A*	*Avena/Bromus, Chenopodium* sp., *Triticum* sp., *Hordeum vulgare*
1299	1301	65	33	150	A	*Avena/Bromus, Vicia/Lathyrus, Rumex* sp., *Poa/Phleum, Galium* sp., *Triticum* sp., *Hordeum vulgare*
1349	1331	64	18	20	B	*Corylus avellana, Galium* sp., *Vicia/Lathyrus, Brassica* sp., *Triticum* sp.
1725	1726	133	8	180	B	*Corylus avellana, Triticum* sp.
1894	1895	145	4	5	–	–
1450	1451	88	10	40	B	*Prunus spinosa, Valerianella* sp., *Chenopodium* sp., *Triticum* sp.
Well						
1936	1108	40	16	10	B	*Vicia/Lathyrus, Avena/Bromus, Rumex* sp., *Triticum* sp.
	1109	42	8	10	B	*Vicia/Lathyrus, Triticum* sp.
	1110	41	18	30	B	*Rumex* sp., *Corylus avellana, Triticum* sp.
Postholes						
1040	1046	13	4	110	B	*Triticum* sp.
1042	1043	14	2	15	B	*Sherardia arvensis, Arrhenatherum elatius* subsp. *bulbosum, Triticum* sp.
1044	1045	15	10	70	A	*Avena/Bromus, Vicia/Lathyrus, Polygonum, Triticum* sp., *Hordeum vulgare*
SFB	–	–	–	–	–	–
1924	1236	43	16	50	A*	*Avena/Bromus, Vicia/Lathyrus, Lolium/Festuca, Triticum* sp., *Hordeum vulgare*
Postholes within SFB						
1328	1238	39	18	100	A*	*Avena/Bromus, Brassica* sp., *Lolium/Festuca, Triticum* sp., *Hordeum vulgare*
1924	1258	45	8	50	A*	*Avena/Bromus, Galium* sp., *Triticum* sp.
Layer						
	1602	136	20	35	C	*Vicia/Lathyrus, Triticum* sp.
Hollow-way						
1932	1873	143	18	2050	B	*Hordeum vulgare*
Robber trench						
1923	1096	79	10	50	B	*Avena/Bromus, Vicia/Lathyrus, Raphanus raphanistrum, Triticum* sp.

affecting the type of features sampled and published exist (Lodwick 2016).

The main crops, as represented in the charred macro-remain record (with its own differential representation biases; eg, van der Veen 2007), were cereals. Spelt was the dominant crop, both in chaff and grains, followed by less numerous barley grains and oats (which might be further under-represented, as only floret bases, but not isolated grains, can be identified to a domestic species).

The interpretation of germinated grain is a problematic issue (van der Veen 1989; Carruthers 2011; Stevens 2011), particularly given the poor preservation of some assemblages, and the evidence for grain germination at Beanacre is not sufficient to demonstrate intentional malting at this site. The ovens and other features from which the assemblages were recovered could have been used for a number of different crop processing activities undertaken throughout the year (Hillman 1982), and these may also have produced germinated grains (van der Veen 1989). For example, drying sheaves of harvested cereals, parching threshed spikelets to help dehusking by pounding, parching grain to facilitate grinding for flour, and drying grain to prevent mould and kill insects prior to storage. Grain sprouting is, therefore, a relatively common phenomenon which is not necessarily associated with malting, and many other conditions, both accidental and intentional, can also produce sprouting. In wet summers, spelt grains can sprout in the ears whilst still unharvested in the field, so drying them would have become a necessary step before threshing (Hillman 1982). Also, sprouting could be a consequence of poor storage conditions, such as 'a leaky roof and a soggy floor' (Helbaek 1964, 163). However, one of the most common situations where sprouting takes place is the result of storage in 'airtight containers' such as pits. This type of feature provides ideal preservation conditions because of the germination of the exterior layers of the grain utilising the existing oxygen in the pit, with the resulting anaerobic environment ensuring the survival of the interior layers (Reynolds 1974). Sites with evidence of sprouted spelt grain but considered accidental and not indicative of malting include, for example, Castle Copse (Great Bedwyn), Wiltshire, Billesley, Warwickshire and Fengate, Peterborough (Clapham and Gleason 1997; Monckton 1999; Murphy 1984). On the other hand, the abundance of sprouted grain at Catsgore (Hillman 1982), the uniform length of the coleoptiles at Silbury Hill (Pelling 2013), various lengths of coleoptile at Springhead (Stevens 2011) and Northfleet villa (Smith 2011) in Kent, and other evidence at Mother Anthony's Well, Wiltshire (R. Pelling pers. comm.; Dando and Andrews 2017) have all suggested malting as the most likely explanation for some of the assemblages from these sites, without conclusively excluding other reasons. A number of germinated grain assemblages have been identified across Romano-British Wiltshire in recent years (Ruth Pelling, pers. comm.), not only from crop drying ovens but from other features which might have predated them (for example Kellaways; Adams 2016).

Other crops identified were broad bean (*Vicia faba*), pea (*Pisum sativum*) and flax (*Linum ussitatissimum*), all but the latter probably cultivated for food or fodder, with the likely use of by-products such as straw and chaff for thatching or fuel, for example. Although it is possible that the cultivation of flax was carried out for fibre exploitation, the presence of capsules suggests the most likely explanation was for the use of the seeds, which could have been added to food or pressed for the extraction of oil (Fern 1996–2012).

Several edible fruits or nuts were identified, such as sloe (*Prunus spinosa*) and hawthorn berries (*Crataegus monogyna*) and hazel nuts (*Corylus avellana*), which may have been gathered from wild or possibly managed stands and consumed in a variety of ways (Fern 1996–2012).

Interestingly, exotic plants such as stone pine (*Pinus pinea*), olive (*Olea europaea*) and fig (*Ficus carica*), typical introductions of this period (van der Veen *et al.* 2008) that spread along major routes (Orengo and Livarda 2016; Pelling 2008; Stevens 2011), were not recorded. Although there is possibly a bias related to the type of preservation (charring, rather than waterlogging), the different ways in which plants were prepared (many do not need processing that involves heat, and thus are usually under-represented) and to the type of features present on the site (no cess pits, for example, were identified), the lack of new or exotic plant remains might reflect a real absence of use. Whilst some Romano-British sites in the area have provided evidence for the presence of exotic products, such as Castle Copse, Great Bedwyn (Clapham and Gleason 1997), there are other sites in which only products of probable local origin have been identified, such as Silbury Hill (Pelling 2013), despite being on a major road.

Several wild plants, probably weeds introduced in the Late Iron-Age or Romano-British period, were identified, for example yellow vetchling (*Lathyrus aphaca*; Preston *et al.* 2004) and corncockle (*Agrostemma githago*) (Helbaek 1964). Many of the other remains from herbaceous wild plants could have been weeds of agricultural fields (see Table 4.1), as well as being intentionally exploited for a variety of purposes, including food, beverages or medicines (Fern 1996–2012). Although charred preservation is necessarily biased (eg, van der Veen 2007), there are particularly abundant taxa which might have been utilised, such as docks (*Rumex* spp.) and medium-seeded grasses including ryegrass and fescue (*Lolium/Festuca*).

The substantial deposit of sprouted brome noted above is particularly interesting, as this is a phenomenon rarely reported in the literature. Large quantities of brome at Prickwillow in Cambridgeshire (Carruthers 2003) and of sprouted brome at Westhawk Farm, Kent (Pelling 2008) suggested the possibility of cultivation, or at least of it being a 'tolerated weed'. The brome grains, which are edible and also difficult to pick out from spelt due to their similar size, could have been left to bulk out the spelt harvest. Whilst it is possible that brome was used as fuel with the other cereal crop by-products (Monckton 1999), other possibilities can also explain its presence. For example, although barley has been the grain preferred for malting across history and cultures, there are many examples (including from classical sources) of wheat malting in the past (eg, Helbaek 1964). In fact, any cereal can be malted for brewing purposes, and a diversity of malts have been potentially identified in the archaeological record, including spelt and rye (eg, Helbaek 1964; van der Veen 1989), other grasses such as oats and darnel (*Lolium temulentum*; Campbell 2006), and even peas and beans (Campbell 2006; Hillman 1982).

Wood Charcoal

by Dana Challinor

A selection of the samples assessed by Sarah Wyles (2015) were provided for charcoal analysis, with a view to examining the use of fuelwood in the ovens; to determine any functional differences; to examine any context-related variation between the ovens and other activities; and whether there were any changes in fuel use patterns within the Romano-British period. Twenty-seven samples were examined, from 10 ovens and 12 other features including hollow-ways, ditches and pits. At one of the latter was associated with iron working activities, while the others represent probable mixed domestic cooking and crop processing debris. Where possible, samples were selected to reflect both the spatial and chronological features of the site.

Methods

Twenty samples were analysed to provide quantified data; the remaining seven were scanned to determine if the assemblages were comparable to those from the same feature or adjacent features. Charcoal > 2 mm in transverse section was considered for identification with up to 50 fragments (of variable size) randomly selected for identification from each sample. This was considered adequate to characterise the fuel used in the ovens and to determine any significant differences between them. The charcoal was fractured and sorted into groups based on the anatomical features observed in transverse section at x7 to x45 magnification. Representative fragments from each group were then selected for further examination using a Meiji incident-light microscope at up to x400 magnification. Identifications were made with reference to Schweingruber (1990), Hather (2000) and modern reference material. Classification and nomenclature follow Stace (1997). Identifications are provided to the highest taxonomic level possible according to the native British flora, ie, where there is only a single native species, this is named, but where there are several native species, the genus or subfamily is given. Observations on maturity and character of the wood were recorded where visible.

Results

Preservation of charcoal was variable, with some assemblages comprising clean and large fragments, while others contained small, friable, infused pieces. In some instances this may relate to the cleaning out of the oven post-firing. High levels of vitrification were rare, noted only in a few fragments, but radial cracks were more common, especially in oak fragments. Eight taxa were positively identified from a total of 690 fragments (Table 4.3). Results by sample are given in Tables 4.4 and 4.5.

Table 4.3 Charcoal taxa identified in the excavated assemblage

Family	*Genus/species*	*Notes*
Pinaceae/Cupressaceae	*Pinus sylvestris* L. (pine) *Juniperus communis* L. (juniper) *Taxus baccata* L. (yew)	These three are native species; however, it is possible that the single fragment came from a non-native genus such as *Abies* (fir), *Larix* (larch) or *Picea* (spruce).
Ulmaceae	*Ulmus* spp. (elm)	Large tree, several native species, not distinguishable anatomically.
Fagaceae	*Quercus* spp. (oak)	Large tree, two native species, not distinguishable anatomically.
Betulaceae	*Corylus avellana* L. (hazel)	Shrub or small tree, sole native species.
Rosaceae	Prunoideae: *P. spinosa* L. (blackthorn) *P. avium* L. (wild cherry) *P. padus* L. (bird cherry)	Trees or shrubs, native species. In most fragments, large rays widths were confirmed, which is characteristic of *P. spinosa,* and it is likely, given the presence of sloe stones in the charred plant remains (López-Dóriga, see above) that this species is represented. However, it should be noted that this species is anatomically indistinguishable from the Roman introduction *P. domestica* (plum).
	Maloideae: *Pyrus cordata* Desv. (Plymouth pear) *Malus sylvestris* Mill. (crab apple) *Sorbus* spp. (rowan, service, whitebeam) *Crataegus* spp. (hawthorn)	Subfamily of various shrubs/small trees rarely distinguishable by anatomical characteristics. *Crataegus* is likely as *C. monogyna* fruits were found in the charred plant material (López-Dóriga, see above), but is possible that more than one species was represented as some variability was recorded (such as occasional presence of spiral thickenings).
Aceraceae	*Acer campestre* L. (field maple)	Tree, sole native species.
Oleaceae	*Fraxinus excelsior* L. (ash)	Tree, sole native species.

Table 4.4 Results of the charcoal analysis from Romano-British ovens (by fragment count)

	Area	A								B	C
	Feature number	1014	1054	1028		1136	1223	1293	1225	1806	1732
	Context number	1015	1056	1029	1029	1138	1269	1292	1312	1808	1733
	Sample number	7	12	17	18	32	50	55	59	140	134
Quercus sp.	oak	–	–	14r	–	18 (r)	26 (r)	10 (r)	–	9rs	5r
Corylus avellana L.	hazel	–	–	–	–	2r	13r	1	–	–	24r
Prunus sp.	blackthorn/cherry	30r	–	–	3r	2	–	v	–	–	1r
Maloideae	hawthorn group	–	2	6r	22r	4 (r)	–	–	30r	–	–
Acer campestre L.	field maple	–	–	2	–	2	–	1	–	–	–
Fraxinus excelsior L.	ash	–	28 (h)	–	–	–	11 (rs)	38r	–	21 (sr)	–
Indeterminate	diffuse	–	–	3r	–	2	–	–	–	–	–

r=roundwood; s=sapwood; h=heartwood: (brackets denote recorded in some fragments only)

Table 4.5 Results of the charcoal analysis from other Romano-British features (by fragment count)

	Area	A				B				C	
	Feature type	pits				pit	hearth	SFB	hollow-way	pit	ditch
	Feature number	1011	1060	1323	1387	1299	1653	1177	1932	1434	1443
	Context number	1012	1059	1351	1373	1301	1654	1296	1873	1429	1445
	Sample number	2	9	67	78	65	122	57	143	82	87
Pinaceae/Cupressaceae		–	–	–	1	–	–	–	–	–	–
Ulmus sp.	elm	–	–	–	–	–	–	–	–	–	1
Quercus sp.	oak	36r	–	30r	20(r)	23(hr)	29(rhb)	30(hr)	41(rs)	–	18 (hsr)
Corylus avellana L.	hazel	–	–	–	–	–	–	–	–	21r	–
Prunus sp.	cherry type	11r	–	–	–	–	(1)	–	–	–	–
Maloideae	hawthorn group	1r	4r	–	–	–	–	–	3r	–	(1)
Acer campestre L.	field maple	–	–	–	–	–	–	–	4(r)	–	4(r)
Fraxinus excelsior L.	ash	2	26(r)	–	9(r)	3r	–	–	2	29r	6(3r)
Indeterminate	bark	–	–	–	–	4	–	–	–	–	–

r=roundwood; s=sapwood; h=heartwood, b=burrwood: (brackets denote recorded in some fragments only or cf. id)

A particularly notable feature of the assemblage as a whole was the dominance of roundwood fragments; whole stems were recorded in the better preserved samples, with moderate to strong ring curvature recorded in more fragmented material. With the exception of those samples where the charcoal (usually oak) was heavily comminuted and maturity could not be assessed, it was clear that either sapwood or young roundwood was commonly utilised. Most of the roundwood was between 7 and 15 years in age at felling, with rarer pieces of up to 26 years. Diameters varied between 16 mm and 30 mm, with occasional twigs. Small, roundish insect tunnels were recorded in hazel fragments in contexts 1269, 1429 and 1733 and some Maloideae fragments in context 1312.

Discussion

Functional differences

There was significant variability in the taxonomic composition of the oven assemblages; some were dominated by oak, others by ash, Maloideae group or hazel, and some were more mixed (Fig. 4.2). There was no apparent correlation in taxa use between those which produced large quantities of germinated grain, such as oven 1136, which was quite mixed (comprising five taxa) and oven 1225 which was exclusively composed of oak. No definitive evidence for deliberate malting was found in the charred plant analysis, which concluded that the assemblages could have derived from a variety of crop processing activities (see López-Dóriga, above), and this lack of functional attributions is reflected in the wood fuel. The assemblages were dominated by roundwood of relatively small diameter and narrow age ranges, consistent with the use of coppiced stems and branchwood from deciduous woodland. Only oven 1028 produced fills with notably different assemblages (Fig. 4.2); this suggests that the oven had not been cleaned out regularly (and several firings were represented). No conclusions could be drawn on temporal variations, nor were any significant spatial patterns noted in relation to fuel type and oven location.

Some interesting functional differences can be discerned, however, in comparing the oven assemblages to features associated with other activities (Fig. 4.3). The diversity of the oven assemblages is similar to the mixed/cooking category,

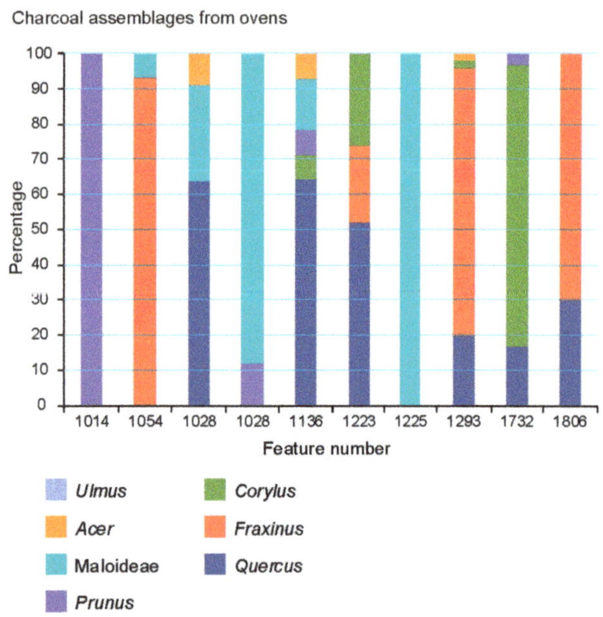

Figure 4.2 Taxonomic composition of charcoal assemblages from ovens (based upon fragment count; N = 325)

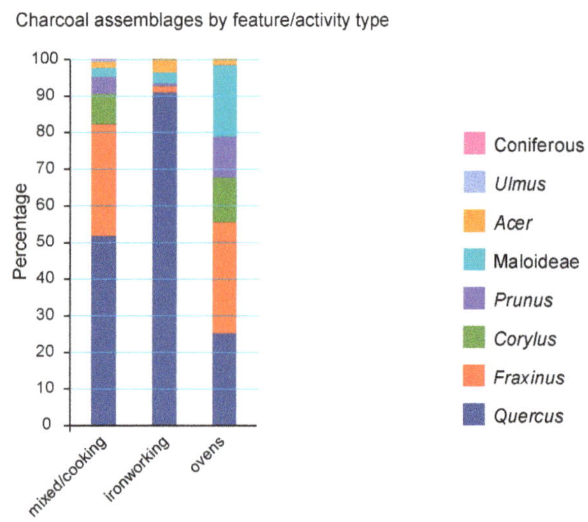

Figure 4.3 Comparison of charcoal assemblages by feature/activity type (based upon fragment count; N = 681)

which is perhaps unsurprising given that there may be some mutual domestic/agricultural activities represented. The assemblages from the ovens are largely single-event, representing the fuel remnants of the last firing, while the charcoal from the mixed/cooking category includes multiple events and longer-term accumulation of material into ditches, along with some dumps of cooking waste (associated with burnt pig bone, see Higbee, Chapter 3). It is notable that, in contrast, the charcoal assemblages found in association with smithing waste (both *in situ* and redeposited), were more than 90% dominated by oak, with minimal components of other taxa. In addition, the character of the wood from these assemblages was not the same, as there was notably less roundwood (insofar as it was possible to determine given the comminuted nature of the material) and they included some mature oak wood, both heartwood and, even burrwood (in hearth 1653). The results are consistent with a more focused selection of fuel for smithing, rather than the more diverse assemblages from domestic type activities. Romano-British ironworking commonly used oak charcoal as fuel; for instance, in smelting-associated assemblages at Devizes (Cramp 2013), and further afield at Calstock Roman fort, Cornwall (Challinor 2014).

Temporal changes

Analysis by phase shows that oak was the main fuelwood in the early Romano-British phase, while increased diversity is recorded by the 2nd to 3rd centuries AD. Samples which could not be confidently ascribed to either phase are likely to include a large component of mid-Romano-British (or possibly later) dates as most of these were ovens located in Area 1A, in proximity to other, securely dated ovens. It is tempting to speculate that the analysis shows that supplies of oak may have decreased throughout the life of the settlement, and an increased use of ash and blackthorn (which are light-demanding and coloniser type trees) indicates clearance and regeneration. However, this does not take into account any functional influences on fuelwood selection; added to which, the numbers of samples for each phase were considerably divergent (ERB=3; MRB=10). Likewise, any spatial analysis was hampered for the same reasons.

Woodland supplies

The charcoal shows that wood fuel used at this rural site was drawn mostly from mixed deciduous woodland, with oak, ash and hazel, field maple and occasional elm. Elm has a tendency to smoulder (Edlin 1949) and may have been deliberately avoided. Blackthorn and Maloideae-type are indicative of woodland margins or hedgerow/scrub, but also coppice well. The dominance of small diameter roundwood and consistency in age ranges suggest that fuel was supplied from coppiced woodland (albeit evidence for coppicing from charcoal remains is tentative at best). The character of the wood is also indicative of the type of fire required – bundles of branchwood or narrow stems would have produced a fast, high heat, rather than the slow, steady heat produced by heartwood or larger trunkwood. This is appropriate for ovens that may have been used for crop parching and is consistent with other results from nearby sites, for example Romano-British ovens at Bath Road, Melksham (Challinor 2018). The presence of insect tunnels in the material indicates that some time had elapsed between the felling of the tree and its use for fuelwood, which suggests that the wood supplies had been seasoned prior to use.

Conclusions

The analysis of the charcoal suggests that the Romano-British ovens were fuelled by a supply of seasoned firewood, probably sourced from managed woodlands. The use of taxa varied, although no significant relationship to function could be determined. Deposits of cooking and domestic waste produced similar fuel residues, in the character and types of wood used. There was a difference in the assemblages associated with iron-working activities, which would have used charcoal rather than wood for fuel, for which mature oak was utilised. Charcoal-making activities could have taken place in the local woodland (on a small scale) but it may also have been brought in from further afield.

Chapter 5
Discussion

Prehistoric

There have been relatively few previous archaeological investigations within the Avon Valley between Melksham and Chippenham. As a result, the nature of prehistoric activity in the area is poorly understood.

In common with many sites in the region, the evidence for probable Mesolithic and earlier Neolithic activity on the site is restricted to scatters of worked flint, found in the topsoil and residually in later features. These flint scatters are thought to be indicative of temporary camps utilising woodland and riverine resources (Bateman and Enright 2000, 237).

Excavations to the south of Chippenham have shown that the gravel terraces overlooking the Avon floodplain were farmed and occupied from the Neolithic onwards, whilst the presence of Bronze Age funerary monuments both within and around the valley is testament to a relatively large settled population by this date.

The excavation uncovered a pit and posthole of broad, probably later Bronze Age date which, together with a cluster of undated postholes, are tentatively identified as evidence for some form of occupation on or near the site during this period. Their location, on a low terrace above the floodplain, fits with the general pattern found near Chippenham, and it seems probable that there are many more undiscovered late prehistoric settlements in similar locations within the Upper Avon Valley.

A Romano-British 'Small Town' in the Upper Avon Valley

Origin and Function

Prior to the Roman invasion, Gloucestershire, north-west Wiltshire and the catchment of the Bristol Avon are all thought to have lain within the territory of a tribal group known as the *Dobunni*. This tribe's territory straddled the boundary between lowland and upland regions of Britain, and as such shared characteristics of both. For example, whilst there are several strongly fortified hillforts, particularly towards the west, there were also proto-towns, or *oppida*, in the Upper Thames Valley (eg, Bagendon, Salmondsbury and Grim's Ditch). The *Dobunni* also minted coins and were connected to wider European trading networks, probably via the neighbouring *Catuvellauni* tribe (Salway 1993, 35, 42–4).

The Roman army invaded Britain in AD 43 and defeated the main resistance, led by the Catuvellaunian leaders, Caratacus and Togodumnus, the same year. Most of the *Dobunni* subsequently surrendered, but those living in the western areas may have held out until *c.* AD 47 (Salway 1993, 62–3, 70). The transition of power from *Dubonnic* to Roman rule appears to have been relatively peaceful in the eastern part of their territory, and it has been suggested that the southern Cotswolds and the Thames Valley may initially have been governed by a local client king (Miles *et al.* 2007, 385; Simmonds *et al.* 2008, 1).

There is no evidence for an Iron Age precursor to the Romano-British settlement at Beanacre, and it seems probable that the spur for its development was the construction of the Roman road between *Aquae Sulis* and *Cunetio*. The earliest features on the Beanacre site appear to date from the second half of the 1st century AD, which is broadly contemporary with the earliest evidence for occupation at nearby *Verlucio*, *Cunetio* and *Aquae Sulis* (Wiltshire Council Archaeology Service (WCAS) 2004, 8; Wessex Archaeology 2011, 2; Davenport 2000, 8, 16).

The strategic location of the Beanacre settlement, on a main road, close to a major river crossing, could point to a military origin. However, the absence of supporting artefactual or other evidence, and the general paucity of Roman military sites in the eastern half of the *Civitas Dobunnorum*, make this unlikely.

Roman altars such as those found at Beanacre are not common finds, and although they are known from domestic contexts, they are more frequently associated with sites of religious significance (Allason-Jones 2011, 273). However, based on present evidence, it is impossible to be certain if Beanacre was such a site, and it could well have had a more mundane beginning, perhaps as a trading post serving the needs of local farmers and passing travellers. In this context, the find-spot of the altars immediately to the north of the road, and the proximity of a well, a double dog burial and a roughly paved surface, may be significant, raising the possibility of a roadside shrine.

Size, Morphology and Status

The excavation uncovered a 0.4 ha strip through what appears to have been the western end of a substantial roadside settlement. The geophysical survey confirmed that it encompassed an area of at least 3 ha. However, when evidence from satellite imagery (showing a spread of dark soil flanking the roadside), field walking and metal detecting is considered, it seems probable that the occupied area extended for at least 0.9 km along the road frontage (Fig. 5.1); this increases the settlement's potential size to 12 ha. This should, however, probably be considered as a minimum, for the features in Area 1A demonstrate that there are areas of occupation set further back from the road frontage that are not apparent from other sources such as field walking. Taking this and the presence of 'Blacklands' field names away from the road into account, it could indicate a larger area of occupation, and a figure of 20 ha is certainly possible. Even at the lower end of the size range, Beanacre falls within Burnham's (1987) 'small town' category, though in reality it was probably more akin to a large village. At 12–20 ha, the settlement at Beanacre is of a similar size to the roadside settlements at Camerton and White Walls (both at least 10 ha) (Wedlake 1958, fig. 2; Wilmott and Shipp 2006, fig. 3) and possibly Silbury Hill (20 ha) (Allen *et al.* 2016; Crosby and Hembrey 2013, fig. 2), but probably smaller than Fosse Lane, Shepton Mallet (30 ha) (Leach 2001, 315).

Morphologically, Beanacre appears to have been a linear settlement with occupation focused along a main road, with trackways and zones of development to the rear. Settlements of this form are widespread throughout Roman Britain and local parallels can be found at Shepton Mallet, Camerton and White Walls. The roadside settlements at Nettleton and Silbury Hill are of a similar size, though there are significant morphologically differences: Nettleton had a compact nucleated core focused around a temple complex (Wedlake 1982, fig. 2), whilst at Silbury Hill there are extensive enclosures and areas of occupation set well back from the main road (Crosby and Hembrey 2013, fig. 2).

The road from *Cunetio* to *Aquae Sulis* is listed in the 3rd/4th-century *Antonine Itinerary* (see Rivet and Jackson 1970), but the only recorded settlement listed between these towns is *Verlucio*, which is considered to have been located in the Sandy Lane area, 6 km to the east of the site (Fig. 1.1). If this attribution is correct, then the fact that the Beanacre site was omitted from the *Itinerary* suggests that it was a relatively minor settlement at this date.

The Romano-British settlement at Beanacre is situated 15 km to the east of *Aquae Sulis*, and 6 km to the west of *Verlucio*. Nettleton is a similar distance from *Aquae Sulis*, whilst Camerton and *Trajectus* (Somerdale, Keynsham) are both slightly closer. All of these settlements are approximately half a day's walk or slightly less than half a day's ride from *Aquae Sulis*. This may not be coincidental, and although they are likely to have had other functions, the provision of refreshments to travellers is likely to have been a significant part of their *raison d'être*.

Hodder (1975) suggested that the administrative, economic and social needs provided by urban centres were not adequately served away from civitas capitals; a want he considered to have benefitted smaller settlements on the periphery (Leach 2001, 318). The Beanacre settlement is similar to Shepton Mallet in this regard, in that it was 55 km by road from the civitas capital at *Corinium Dobunnorum* (Cirencester). However, the proximity of *Aquae Sulis* and *Verlucio* is likely to have mitigated any effects of isolation from the administrative capital.

The status of the Beanacre site remains uncertain, and although there was no evidence for a specific official purpose, it seems probable that some form of administrative activity, most likely related to the functioning of the local agricultural economy, occurred within the settlement.

Trade and Economy

Farming is likely to have been an important, if not dominant, focus of the settlement's economy, and the inhabitants appear to have practiced a mixed farming regime, typical of Romano-British roadside settlements, and indeed rural settlements in general. Wheat, primarily spelt, but also emmer, were the main cereal crops, with some variation provided by the cultivation of oats, barley, broad beans, pea and flax, though the latter may have been grown for its fibres. Sheep were the most common domestic animal, followed by cattle and pig. Cattle would also have provided traction for ploughing and haulage. Horses would have been used for transport, whilst cats and dogs were kept for vermin control. Animals would have been slaughtered and butchered on site, both for local consumption or for sale to passing travellers. The latter were presumably also supplied with pork from young pigs roasted in the site's numerous ovens. In addition to farmed produce, wild resources were also exploited. Firewood was sourced from mixed deciduous woodland containing oak, ash, hazel, field maple and elm. The diameter of some of the roundwood charcoal is suggestive of coppiced woodland, which, along with hedgerows, would have provided a source of hazelnuts, sloes, hawthorn berries and other edible plants. Woodland would also have provided shelter for deer, which are likely to have been hunted for meat, thought these do not

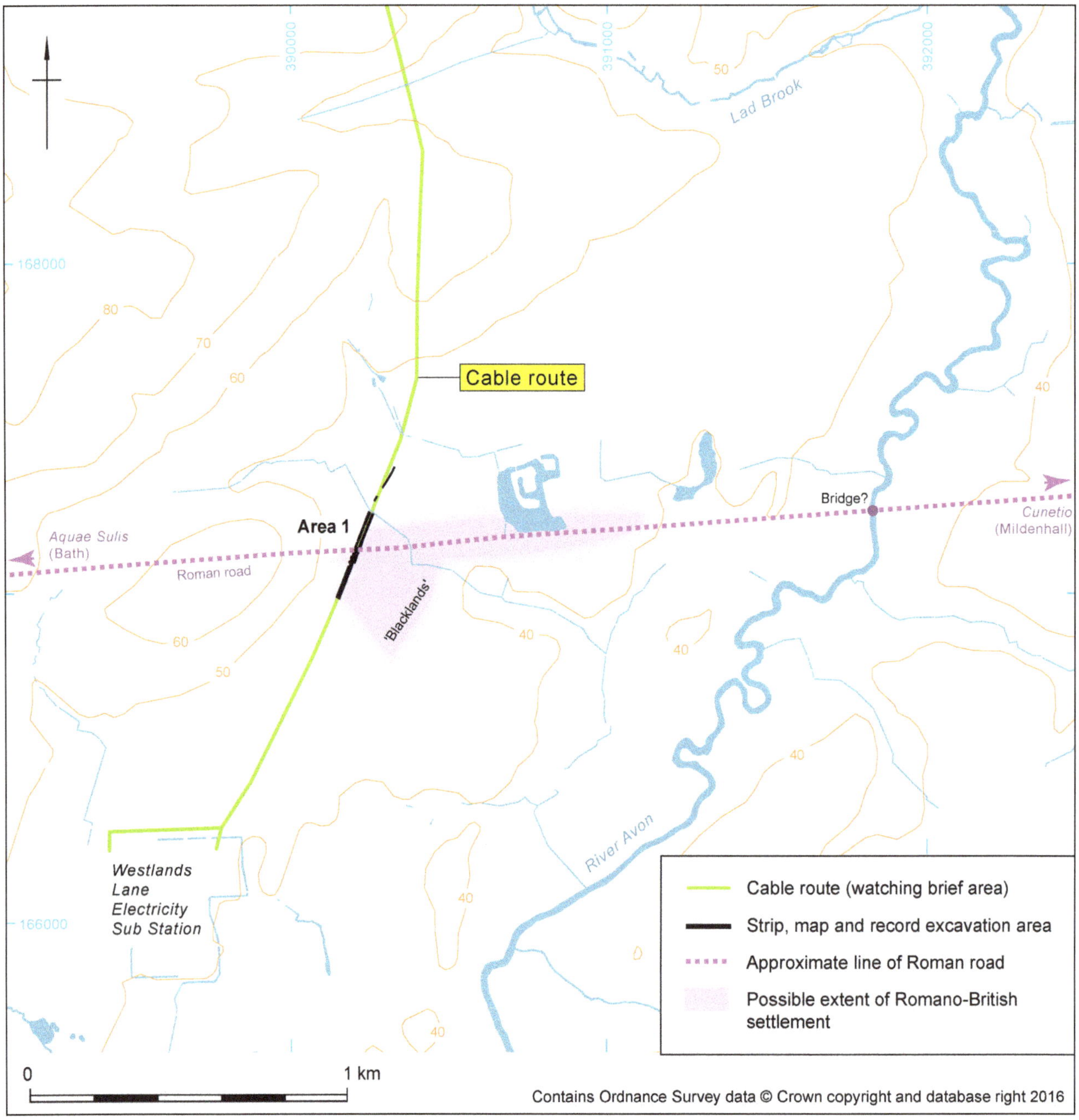

Figure 5.1 Postulated extent of the Romano-British roadside settlement at Beanacre

appear to have been a significant element of the local population's diet.

Evidence of industrial activity is provided by finds of iron smelting and smithing slag, which was recovered from several contexts across the site. There was no evidence for smelting on the site itself, which could indicate that the slag was imported from elsewhere, possibly for use as hardcore. The source of the smelting slag remains unknown, though given its weight, it seems unlikely that it was transported more than a few kilometres. Most the smithing slag was recovered from a mid-Romano-British hearth and an adjacent pit, and is indicative of small-scale, and probably short lived, smithing to meet the day-to day needs of an agricultural community. Similarly, the presence of small pieces of melted lead and off-cuts of lead and copper alloy may be related to small-scale manufacture or repair of metal items. Bone pins and needles provide evidence for textile manufacture, though this is likely to have been of a domestic rather than commercial nature.

Most of the ceramics were sourced from local potteries, with some variety provided by imports from elsewhere in Britain and the Continent. The other finds categories, in addition to those noted above, provide evidence for limited trade and exchange of objects (eg, objects of personal adornment and household utensils), as well as economic activities (eg, grain processing). The majority of the material relates to a range of day-to-day tasks but, certain objects, specifically the stone altars and possible face pot, are associated with religious beliefs and practices, suggesting that religious activities were part and parcel of everyday life. In general, these materials reflect a typical range of activities that could be associated with a Romano-British roadside settlement of this size and with good road access to nearby towns and the wider Roman world.

Buildings and Structures

Building 1 is somewhat unusual in that it appears to have been a wooden sunken-featured building (SFB) dating from the late 1st or early 2nd century AD. The building was constructed with posts and beamslots set around a sub-rectangular hollow. So-called SFBs were once considered to be unequivocal markers of post-Roman Germanic settlers, and early medieval examples are still occasionally referred to as *Grubenhäuser*, after their continental equivalents (Gardiner 2012, 235). However, excavations over the last 30 years have uncovered a moderately large number of SFBs that unequivocally date from the Romano-British period. The SFBs of this date have been found in disparate locations across lowland Britain, but are most numerous in Kent, particularly on the Isle of Thanet (Allen *et al.* 2016; Bennet *et al.* 2008; Clarke 2010; Andrews *et al.* 2015). The SFBs from Thanet primarily date from the 3rd and 4th centuries AD, though Iron Age and early–mid-Romano-British examples have also been identified (Andrews *et al.* 2015). Several 3rd–4th-century examples and one dating from the 2nd–3rd-century have also been excavated in Leicestershire (Clarke 2010, 220).

Regional parallels for Building 1 can be found in a partially excavated feature from a Romano-British roadside settlement in Dymock, Gloucestershire, which comprised a sub-rectangular sunken area, 2.6 m by over 1.8 m wide, and 0.4 m deep, with two surviving stakeholes around the sides. Pottery evidence suggested that the Dymock feature dated from the late 1st or early 2nd century AD (Catchpole 2007, 146, 215). The excavators interpreted this feature as an SFB, however the report's author considered this unlikely given the early date. The size, morphology and date of the Dymock feature are comparable with the SFB at Beanacre, which suggests that they may have been similar structures.

The Romano-British SFBs from Leicestershire are considered to have been non-domestic buildings connected with crop-processing activities, due to their association with fragments of quernstone, possible threshing floors and nearby crop drying ovens (Clark 2010, 216–17). Similarly, ovens or hearths have been found in many of the Romano-British SFBs from Thanet (Andrews *et al.* 2015, 249–50, 278–9, 316–7, 320, 323–4, 337–9; Hicks 2008, 276) and a significant number were used for the burial of infants, mostly along the edges of the buildings (Andrews *et al.* 2015, 355).

There are many parallels between the SFBs of Thanet, Leicestershire and Beanacre, notably, the proximity of ovens – some for crop drying, and the burial of infants along the edge of the building. The latter was the case in Building 1 and with those excavated on Thanet. This location, tucked away on the edge of the room, rather than being dug through the infill of the sunken area, suggests that they were probably buried while the building was in use. The presence of at least one hearth and the infant burials suggest that the building is unlikely to have been used as a shelter for animals, for example, and a domestic function is more likely, though perhaps as an outbuilding used for craft, crop-processing or other activities.

The late Romano-British stone-founded buildings and structures (Building 2, walls 1922 and 1032/1064) were all constructed in a similar manner, comprising a construction trench with a layer of pitched locally-quarried ragstone in the bottom, which provided a base for drystone foundations. Where the foundations survived, they comprised irregular courses of ragstone. There were no upstanding walls, and it is unclear if the foundations were footings for masonry walls, or dwarf walls for timber-framed buildings. What is clear, however, is that the foundations for Building 1 and wall 1922 (possibly also part of a building) were designed to support a considerable weight, which suggests that the building(s) are likely to have had more than one storey. The relative paucity of Romano-British CBM indicates that the excavated buildings were roofed with thatch or stone tiles. Indeed, a dump of broken hexagonal sandstone tiles to the rear of the Building 2 may be construction waste from the earliest part of this building. The foundations of Building 2 and wall 1922 were both systematically robbed, which suggests controlled demolition and the salvaging of materials, presumably for use nearby. Finds evidence suggests that the demolition probably occurred in the 4th century AD. However, the possibility that it occurred during the 5th century or later cannot be entirely discounted.

Perhaps the most notable aspect of the Beanacre site was the profusion of clay and stone-lined ovens, which were generally of figure-of-eight or keyhole-shaped, a form which is common throughout the Roman world. Ovens are frequently uncovered on

Romano-British settlements, but what is more unusual is the number, 41 in total, all clustered in a relatively small area. A comparison with other nearby roadside settlements, such as the extensively-excavated site at Fosse Lane, Shepton Mallet (Leach 2001), shows that the density of ovens at Beanacre is much higher than has been recorded elsewhere. In fact, the density of ovens is closer to that found at a possible 1st-century military construction camp at Ysgol yr Hendre near the Roman fort of *Segontium* in Gwynedd (Kenny and Parry 2013, 4) and at a Roman marching camp at Kintore, Aberdeenshire (Cook and Dunbar 2008, 133). Although there is no evidence that the ovens at Beanacre are related to military encampment, the Ysgol yr Hendre and Kintore sites serve to highlight how unusual this density of ovens is, and that it probably indicates food production above and beyond what would have been needed by the resident population. The use of ovens at Beanacre appears to have spanned the entire Romano-British period, but there was a notable *flourit* of activity in the mid-Romano-British period, perhaps indicating an increase in the provision of food around this date. The number of ovens dated to the 1st and later 3rd–4th centuries is more in line with the numbers that might be expected at a 'typical' Romano-British settlement, perhaps indicating that the period of increased food provision was a particular episode in the settlement's history.

The T-shaped crop drying oven is a typical, though heavily truncated, example of its type, and its presence on a site with a strong agricultural focus is unsurprising. Excavated examples of crop drying ovens elsewhere have produced evidence for malting, in the form of germinated cereal grains, and it would not be unexpected to find evidence of this in a roadside settlement. There were sprouted grains in the charred plant assemblage at Beanacre, but the evidence for malting is equivocal and other explanations, such as poor crop storage, may account for its presence.

The End of the Romano-British Settlement

Building 2 was constructed after the late 2nd–3rd century and it, along with wall 1922, were probably demolished in the 4th century. The latest coin, which was recovered from a post-medieval context, dates from AD 388–402. The excavation site's location on the periphery of the settlement, a location which is likely to have been abandoned earlier than the core, means that any discussion as to the date of the settlement's abandonment must be heavily caveated. However, the absence of any unequivocally post-4th century finds, suggests that the settlement was probably abandoned by *c.* 400 AD. Evidence from the Romano-British roadside settlements at Silbury Hill, White Walls and Nettleton indicate abandonment at around the same date, which suggests that this was a regional phenomenon. This contrasts with the evidence from sites further to the west, such as Camerton and Shepton Mallet, where occupation appears to have persisted into 5th century or later. Evidence of possible post-Roman occupation has also been noted at the nearby villas in Atworth (Erskine and Ellis 2008, 121), Budbury (Allen *et al.* 2016) and Marshfield (Blockley 1985), though many others in the region appear to have been abandoned by the close of the 4th century. The apparent abandonment of roadside settlements, whilst some nearby villas remain occupied, may have been due to the collapse of the market economy, and the perceived or real threat felt by inhabitants along major thoroughfares during periods of instability.

Conclusions

The Romano-British settlement at Beanacre is one of a widely-distributed class of roadside settlement, which are often referred to as 'small towns', though in scale, and perhaps status, they were probably not at the same level.

The excavation sampled a relatively small area on the western periphery of the settlement, therefore any conclusions as to the date of its establishment, function or status must be treated with some caution. With these caveats in mind, there are some conclusions which can be drawn from the available evidence.

There was some form of activity, probably occupation, on the site by the second half of the 1st century AD, and the settlement appears to have been continually occupied until the end of the Romano-British period. There is no evidence for post-Roman occupation.

The finds from Beanacre are typical of 'highly Romanised' sites such as towns, villas, religious and military sites, indicating that it was well integrated into the wider Roman cultural sphere. The profusion of ovens and evidence for pig roasting indicates that food provision, probably above and beyond that needed for the local population, was an important part of settlement's function. The reason for this remains unknown, however there are several possible, and not necessarily mutually exclusive, explanations. The settlement's strategic location near a river crossing could point to a military origin, but there is no evidence to support this suggestion. River crossings could also be a focus for religious activity (eg, Nettleton and Silbury Hill) and the presence of a pair of altars, an unusual dog burial and a possible face pot provide some evidence for a religious aspect to the site. However, in the absence of other overtly religious finds (eg, bent pins, votive figurines etc.), this suggestion must remain speculative. Perhaps the most plausible explanation is that the evidence of relatively large-scale food production is simply a reflection of the site's roadside location, where the passing travellers would have provided a ready market for such goods.

Romano-British settlements are one of the most 'visible' types of archaeological site, which often contain stone buildings and a profusion of finds. As such, the discovery of a large, previously unknown settlement serves to highlight how some areas that are apparently 'blank' in archaeological terms, simply may reflect a lack of archaeological investigation, rather than an indication of past occupation patterns. The settlement at Beanacre is clearly much larger than the excavated area, and future research will no doubt modify and perhaps refute some of the suggestions made in this publication.

Bibliography

Adams, S 2016 *Kellaways Farm, Wiltshire: archaeobotanical remains*. Portsmouth, Historic England

Allason-Jones, L (ed) 2011 *Artefacts in Roman Britain: their purpose and use*. Cambridge University Press

Allason-Jones, L and Bishop M C 1988 *Excavations at Roman Corbridge: the Hoard*. English Heritage Archaeological Report 7. London

Allen M, Blick, N, Brindle, T, Evans, T, Fulford, M, Holbrook, N, Richards, J D, Smith, A 2016 *The Rural Settlement of Roman Britain: an online resource,* http://archaeologydataservice.ac.uk/archives/view/romangl/index.cfm [accessed 26 January 2017]

Allen, M 2011 *Animalscapes and Empire: new perspectives on the Iron Age to Romano-British transition*. University of Nottingham PhD thesis, unpubl

Anderson, A S 1979 *The Roman Pottery Industry in North Wiltshire*. Swindon, Swindon Archaeol Soc Rep 2

Anderson, A S 1980 Romano-British pottery kilns at Purton, *Wilts Archaeol Natur Hist Mag* 72/73 (1977/1978), 51–58

Anderson, A S, Wacher J S and Fitzpatrick A P 2001 *The Romano-British 'Small Town' at Wanborough, Wiltshire*. London, Britannia Monogr Ser 19

Andrews, P, Booth, P, Fitzpatrick, A P, Welsh, K 2015 *Digging at the Gateway: Archaeological landscapes of south Thanet. The Archaeology of the East Kent Access (Phase II) Volume 1: the sites.* Oxford, Oxford Wessex Archaeology Mongr 8

Andrews, P and Little, A 2016 The stone roof-tiles from Truckle Hill, *Bull Assoc Roman Archaeol* 23 (2015–2016), 29–31

Annable, F K 1962 A Romano-British pottery industry in Savernake Forest, kilns 1–2, *Wilts Natur Hist Archaeol Mag* 58, 143–55

Antolín, F and Buxó, R 2011 Proposal for the systematic description and taphonomic study of carbonized cereal grain assemblages: a case study of an early Neolithic funerary context in the cave of Can Sadurní (Begues, Barcelona province, Spain), *Vegetation Hist Archaeobotany* 20, 53–66

Antolín, F and Jacomet, S 2015 Wild fruit use among early farmers in the Neolithic (5400–2300 cal BC) in the north-east of the Iberian Peninsula: an intensive practice? *Vegetation Hist Archaeobotany* 24, 19–33

Atkinson, D 1914 A hoard of Samian ware from Pompeii, *J Roman Stud* 4(1), 26–64

Atkinson, D 1942 *Report on the excavations at Wroxeter 1923–1927*. Birmingham Archaeol Soc

Aufderheide, A C and Rodríguez-Martín, C 1998 *The Cambridge Encyclopaedia of Human Palaeopathology*. Cambridge, Cambridge Univ Press

Baker, P 2013 The animal bones, 136–45 in V Crosby and N Hembrey, An evaluation in the fields south of Silbury Hill in 2010: Romano-British settlement, later alluviation and water meadows, *Wiltshire Archaeol Natur Hist Mag* 106, 101–66

Barber, A, Schuster, J and Holbrook, N 2013 Prehistoric activity and Roman rural settlement at Blacklands, Staverton: excavations in 2007, *Wiltshire Archaeol Natur Hist Mag* 106, 16–51

Barnett, C, McKinley, J I, Stafford, E, Grimm, J and Stevens, C J 2011 *Settling the Ebbsfleet Valley: High Speed 1 Excavations at Springhead and Northfleet, Kent.* The Late Iron Age, Roman, Saxon and Medieval Landscape, Volume 3: late Iron Age to Roman human remains and environmental reports. Oxford Wessex Archaeology

Bass, W M 1987 *Human Osteology*. Columbia, Missouri Archaeol Soc

Bateman C and Enright D 2000 Excavations of Bronze Age and Romano-British Sites along the Chippenham Western Bypass A4 to A350 Link, *Wiltshire Archaeol Natur Hist Mag* 93, 233–8

Bennett, P, Clark, P, Hicks, A, Rady, J and Riddler, I 2008 *At the Great Crossroads: prehistoric, Roman and medieval discoveries on the Isle of Thanet 1994–1995*. Canterbury, Canterbury Archaeological Trust

Berry, A C and Berry, R J 1967 Epigenetic variation in the human cranium, *J Anatomy* 101(2), 261–379

Bird, J 1986 Samian wares, in L Miller, J Schofield and M Rhodes *The Roman Quay at St Magnus House, London. Excavations at New Fresh Wharf, Lower Thames Street, London 1974–78*, 139–85. London, LAMAS Special Paper 8

Bird, J 1993 Third-century samian ware in Britain, *J Roman Pottery Stud* 6, 1–14

Blockley K 1985 *Marshfield Ironmongers Piece Excavations 1982–3. An Iron Age and Romano-*

British settlement in the South Cotswolds. Oxford, BAR 141

Boardman, S and Jones, G E M 1990 Experiments on the effects of charring on cereal plant components, *J Archaeol Sci* 17, 1–11.

Boessneck, J 1969 Osteological differences between sheep (*Ovis aries*) and goat (*Capra hircus*), in D Brothwell and E S Higgs (eds), *Science in Archaeology* (2nd edition), 331–58. London, Thames and Hudson

Braithwaite, G 1984 Romano-British Face Pots and Head Pots, *Britannia* 15, 99–131

Brickley, M and McKinley, J I 2004 (eds) *Guidelines to the Standards for Recording Human Remains*. Brit Ass for Biological Anthropol and Osteoarchaeol and Inst for Fld Archaeol

Brindle, T 2014 *Portable Antiquities Scheme and Roman Britain*. London, British Museum Press

British Geological Survey 2017 *Geology of Britain Viewer*, http://mapapps.bgs.ac.uk/geologyofbritain/home.html [accessed 12 January 2017]

Brook, E and Seager Smith, R H 2017 Romano-British pottery, in L Higbee and L Mepham *Living on the Edge. Archaeological investigations at Steart Point, Somerset*, 33–39. Salisbury, Wessex Archaeology Occ Paper

Brothwell, D R 1972 *Digging Up Bones*. London, British Museum Natural History

Brothwell, D and Zakrzewski, S 2004 Metric and non-metric studies of archaeological human remains, in Brickley and McKinley 2004, 24–30

Buikstra, J E and Ubelaker, D H 1994 *Standards for Data Collection from Human Skeletal Remains*. Fayetteville (AR), Arkansas Archaeological Survey Res Ser 44

Butcher, S 1993 Brooches of copper alloy, in Woodward and Leach 1993, 149–159

Burn, A H 1944 Discovery of a Roman coffin at Corsham, October 1942, *Wiltshire Archaeol Natur Hist Mag* 50, 371–2

Burnham, B 1987 The morphology of Romano-British small towns, *Archaeol J* 144, 156–90

Campbell, G 2006 Plant Remains, in K Parfitt, B Corke and J Cotter *Townwall Street, Dover, Excavations 1996*, 378–90. Canterbury, The Archaeology of Canterbury New Series 3

Campbell, G 2016 Market forces – a discussion of crop husbandry, horticulture and trade in plant resources in southern England, in D Bird (ed) *Agriculture and Industry in South-Eastern Roman Britain*, 134–55. Oxford, Oxbow

Carruthers, W 2003, The charred plant remains, in R Atkins and A Mudd, An Iron Age and Romano-British settlement at Prickwillow Road, Ely, Cambridgeshire: excavations 1999–2000 *Proc Cambridgeshire Antiq Soc* 92, 44–8

Carruthers, W 2011 Charred plant remains from Northfleet, in Barnett *et al.* 2011, 105–113

Catchpole, T 2007 Roman Dymock: Excavations at the Sewage Treatment Works, Dymock, Gloucestershire, 1995, *Trans Bristol Gloucestershire Archaeol Soc* 125, 137–219

CBA Wessex and CBA South West 1969 *Archaeol Rev*, 49

Challinor, D 2014 Wood charcoal, in C Smart *A Roman Military Complex and Medieval Settlement on Church Hill, Calstock, Cornwall: survey and excavation 2007–2010*, 101–4. Oxford, BAR 603

Challinor, D 2018, Wood charcoal, in A Powell 2018, 225–227

Charlier, P, Brun, L, Pretre, C and Huynh-Charlier, I 2012 Toilet hygiene in the classical era, *Brit Medical J* 2012, 345, e8287

Chettle, H F, Powell, W R, Spalding, P A and Tillott, P M 1953 Parishes: Melksham, in R B Pugh and E Crittall (eds) *A History of the County of Wiltshire: Volume 7*. London, 91–121

Clapham, A and Gleason, K L 1997 Archaeobotanical evidence, in E Hostetter and T N Howe (eds) *The Romano-British villa at Castle Copse, Great Bedwyn*, 345–54. Indiana Univ Press

Clarke, S. 2010. Sunken-featured buildings on a late Romano-British farmstead, Rectory Lane, Appleby Magna, Leicestershire, *Trans Leicestershire Archaeol Hist Soc* 84, 213–22.

Cohen, A, and Serjeantson, D 1996 *A Manual for the Identification of Bird Bones from Archaeological Sites*. London, Archetype

Cool, H E M 1990 Roman metal hair pins from Southern Britain, *Archaeol J* 147, 148–82

Cool, H E M 2008 Small finds of bone, jet, shale, stone, fired clay and glass, 91–100 in J G P Erskine and P Ellis, Excavations at Atworth Roman Villa, Wiltshire 1970–1975, *Wiltshire Archaeol and Natur Hist Mag* 101, 51–129

Cooper, N 1998 The supply of pottery to Roman Cirencester, in N Holbrook (ed) *Cirencester Excavations V, Cirencester the Roman Town Defences, Public Buildings and Shops*, 324–350. Cirencester, Cotswold Archaeological Trust

Cotswold Archaeological Trust 1999 *Land at Showell Farm, Chippenham, Wiltshire. Cultural Heritage Assessment, Technical Appendix Archaeological Evaluation*. Cirencester, unpubl rep 991001

Cotswold Archaeology 2003 *Land at Showell Farm, Chippenham, Wiltshire. Post-Excavation Assessment and Updated Project Design*. Cirencester, unpubl rep 03135

Cotswold Archaeology 2014 *Rowden Park, Chippenham, Wiltshire, Archaeological Evaluation*. Cirencester, unpubl rep 14584

Cramp, L 2013 Carbonized plant remains, 78 in A Taylor, A Roman building at Southbroom School, Devizes, *Wiltshire, Wiltshire Archaeol Natur Hist Mag* 106, 66–80

Crosby V and Hembrey N 2013 An evaluation in the fields South of Silbury Hill in 2010: Romano-British settlement, later alluviation and water meadows, *Wiltshire Archaeol Natur Hist Mag* 106, 101–66

Crummy, N 1983 *Colchester Archaeological Report 2: the Roman small finds from excavations in Colchester 1971–9*. Colchester, Colchester Archaeological Trust

Crummy, N and Eckardt, H 2003 Regional identities and technologies of the self: nail-cleaners in Roman Britain, *Archaeol J* 160, 44–69

Cunliffe, B and Davenport, P 1985 *The Temple of Sulis Minerva at Bath: Vol 1(i). The Site*. Oxford Univ Comm Archaeol Monogr 7, Oxford

Dando, J and Andrews, P 2017 Bromham–Rowdefield Project 2014–18: an interim note, *Wiltshire Archaeol Natur Hist Mag* 110, 224–29

Dannell, G B Dickinson, B M, Hartley, B R, Mees, A W, Polak, M, Webster, P V and Vernhet, A, *Samian Research*. http://www.rgzm.de/samian/home/frames.htm

Darby, H C and Welldon Finn, R 1967 *The Domesday Geography of South-West England*. Cambridge, Cambridge Univ Press

Davenport, P 2000 *Aquae Sulis*: the origin and development of a Roman town, *Bath Hist* 8, 7–26

Davies, B, Richardson, B and Tomber, R, 1994 *The Archaeology of Roman London. Volume 5: a dated corpus of early Roman pottery from the City of London*. London, CBA Res Rep 98

Dickinson, B and Hartley, B R 2000 The samian, in Rush *et al.* 2000, 5–88

Dobney, K 2001 A Place at the Table: the role of vertebrate zooarchaeology within a Roman research agenda, in S James and M Millet (eds) *Britons and Romans: advancing an archaeological agenda*, 36–45. York, CBA Res Rep 125

Dobney, K, Jacques, D and Irving, B 1996 *Of Butchery and Breeds: report on the vertebrate remains from various sites in the City of Lincoln*. Lincoln Archaeol Stud 5

Draper, S A 2006 *Landscape, Settlement and Society: Wiltshire in the first millennium AD*. Oxford, BAR 419

Duval, P M 1952 *La Vie Quotidienne en Gaul pendant la Paix Romaine*. Hachette

Edlin, H L 1949 *Woodland Crafts in Britain: an account of the traditional uses of trees and timbers in the British countryside*. London, Batsford

Egging Dinwiddy, K 2011 Unburnt bone, in Egging Dinwiddy and Bradley 2011, 110–32

Egging Dinwiddy, K and Bradley, P 2011 *Prehistoric activity and a Romano-British settlement at Poundbury Farm, Dorchester, Dorset*, 142–58. Salisbury, Wessex Archaeology Rep 28

Ellis, P 2001 *Roman Wiltshire and After: papers in Honour of Ken Annable*. Devizes, Wiltshire Archaeol Natur Hist Soc

Erskine, J G P and Ellis P 2008 Excavations at Atworth Roman villa, Wiltshire 1970–1975, *Wiltshire Archaeol and Natur Hist Mag* 101, 51–129

Fenton, A 1978 *The Northern Isles: Orkney and Shetland*. Edinburgh, John Donald.

Fern, K 1996–2012 *Plants for a Future: Plant Species Database* http://www.pfaf.org/ [accessed 23 January 2017]

Finnegan, M 1978 Non-metric variations of the infracranial skeleton, *J Anatomy* 125(1), 23–37

Fulford, M 2001 Links with the past: pervasive 'ritual' behaviour in Roman Britain, *Britannia* 32, 199–218

Fuller, D Q, Stevens, C J and McClatchie, M 2014 Routine activities, tertiary refuse and labor organization: social inference from everyday archaeobotany, in M Madella and M Savard (eds) *Ancient Plants and People. Contemporary Trends in Archaeobotany*, 174–217. University of Arizona Press

Gardiner, M 2012 An Early Medieval tradition of building in Britain, *Arqueología de la Arquitectura* 9, 231–46

Ghey, E, 2015 IARCH-98AA74 *A Roman Hoard* https://finds.org.uk/database/hoards/record/id/2202 [accessed 17 January 2017]

Gover, J E B, Mawer, A, Stenton, F M and Smith, A H 1939. *The Place-names of Wiltshire*. Cambridge, Cambridge Univ Press

Graham, E-J 2011 From fragments to ancestors: re-defining the role of os resectum in rituals of purification and commemoration in republican Rome, in M Carroll and J Rempel *Living Through the Dead: burial and commemoration in the Classical world*, 91–109, Studies in Funerary Archaeology vol. 5, Oxbow Books

Grant A, 1982 The use of tooth wear as a guide to the age of domestic animals, in B Wilson, C Grigson and S Payne (eds) *Ageing and Sexing Animal bones from Archaeological Sites*, 91–108. Oxford, BAR 109

Grant, A 1984 Animal husbandry, in B Cunliffe *Danebury: an Iron Age Hillfort in Hampshire. Volume 2. The Excavations 1969–1978: the finds*, 496–548. London, CBA Res Rep 52

Grundy, G B 1939 The Ancient Woodland of Wiltshire, *Wiltshire Archaeol Natur Hist Mag* 48, 540–79

Guido, M 1978 *The Glass Beads of the Prehistoric and Roman Periods in Britain and Ireland*. London, Rep Res Comm Society Antiq London 35

Halstead, P 1985 A study of mandibular teeth from Romano-British contexts at Maxey, in F Pryor and C French *Archaeology and Environment in the Lower Welland Valley, Volume 1*, 219–24. East Anglian Archaeol Rep 27

Halstead, P, Collins, P and Isaakidou, V 2002 Sorting the sheep from the goats: morphological distinctions between the mandibular teeth of adult *Ovis* and *Capra*, *J Archaeol Sci* 29(5), 545–53

Hambleton, E 1999 *Animal Husbandry Regimes in Iron Age Britain: a comparative study of faunal assemblages from British archaeological sites.* Oxford, BAR 282

Hammon, A 2006 Vertebrate remains, 184 in T Wilmott and D Shipp, The Romano-British roadside settlement of Whitewalls, Easton Grey, Wiltshire. *Wiltshire Archaeol Nat Hist Mag* 99, 165–89

Hartley, B R and Dickinson, B M 2008 *Names on Terra Sigillata. An Index of Makers' Stamps and Signatures on Gallo-Roman Terra Sigillata (Samian Ware). Volume 3 (CERTAINUS to EXSOBANO).* Bull Institute Classical Stud Suppl 102–3. University of London

Hartley, K F 1998 The incidence of stamped mortaria in the Roman Empire, with special reference to imports to Britain, in J Bird (ed) *Form and Fabric: studies in Rome's material past in honour of B R Hartley*, 199–218. Oxford, Oxbow Monogr 80

Hartley, K F 2001 Mortaria, in Anderson *et al.* 2001, 220–31

Harvey, R B 1998 Shaftesbury Abbey's 12th-century Rentals for Bradford-on-Avon, *Wiltshire Archaeol Natur Hist Mag* 91, 76–89

Hather, J G 2000 *The Identification of Northern European Woods; a guide for archaeologists and conservators.* London, Archetype

Hattatt, R 2000 *A Visual Catalogue of Richard Hattatt's Ancient Brooches.* Oxford, Oxbow

Helbaek, H 1964 The Isca grain, a Roman plant introduction in Britain, *New Phytologist* 63, 158–64

Henig, M 1993 Votive objects: images and inscriptions, in Woodward and Leach 1993, 88–112

Henig, M 2007 *A Corpus of Engraved Gemstones from Romano-British Sites.* Oxford, BAR 8, 3rd edition, Archaeopress

Henry, R and Ellis-Schön, J 2017 The Finding Pitt-Rivers project: a reassessment of the numismatic assemblage from Woodcutts in context, *Wilts Archaeol Natur Hist Mag* 110, 179–90

Hermet, F 1934 *La Graufesenque (Condatomago)*, Paris

Hicks, A 2008 The Roman settlement, in Bennett *et al.* 2008, 101–278

Higbee, L 2007 *The Animal Bones from Two Sites Along the Fosse Way in Shepton Mallet, Somerset,* unpubl client report for C and N Hollinrake

Hillman, G C 1982 Evidence for spelting malt, in R Leech (ed) *Excavations at Catsgore 1970–1973: a Romano-British village,* 137–41. Western Archaeol Trust Excavation Monogr

Hinds, K 2007 *WILT-6DF737: A Roman Finger Ring* https://finds.org.uk/database/artefacts/record/id/161752 [accessed 16 January 2017]

Hinds, K 2008 *WILT-B942F7: A Roman Brooch* https://finds.org.uk/database/artefacts/record/id/224586 [accessed 17 January 2017]

Historic England 2017a *Catridge Farmhouse* https://historicengland.org.uk/listing/the-list/list-entry/1022205 [accessed 17 Jan 2017]

Historic England 2017b *Westlands Farmhouse* https://historicengland.org.uk/listing/the-list/list-entry/1021774 [accessed 17 Jan 2017]

Historic England 2017c *New Farmhouse* https://historicengland.org.uk/listing/the-list/list-entry/1022157 [accessed 17 Jan 2017]

Historic England 2017d *Upper Beanacre Farmhouse* https://historicengland.org.uk/listing/the-list/list-entry/1021757 [accessed 17 Jan 2017]

Hodder, I 1975 The spatial distribution of Romano-British small towns, in W Rodwell and T Rowley *The Small Towns of Roman Britain*, 67–74. Oxford, BAR 15

Ingram, C 2007 Animal bone, 123–25 in C Malim and A Martin, A Romano-British roadside settlement on Chapperton Down, Salisbury Plain Training Area, *Wilts Archaeol Natur Hist Mag* 100, 104–30

Iwaaki, N and Minami, A 2008 Osteochondritis dissecans of the elbow, *Current Orthopaedic Practice* 19(6), 608–11

Kenney, J and Parry L W 2013 *Ysgol yr Hendre, Llanbeblig, Caernarfon, Report on Archaeological Excavation.* Bangor, Gwynedd Archaeological Trust, unpubl rep 1103

King, A 1978 A comparative survey of bone assemblages from Roman sites in Britain, *Bull. Instit Archaeol* 15, 207–32

King, A 1984 Animal bones and the dietary identity of military and civilian groups in Roman Britain, Germany and Gaul, in T F C Blagg and A King (eds) *Military and Civilian in Roman Britain: cultural relationships in a frontier province*, 187–218. Oxford, BAR 136

King, A 1999 Diet in the Roman world: a regional inter-site comparison of the mammal bones, *J Roman Archaeol* 12, 168–202

Lake, J and Edwards, B 2014, *Wiltshire and Swindon Farmsteads Guidance. Wiltshire and Swindon Farmsteads Character Statement.* English

Heritage, Wiltshire Buildings Record, Wiltshire Council and Swindon Borough Council

LRBC = Carson, R A G, Hill, P V and Kent, J P C, 1960 *Late Roman Bronze Coinage*. London, Spink

Lauwerier, R C G M, 1988 *Animals in Roman Times in the Dutch Eastern River Area*. Amersfoort, Nederlanse Oudheden 12/Projest Oostelijk Rivierengebied 1

Lawson, A J 1976 Shale and jet objects from Silchester, *Archaeologia* 105, 241–75

Leach, P 1993 The Pottery, in Woodward and Leach 1993, 219–249

Leach, P 2001 *Fosse Lane Shepton Mallet 1990: excavation of a Romano-British Roadside Settlement in Somerset,* Soc Promotion Roman Stud Monogr 18

Lewis, M E 2007 *The Bioarchaeology of Children. Perspectives from Biological and Forensic Anthropology.* Cambridge, Cambridge Univ Press

Lewis, M E, 2010 Life and death in a Civitas Capital: metabolic disease and trauma in the children from late Roman Dorchester, Dorset. *American J Physical Anthropol* 142, 405–16

Lewis, M and Roberts, C 1997 Growing pains: the interpretation of stress indicators, *Int J Osteoarchaeol* 7, 581–6

Lodwick, L A 2016 The recovery, reporting and analysis of plant macrofossils, in M Fulford and N Holbrook *Approaches to the Investigation, Analysis and Dissemination of Work on Romano-British Rural Settlements and Landscapes – a Review,* Cotswold Archaeology http://cotswoldarchaeology.co.uk/community/discover-the-past/developer-funded-roman-archaeology-in-britain/methodology-study/ [accessed 27 March 2018]

Lowther, A W G 1935 An early Iron Age oven at St Martha's Hill, near Guildford, *Surrey Archaeol Collections* 43, 113–5

Lyne, M A B and Jefferies, R S 1979 *The Alice Holt/Farnham Roman Pottery Industry*. London, CBA Res Rep 30

Maggs, C 1982 *The Bath to Weymouth Line*. Usk, Oakwood Press

Manchester, K 1983 *The Archaeology of Disease*. Bradford, Bradford Univ Press

Manning, W 1985 *Catalogue of the Romano-British Iron Tools, Fittings and Weapons in the British Museum*. London, British Museum Press

Marquess of Lansdowne 1929 A Roman villa at Nuthills, near Bowood, *Wiltshire Archaeol Natur Hist Mag* 44, 49–58

Marsh, G 1978 Early second century fine wares in the London area, in P Arthur and G Marsh (eds) *Early Fine Wares in Roman Britain*, 119–223. Oxford, BAR 57

Marsh, G and Tyers P 1978 The Roman pottery from Southwark, in J Bird, A H Graham, H L Sheldon and P Townend (eds) *Southwark Excavations 1972–74*, 530–607. London, LAMAS and Surrey Archaeol Soc joint publ 1

Marter-Brown, K and Seager Smith, R 2012 What did the Apocrypha know? Glued pottery vessels from Springhead and other Romano-British Sites in South and Eastern England, in B Jervis and A Kyle (eds) *Make-do and Mend: Archaeologies of Compromise, Repair and Reuse*, 5–12.Oxford, BAR Int Ser 2408

McKinley, J I 2004 Compiling a skeletal inventory: disarticulated and co-mingled remains, in Brickley and McKinley 2004, 13–16

McKinley, J I 2011 Human bone, in Barnett *et al.* 2011, 1–15

McMahon, P 2004 *The Archaeology of Wiltshire's Towns: an extensive urban survey, Melksham*. Trowbridge, Wiltshire County Archaeology Service

Mees, A 1995 *Modelsignierte Dekorationen auf südgallischer Terra Sigillata*. Stuttgart

Miles, D, Palmer, S, Smith, A and Jones, G P, 2007 *Iron Age and Roman Settlement in the Upper Thames Valley*. Thames Valley Landscapes Monogr 26, Oxford Archaeology

Mills, P S 1984 Excavations at Roman Road/Parnell Road, Old Ford, London E3, *Trans London Middlesex Archaeol Soc* 35, 25–36

Mills, J M forthcoming, The samian pottery, in R Bradley, C J Evans, E Pearson, S Richer and S Sworn, *Excavation at the Site of The Hive, The Butts, Worcester*. Worcestershire Archaeol Res Rep

Molleson, T I 1993 The human remains, in D E Farwell T I Molleson *Excavations at Poundbury 1966–80. Vol. II: the cemeteries*, 142–214. Chichester, Dorset Natur Hist Archaeol Soc

Monckton, A 1999 *Charred plant remains from corn driers and other contexts of a Romano-British settlement site at Billesley Manor Farm, Warwickshire*. Ancient Monuments Laboratory, English Heritage Rep 25/99

Monk, L 2001 Glass, in Anderson *et al.* 2001, 162–72

Moorhead, T S N 2001a *Roman Coin finds from Wiltshire*. MPhil Thesis, University College London

Moorhead, T S N 2001b Roman coin finds from *Wiltshire, in P. Ellis (ed) Roman Wiltshire and After: Papers in Honour of Ken Annable*, 85–105 Devizes, Wilts Archaeol Natur Hist Soc

Moorhead, T S N 2009 Three Roman coin hoards from Wiltshire terminating in coins of Probus (AD 276–82), *Wilts Archaeol Natur Hist Mag* 102, 150–59

Moorhead, T S N 2011 *Silbury Hill, Wiltshire. Roman coins from the Silbury region*. English Heritage

Res Dept Rep Ser 102. Portsmouth, English Heritage

Moorhead, T S N and Stuttard D 2012 *The Romans Who Shaped Britain.* London, Thames and Hudson

Morris, E L 1992 *The Analysis of Pottery.* Salisbury, Wessex Archaeol Guideline 4

Morris, J 2008 *Re-examining Associated Bone Groups from Southern England and Yorkshire, c. 4000 BC to AD 1550.* Bournemouth Univ PhD Thesis

Morris, J 2010 Associated bone groups; beyond the Iron Age, in J Morris and M Maltby (eds) *Integrating social and Environmental Archaeologies: reconsidering deposition* 7, 12–23. Oxford, BAR 207

Morris, J 2011 *Investigating Animal Burials: ritual, mundane and beyond.* Oxford, BAR 535

Mulkeen, S and O'Connor, T 1997 Raptors in towns: towards an ecological model, *Int J Osteoarchaeol* 7, 440–9

Murphy, P 1984 *Fengate Farm, Weeting, Norfolk: plant remains.* Archive report

Neito, X and Puig, A 2001 *Excavacions arqueològiques subaquàtiques a Cala Culip 3. Culip 4: la Terra Sigillata decorada de La Graufesenque.* Girona

O'Connor, T P 1989 *Bones from Anglo-Scandinavian Levels at 16–22 Coppergate.* The Archaeology of York 15 (3), 137–207. London, CBA

Oliver, H A 1881 Some account of the remains of a Roman villa in the Parish of Bromham, *Wiltshire Archaeol Natur Hist Mag* 19, 299–302

Orengo, H A and Livarda, A 2016 The seeds of commerce: A network analysis-based approach to the Romano-British transport system, *J Archaeol Sci* 66, 21–35

Oswald, F 1936–1937. *Index of Figure-Types on Terra Sigillata ("Samian Ware").* Liverpool

Oxford Archaeological Unit 1991 *Milbourne Farm and Showell Nurseries, Chippenham, Wiltshire, Field Evaluation.* unpubl rep

Palmer, C 1998 The role of fodder in the farming system: a case study from northern Jordan, *Environmental Archaeol* 1, 1–10

Papadopoulos, J K 2002 A contextual approach to *pessoi* (gaming pieces, counters, or convenient wipes?), *Hesperia* 71, 423–27

Payne, S 1973 Kill-off patterns in sheep and goats: the mandibles from Asvan Kale, *Anatolian Stud* 23, 281–303

Payne, S 1985 Morphological distinction between the mandibular teeth of young sheep Ovis and goats Capra, *J Archaeol Sci* 12, 139–47

Payne, S and Bull, G 1988 Components of variation in measurements of pig bones and teeth, and the use of measurements to distinguish wild from domestic pig remains, *Archaeozoologia* 2, 27–65

Peacock, D P S and Williams, D F 1986 *Amphorae and the Roman Economy: an introductory guide.* London, Longman

Pelling, R 2008 Charred and waterlogged plant remains, in P Booth, A M Bingham and S Lawrence (eds) *The Roman roadside settlement at Westhawk Farm, Ashford, Kent, Excavations 1998–9*, 349–56. Oxford Archaeology Monogr 2

Pelling, R 2011a Charred plant remains, in Powell 2011, 79–91

Pelling, R 2011b Charred plant remains, in Egging Dinwiddy and Bradley 2011, 142–58

Pelling, R 2013 The charred plant remains in Crosby and Hembury 2013, 145–51

Peña, J T 2007 *Roman Pottery in the Archaeological Record.* Cambridge, Cambridge Univ Press

Pengelly, H, Hartley, B R and Dickinson, B 2001 The samian, in Anderson *et al.* 2001, 179–209

Perrin, J R, 1999 *Roman Pottery from excavations at and near to the Roman Small Town of Durobrivae, Water Newton, Cambridgeshire, 1956–58.* Oxford, J Roman Pottery Stud 8

Philpott, R 1991 *Burial Practices in Roman Britain.* Oxford, BAR 219

Poole, C 1995 Loomweights versus oven bricks, in B Cunliffe *Danebury: an Iron Age hillfort in Hampshire. Volume 6*, 285-6. London, CBA Res Rep 102

Poole, C 2015 Fired clay and briquetage, in Andrews *et al.* 2015 [Vol 2], 289–323

Powell, A B 2011 *An Iron Age Enclosure and Romano-British Features at High Post, near Salisbury.* Salisbury, Wessex Archaeology

Powell, A B 2018, Romano-British edge-of-settlement activity and landscape organisation, north of Bath Road, Melksham, Wiltshire *Archaeol Natur Hist Mag* 111, 211-229

Preston, C D, Pearman, D A and Hall, A R 2004 Archaeophytes in Britain Botanical, *J Linnean Soc* 145, 257–94

Price, J and Cottam S 1998 *Romano-British Glass Vessels: a handbook.* York, CBA

Rawes, B 1972 Roman pottery kilns at Gloucester, *Trans Bristol and Gloucs Archaeol Soc.* 91, 18–59

Rawlings F and Fitzpatrick A P 1996 Prehistoric sites and Romano-British settlement at Butterfield Down, Amesbury, *Wiltshire Archaeol Natur Hist Mag* 89, 1–43

Redknap, M 1998 The small-finds from Kingscote Site 1, in Timby 1998, 93–113

Reece, R 1982 The Roman coins, in Wedlake 1982, 112–18

Reece, R 1988 Numerical aspects of Roman coin hoards in Britain, in J Casey and R Reece (eds) *Coins and the Archaeologist*, XX. London, Seaby

Reece, R 1991 *Roman Coins from 140 Sites in Britain.* Cotswold Studies 4.

Reece, R 1995 Site-finds in Roman Britain, *Britannia* 26, 179–206

Reynolds, P J 1974 Experimental Iron Age storage pits: an interim report, *Proc Prehistoric Soc* 40, 118–31

RIC, *The Roman Imperial Coinage*, vols I–VII. London, Spink

Richardson, R 1996 Field-Names with possible Roman Connections, *Trans Woolhope Natur Fld Club*, 48, 453–69

Rigby, V 1982 The pottery, in A McWhirr, L Viner and C Wells *Cirencester Excavations II, Romano-British Cemeteries at Cirencester*, 112–25. Cirencester, Cirencester Excavation Comm

Rivet, A L F and Jackson, K 1970 The British section of the Antonine Itinerary, *Britannia* 1, 34–82

Roberts, C and Manchester, K 1997 The *Archaeology of Disease*. Stroud, Sutton

Rogers, G B 1974 *Poteries Sigillées de la Gaule Centrale I: Les motifs non figurés*. Paris, Supplément à Gallia 28

Rogers, G B 1999 *Poteries Sigillées de la Gaule Centrale II: Les Potiers* (2 vol.), Premier Cahier du Centre Archéologique de Lezoux collection publiée sous la direction de Philippe Bet et de Richard Delage

Rogers, J and Waldron, T 1995 *A field guide to Joint Disease in Archaeology*. Chichester, Wiley

Rush, P, Dickinson, B M, Hartley, B R and Hartley, K F 2000 *Roman Castleford, Excavations 1974–85. Vol. 3: the Pottery. Leeds*, West Yorkshire Archaeol Service

Salway, R 1993 *The Oxford Illustrated History of Roman Britain*. Oxford, Oxford Univ Press

Samina Research, http://www.rgzm.de/samian/home [accessed March 2017]

Samuel, D 2000 Brewing and baking, in P T Nicholson and I Shaw (eds) *Ancient Egyptian Materials and Technology*, 537. Cambridge, Cambridge Univ Press

Scheuer, L and Black, S 2000 *Developmental Juvenile Osteology*. London, Academic Press

Schuster, J 2011 Springhead metalwork, in E Biddulph, R Seager Smith and J Schuster *Settling the Ebbsfleet Valley: CTRL Excavations at Springhead and Northfleet, Kent. The late Iron Age, Roman, Saxon, and Medieval Landscape, Volume 2: late Iron Age to Roman finds reports*, 189–291. Salisbury, Oxford Wessex Archaeology

Schweingruber, F H 1990 *Microscopic wood anatomy* (3rd edition). Swiss Federal Institute for Forest, Snow and Landscape Research

Scott, E 1999 *The archaeology of infancy and infant death*. Oxford, BAR Int Ser 819

Seager Smith, R H 1996 Pottery, in A B Powell, M J Allen and I Barnes *Archaeology in the Avebury Area, Wiltshire: recent discoveries along the line of the Kennet Valley foul sewer pipeline, 1993*, 43–48. Salisbury, Wessex Archaeology Rep 8

Seager Smith, R H 2001 The coarse pottery, in Anderson *et al.* 2001, 232–300

Seager Smith, R H 2015 Later prehistoric and Roman pottery in Andrews *et al.* 2015 [Vol 2], 193–245

Seager Smith, R H and Davies, S M, 1993 Roman pottery, in P J Woodward, A H Graham, and S M Davies *Excavations at Greyhound Yard, Dorchester 1981–4*, 202–89. Dorset Natur Hist Archaeol Soc Monogr 12

Seetah, K 2006 A multidisciplinary approach to Romano-British cattle butchery, in M. Maltby (ed) *Integrating Zooarchaeology*, 109–16. Oxford, Oxbow

Serjeantson, D 1996 The animal bone, in S Needham and T Spence (eds) *Refuse and disposal at Area 16 East Runnymede: Runnymede Bridge research excavations, Vol 2*, 194–224. London, British Museum

Shaffrey, R 2015a Intensive milling practices in the Romano-British landscape of Southern England: Using newly established criteria for distinguishing millstones from rotary querns, *Britannia* 46, 55–92

Shaffrey, R 2015b Worked stone in Andrews *et al.* 2015 [Vol 2], 135–149

Shaw Mellor, A and Goodchild, R 1942 The Roman villa at Atworth, Wilts, *Wiltshire Archaeol Natur Hist Mag* 49, 46–95

Sheldon, H 1971 Excavations at Lefevre Road, Old Ford E3, *Trans London Middlesex Archaeol Soc* 23, 42–77

Shoemark, J 2014 *PAS WILT-596884* https://finds.org.uk/database/artefacts/record/id/654162

Silver I A 1969 The ageing of domestic animals, in D R Brothwell and E S Higgs (eds) *Science in Archaeology: a survey of progress and research*, 283–301. London, Thames and Hudson

Simmonds, A, Marquez-Grant, N and Loe, L 2008 *Life and Death in a Roman City: Excavation of a Roman cemetery with a mass grave at 120–122 London Road*, Gloucester. Oxford Archaeology Mongr 8

Smith, W 2011 Charred plant remains from Northfleet, in Barnett *et al.* 2011, 105–13

Stace, C 1997 *New Flora of the British Isles* (2nd edition), Cambridge, Cambridge Univ Press

Stanfield, J A and Simpson, G 1990 *Les Potiers de la Gaule Centrale*. Gonfaron, Revue Archéologiques Sites, hors-série 37

Stevens, C J 2006 Charred plant remains, in M G Fulford, A B Powell, R Entwistle and F Raymond (eds) *Iron Age and Romano-British Settlements and Landscapes of Salisbury Plain*, 152–8. Salisbury, Wessex Archaeology Rep 20

Stevens, C J 2011 Charred plant remains from Springhead, in Barnett *et al.* 2011, 95–105

Struck, M 1993 Kinderbestattungen in romano-britischen Siedlungen der archäologische Befund, in M. Struck, (ed.) *Römerzeitliche Gräber als Quellen zu Religion, Bevölkerungsstruktur und Sozialgeschichte*, 313–8. Mainz, Institut für Vorund Frühgeschichte

Swan, V G 1975 Oare reconsidered and the origins of Savernake ware in Wiltshire, *Brittania* 6, 36–61

Sykes, N J 2007 *The Norman Conquest: a zooarchaeological perspective*. Oxford, BAR 1656

Timby, J R 1998 *Excavations at Kingscote and Wycomb, Gloucestershire, A Roman Estate Centre and Small Town in the Cotswolds, with notes on related settlements*. Cirencester, Cotswold Archaeological Trust

Timby, J R 2008 Pottery coarsewares, in Erskine and Ellis 2008, 100–108

Timby, J R 2012 Pottery, 49–54 in A Hood, Prehistoric and Roman Archaeology at Mill Lane, Swindon, *Wiltshire Archaeol Natur Hist Mag* 105, 43–57

Timby, J R 2013a The Roman pottery, in Crosby and Hembury 2013, 126–34

Timby, J R 2013b Roman pottery, 28–34 in A Barber, J Schuster and N Holbrook, Prehistoric activity and Roman rural settlement at Blacklands, Staverton: excavations in 2007, *Wiltshire Archaeol Natur Hist Mag* 106, 16–51

Tipper, J 2004 *The Grubenhaus in Anglo-Saxon England. Analysis and interpretation of the Evidence from a Most Distinctive Building Type*. Landscape Res Centre Archaeol Monogr Ser 2(1). Colchester, Palladian

Thomas, R and Stallibrass, S 2008 For starters: production and supplying food to the army in the Roman north-west provinces, in S Stallibrass and R Thomas (eds) *Feeding the Roman Army: the archaeology of production and supply in NW Europe*, 1–17. Oxford, Oxbow

Tomber, R and Dore, J 1998 *The National Roman Fabric Reference Collection: a handbook*. Museum of London, English Heritage, British Museum

Vann, S and Thomas, R 2006 Humans, other animals and disease: a comparative approach towards the development of a standardised recording protocol for animal palaeopathology, *Internet Archaeol* 20 https://doi.org/10.11141/ia.20.5

van Beek, G C 1983 *Dental Morphology: an illustrated guide* (2nd edition). Bristol, Butterworth-Heinemann

van der Veen, M 1989 Charred grain assemblages from Roman period corn driers in Britain, *Archaeol J* 146, 302–19

van der Veen, M 2007 Formation processes of desiccated and carbonized plant remains – the identification of routine practice, *J Archaeol Sci* 34, 968–90

van der Veen, M, Livarda, A and Hill, A 2008 New plant foods in Roman Britain – dispersal and social access, *Environmental Archaeol* 13, 11

von den Driesch, A 1976 *A Guide to the Measurement of Animal Bones from Archaeological Sites*. Peabody Mus Bull 1. Cambridge (Mass), Harvard Univ

Wainwright, G J 1971 The excavation of prehistoric sites and Romano-British settlements near Durrington Walls, Wiltshire, *Wiltshire Archaeol Natur Hist Mag* 66, 76–128

Walker, P, Bathurst, R, Richman, R, Gjerdrum, T, Andrushko, V 2009 The causes of porotic hyperostosis and *cribra orbitalia*: a reappraisal of the iron-deficiency-anaemia hypothesis, *American J Physical Anthropol* 139, 109–25

Wedlake, W J 1958 *Excavations at Camerton, Somerset: a record of thirty years' excavation covering the period from Neolithic to Saxon times, 1926–56*, Camerton Excavation Club

Wedlake, W J 1982 *The Excavation of the Shrine of Apollo at Nettleton, Wiltshire, 1956–1971*. Soc Antiq Rep 40. London, Thames and Hudson

Wessex Archaeology 2000a *Amesbury Phase 1 Housing, Boscombe Down, Wiltshire*. Salisbury, unpubl rep 43193

Wessex Archaeology 2000b *Land at Pockeridge Farm and Peel Circus, Corsham, Wiltshire: Archaeological Evaluation*. Salisbury, unpubl rep 45958.01

Wessex Archaeology 2006 *Cilfynydd – Melksham 4YX Transmission Line Archaeological Survey*. Salisbury, unpubl rep 61972.01

Wessex Archaeology 2007 *Blacklands, Upper Row Farm, Laverton, Somerset: archaeological evaluation and assessment of results*. Salisbury, unpubl rep 62504.01

Wessex Archaeology 2011 *Cunetio Roman Town, Mildenhall, Marlborough, Wiltshire: archaeological evaluation and assessment of results*. Salisbury, unpubl rep 71509

Wessex Archaeology 2014a *Melksham to Thingley Cable Installation, Wiltshire: Written Scheme of Investigation for an archaeological watching brief* Salisbury, unpubl rep 107350.01

Wessex Archaeology 2014b *Melksham to Thingley Cable Installation, Wiltshire. Written Scheme of Investigation for an Archaeological Strip, Map and Record Excavation*. Salisbury, unpubl rep 107350.03

Wessex Archaeology 2015a *Melksham to Thingley Cable Installation, Wiltshire: post-excavation assessment and updated project design*. Salisbury, unpubl rep 107350.04

Wessex Archaeology 2015b *Melksham Town FC, Melksham, Wiltshire: post-excavation assessment and updated project design.* Salisbury, unpubl rep 102043.02

Wild, J P 2002 The textile industries of Roman Britain, *Britannia*, 33, 1–42

Wilkinson, P 2013 *The Roman Religious Sanctuary at 'Blacklands', School Farm, Graveney Road, Faversham, Kent.* Faversham, Kent Archaeological Field School, unpubl rep

Williams, A and Martin, G H 1992 *Domesday Book: A Complete Translation.* Alecto Historical Editions. London, Penguin

Willis, S 2005 *Samian Pottery. A Resource for the Study of Roman Britain and Beyond: the results of the English Heritage funded Samian Project. An e-monograph. [Supplement to Internet Archaeology 17]*: http://intarch.ac.uk/journal/issue17/willis_index.html

Wilmott, T and Shipp, D 2006 The Romano-British roadside settlement of Whitewalls, Easton Grey, Wiltshire, *Wiltshire Archaeol Natur Hist Mag* 99, 165–89

Wiltshire Archaeological Service 2004 *The Archaeology of Wiltshire's Towns. An Extensive Urban Survey: Verlucio*, Trowbridge

Wiltshire Council 2011a *Wiltshire Community History: Corsham* https://history.wiltshire.gov.uk/community/getcom.php?id=71 [accessed 24 January 2017]

Wiltshire Council 2011b *Wiltshire Community History: Lacock* https://history.wiltshire.gov.uk/community/getcom.php?id=132 [accessed 24 January 2017]

Wiltshire Council 2018 *Wiltshire and Swindon Historic Environment Record* http://www.wiltshire.gov.uk/wiltshireandswindonhistoricenvironmentrecord/wshermap.htm [accessed 3 April 2018]

Woodward, A and Leach, P 1993 *The Uley Shrines. Excavation of a Ritual Complex on West Hill, Uley, Gloucestershire: 1977–9.* London, English Heritage

Wyles, S 2015 Environmental evidence, in Wessex Archaeology 2015. Salisbury, unpubl rep 107350.03

Young, C J, 1977 *The Roman Pottery Industry of the Oxford Region.* Oxford, BAR 43

Young, R and Hancocks, A 2006 Early Bronze Age ring ditches and Romano-British agriculture at Showell Farm, Chippenham. Excavations in 1999, *Wiltshire Archaeol Natur Hist Mag* 99, 10–50

Zohary, D Hopf, M and Weiss, E 2012 *Domestication of Plants in the Old World. The Origin and Spread of Cultivated Plants in West Asia, Europe and the Nile Valley.* Oxford, Oxford Univ Press

Appendix 1
Local Oxidised Sandy Ware Fabrics Q100–Q105

Photographed at x2 magnification.

A1. Q100. Fine oxidised sandy ware

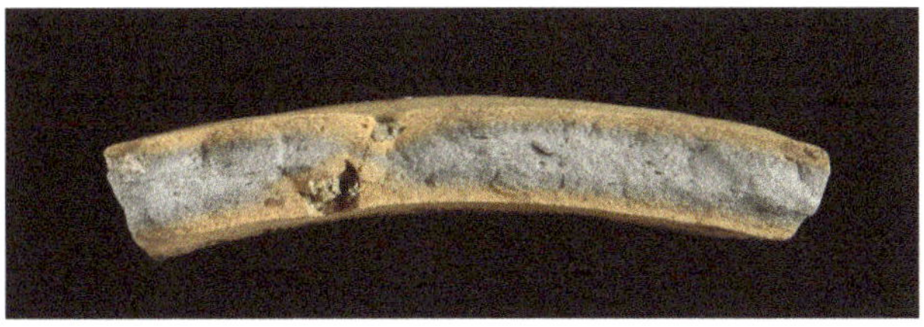

A2. Q100. Fine oxidised sandy ware

A3. Q101. Coarse oxidised sandy ware

A4. Q101. Coarse oxidised sandy ware

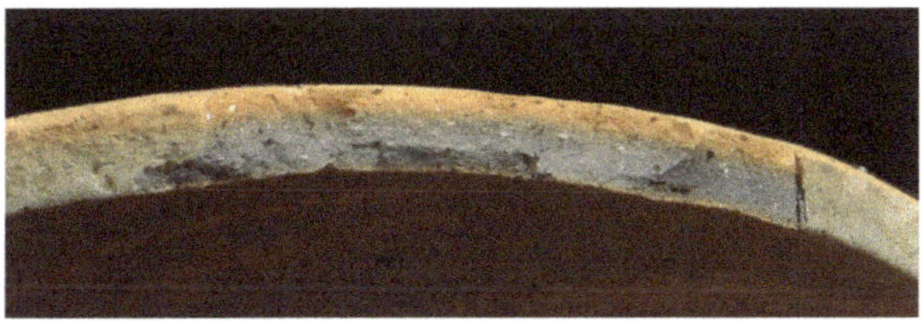

A5. Q102. Fine, white-slipped oxidised sandy ware

A6. Q103. Coarse, white-slipped oxidised sandy ware

A7. Q103. Coarse, white-slipped oxidised sandy ware

A8. Q104. South-West White-slipped ware (Tomber and Dore 1998, 102, NRFRC fabric SOW WS). Coarse, white-slipped oxidised sandy ware mortaria fabric

A9. Q105. Red-brown oxidised ware

Lightning Source UK Ltd.
Milton Keynes UK
UKHW05f0603290818
327977UK00004B/61/P

9 781911 137085